How Schools do Policy

Over the last 20 years, international attempts to raise educational standards and improve opportunities for all children have accelerated and proliferated. This has generated a state of constant change and an unrelenting flood of initiatives, changes and reforms that need to be 'implemented' by schools. In response to this, a great deal of attention has been given to evaluating 'how well' policies are realised in practice – implemented! Less attention has been paid to understanding how schools actually deal with these multiple, and sometimes contradictory, policy demands; how they creatively work to *interpret* policy texts and *translate* these into practices, in real material conditions and with varying resources – how they are *enacted*!

Based on a long-term qualitative study of four 'ordinary' secondary schools, and working on the interface of theory with data, this book explores how schools *enact*, rather than *implement*, policy. It focuses on:

- contexts of 'policy work' in schools;
- teachers as policy subjects;
- teachers as policy actors;
- policy texts, artefacts and events;
- standards, behaviour and learning policies.

This book offers an original and very grounded analysis of how schools and teachers *do* policy. It will be of interest to undergraduate and postgraduate students of education, education policy and social policy, as well as school leaders, in the UK and beyond.

Stephen J. Ball is the Karl Mannheim Professor of Sociology of Education in the Department of Educational Foundations and Policy Studies at the Institute of Education, University of London, UK.

Meg Maguire is Professor of Sociology of Education in the Department of Education and Professional Studies at King's College London, UK.

Annette Braun is a Lecturer in Sociology in the Sociology Department of City University, London, UK.

How Schools do Policy

Policy enactments in secondary schools

Stephen J. Ball, Meg Maguire
and Annette Braun
with Kate Hoskins and
Jane Perryman

 Routledge
Taylor & Francis Group

LONDON AND NEW YORK

First published 2012
by Routledge
2 Park Square, Milton Park, Abingdon, Oxon OX14 4RN

Simultaneously published in the USA and Canada
by Routledge
711 Third Avenue, New York, NY 10017

Routledge is an imprint of the Taylor & Francis Group, an informa business

© 2012 Stephen J. Ball, Meg Maguire and Annette Braun

The right of Stephen J. Ball, Meg Maguire and Annette Braun to be identified as authors of this work has been asserted by them in accordance with sections 77 and 78 of the Copyright, Designs and Patents Act 1988.

British Library Cataloguing in Publication Data
A catalogue record for this book is available from the British Library

Library of Congress Cataloging in Publication Data
Maguire, Meg, 1949-
How schools do policy : policy enactments in secondary schools / by Meg Maguire, Stephen J Ball, and Annette Braun with Kate Hoskins and Jane Perryman.
p. cm.
Includes bibliographical references and index.
1. Education and state. 2. Education, Secondary. 3. Educational change. 4. Educational sociology. 5. Education and state--Great Britain--Case studies. 6. Education, Secondary--Great Britain--Case studies. 7. Educational change--Great Britain--Case studies. 8. Educational sociology--Great Britain--Case studies. I. Ball, Stephen J. II. Braun, Annette, 1973- III. Title.
LC71.M28 2012
379.41--dc23
2011028149

ISBN: 978-0-415-67626-7 (hbk)
ISBN: 978-0-415-67627-4 (pbk)
ISBN: 978-0–203-15318-5 (ebk)

Typeset in Garamond
by GreenGate Publishing Services, Tonbridge, Kent

Contents

Illustrations

Figures

Table

Boxes

Acknowledgements

We would like to thank a number of people for their help, support and encouragement during the preparation of this book, in particular, the staff of the four schools who were so generous with their time during our field-work. Kate Hoskins and Jane Perryman joined the project team as interns and participated in all aspects of the work of the project. We would also like to extend our gratitude to all the educationalists, academics and policy makers who have attended our presentations and given us constructive feedback – in particular Ian Menter and Bob Lingard for their constructive criticism over time. We are also grateful to the PGCE and MA students at the Institute of Education and King's College London who have commented on aspects of the project. We also want to acknowledge the contribution of Clare Sullivan, Clare Thornton, Paul Laluvelin, Giovanna Barzano and Steve Blum. This book would not have been possible without Routledge, and we would like to thank Vicky Parting for all her support and, as always, Anna Clarkson for her editorial advice and generosity of spirit.

We also wish to acknowledge the Economic and Social Research Council whose grant (ref. RES-062-23-1484) made this research possible.

1 Doing enactments research

Where to begin?

This book is one version of our research. In writing collectively and collaboratively about a project that we have researched together, argued about, disagreed over and yet have become passionately attached to over the last three years or so, there are many things we could have done differently and there are many things of interest and importance that we have no room to include here. There certainly could have been different points of emphasis in the text, we could have deployed and discussed different data – we have plenty – and we could have used some different analytic devices. For these and other reasons, we do not regard this writing as closed or finished – this is a set of starting points and openings. This is not the book we imagined we might write when we began the research. To quote Michel Foucault, whose writing will appear at many points in this book: what we have to offer is a set of 'unfinished abutments and lines of dots' (1996: 275).

It is also important to say that our writing has been a process of avoidance and compromise, an exercise of writing around and beyond existing work on policy in schools – sometimes called *implementation* research. We do not want to reject or obliterate this work in toto but we have become profoundly aware of its limitations and omissions. We want to over-write it, to give it greater texture, fuller scope and more theoretical sophistication and in order to do so we draw on sociological theory to 'fill out' the interpretation of 'policy work' in schools.

This first chapter is where we want to lay out the background to the book and to the empirical school-based project from which it emanates. However, we need to be clear that this is not a straightforward empirical research report. It aims to say some useful things about the everyday world of policy in contemporary English schools but we will not be offering you a chapter on the current policy landscape in England or a blow-by-blow account of the relationships between specific policies and specific practices – although this is what happens to some extent in Chapters 4 and 5. This is a book about how schools 'do' policy, specifically about how policies become 'live' and get enacted (or not) in schools. We hope it will have a general relevance and usefulness beyond the specifics of the cases we explore and the data we present and discuss. We are attempting to outline a grounded theory of policy enactments in school, or at least to identify a set of tools and concepts which will provide the elements of such a theory. We also want to present an account of policy enactments in secondary schools that makes sense to practitioners and to people who 'know' schools, that feels as if this is how it is in 'real' schools, while simultaneously adding to and challenging the existing theorising of this complex process. Having said that, while it may seem like it at times, this is not a book about teaching – in the sense that we are not intending to reduce teaching to policy or schools to teaching and learning. Teaching consists of much more than these aspects we address here – a point we return to in the final chapter – and schools are complex and sometimes incoherent social assemblages. Enough preamble, 'This introduction is becoming lengthy: let us begin. Not that we know the beginning, but that a time comes when we have to begin – somewhere' (Sarup 1978: 9). We begin with policy implementation and policy enactment and some of the existing thinking about how schools 'do policy' as a basis for our argument for a different kind of understanding.

Beyond implementation!

In much writing on education policy, the meaning of policy itself is frequently just taken for granted and/or defined superficially as an attempt to 'solve a problem'. Generally, this problem solving is done through the production of policy texts such as legislation or other locally or nationally driven prescriptions and insertions into practice. This kind of 'normative' policy analysis generally 'takes' policy as a 'closed preserve of the formal government apparatus of policy making' (Ozga 2000: 42), or what Taylor *et al.* (1997: 5) describe as the state's 'only plausible response to [the] social and economic changes'. The problem is that if policy is only seen in these terms, then all the other moments in processes of policy and policy enactments that go on in and around schools are marginalised or go unrecognised. The jumbled, messy, contested creative and mundane social interactions, what Colebatch (2002) calls the 'policy activity' of negotiations and coalition building that somehow link texts to practice are erased. Teachers, and an increasingly diverse cast of 'other adults' working in and around schools, not to mention students, are written out of the policy process or rendered simply as ciphers who 'implement'. While many policies 'done' in schools are 'written' by government, their agencies or other influential stakeholders, policy making at all its levels and in all its sites also involves 'negotiation, contestation or struggle between different groups who may lie outside the formal machinery of official policy-making' (Ozga 2000: 113).

Thus, we want to 'make' policy into a process, as diversely and repeatedly contested and/or subject to different 'interpretations' as it is enacted (rather than implemented) in original and creative ways within institutions and classrooms (see also Ball 1997, 2008) but in ways that are limited by the possibilities of discourse. In this book, what is meant by policy will be taken as texts and 'things' (legislation and national strategies) but also as discursive processes that are complexly configured, contextually mediated and institutionally rendered. Policy is done by and done to teachers; they are actors and subjects, subject to and objects of policy. Policy is written onto bodies and produces particular subject positions.

Policy is complexly encoded in texts and artefacts and it is decoded (and recoded) in equally complex ways. To talk of decoding and recoding suggests that policy 'making' is a process of understanding and translating – which of course it is. Nonetheless, policy making, or rather, enactment is far more subtle and sometimes inchoate than the neat binary of decoding and recoding indicates. As Taylor *et al.* (1997: 20) say of policy work in education, 'we need to observe politics in action, tracing how economic and social forces, institutions, people, interests, events and chance interact. Issues of power and interests need to be investigated.' Thus, policy enactment involves creative processes of interpretation and recontextualisation – that is, the translation of texts into action and the abstractions of policy ideas into contextualised practices – and this process involves 'interpretations of interpretations' (Rizvi and Kemmis 1987), although the degree of play or freedom for 'interpretation' varies from policy to policy in relation to the apparatuses of power within which they are set (see Chapter 4) and within the constraints and possibilities of context. Policies are not simply ideational or ideological, they are also very material. Policies rarely tell you exactly what to do, they rarely dictate or determine practice, but some more than others narrow the range of creative responses. This is in part because policy texts are typically written in relation to the best of all possible schools, schools that only exist in the fevered imaginations of politicians, civil servants and advisers and in relation to fantastical contexts. These texts cannot simply be *implemented*! They have to be translated from text to action – put 'into' practice – in relation to history and to context, with the resources available. 'Practice is sophisticated, contingent, complex and unstable' so that 'policy will be open to erosion and undercutting by action, the embodied agency of those people who are its object' (Ball 1994: 10–11).

It is with the diverse and complex ways in which sets of education policies are 'made sense of',[1] mediated and struggled over, and sometimes ignored, or, in another word, *enacted* in schools that this book and our research work is centrally concerned. Enactments are collective and collaborative, but not just simply in the warm fuzzy sense of teamwork, although that is there, but also in the interaction and inter-connection between diverse actors, texts, talk, technology and objects (artefacts) which constitute ongoing responses to policy, sometimes durable, sometimes fragile, within networks and chains. There are minute and mundane negotiations and translations which go on at these points of connection over time and space – sometimes 'virtually' through school intranets. Policy is not 'done' at one point in time; in our schools it is always a process of 'becoming', changing from the outside in and the inside out. It is reviewed and revised as well as sometimes dispensed with or simply just forgotten.

Given all of that, understanding and documenting the myriad ways in which policy is enacted in schools is a somewhat elusive and complicated process. Spillane (2004: 6) argues that in what he describes as 'conventional accounts', there is a tendency to highlight the role of principle policy agents and rational-choice theory. That is, there is a view that policy is implemented, put into practice (or not), based on 'personal interest or utility maximisation'. In this approach, lead policy actors, and Spillane's example is local officials, choose what policies they want to attend to, what they think will be of the most value and sideline any alternatives that do not fit with their agendas. Nevertheless, Spillane (2004: 7) believes that local officials tend to work hard to put mandated policies into practice; 'they do not typically work to undermine policy directives from above'. In addition, he claims that policy implementation is a complex cognitive process. Based on a large-scale empirical study in Michigan, he found that policies were, or were not, implemented because of the 'sense making' schemas of those charged with this task, from School District policy makers, down to classroom practitioners. Spillane (2004: 8) says of policy implementation that 'the story is morphed as it moves from player to player… this happens not because the players are intentionally trying to change the story; it happens because that is the nature of human sense-making.' His point is that taking a cognitive approach towards what he calls policy implementation 'supplements' conventional accounts by allowing for some degree of rational-choice theory but also incorporating a view that includes the sense-making, and thus agency, of policy actors – a difficult issue which we will return to throughout this book (see Chapters 4 and 5). More recently, Supovitz and Weinbaum (2008) have stressed the way in which policies become 'iteratively refracted'. They suggest that policy reforms become 'adjusted repeatedly as they are introduced into and work their way through school environments' (p.153). In many ways though, this kind of approach to the 'doing' of policy remains set within a linear, top-down and undifferentiated conception of policy work in schools. It tells us something about how policies are understood and worked on and recast as they filter into classroom life but it views all policies and all schools and all teachers in the same way. It is an institutionally and socially 'thin' account of policy processes.

Supovitz and Weinbaum's approach, like Spillane's work, stresses the ways in which individual, social and institutionally contextualised factors influence policy implementation and policy adjustments. However, in both cases, the stress is with implementation as a way of describing how a single, unitary policy reform from the centre/top is worked out in practice in schools. These approaches, useful though they are, do not necessarily help with understanding how it is that certain policies, or strands within policies, become picked up and worked on, why they are selected and who selects them and what alternatives are discarded along the way. They do not illuminate the ways in which policies can be clustered together to form new policy ensembles that can have unintended or unexpected consequences in schools. They do not help us understand how and why school leaders and schoolteachers negotiate with, manage and put sometimes conflicting policies into practice simultaneously. Even more crucially, many of the school-based policy implementation studies conceive of the school itself as a somewhat homogenous and de-contextualised organisation that is an undifferentiated 'whole' into which various policies are slipped or filtered into place, either successfully or 'unsuccessfully' – whatever that might mean.

In many of these studies, there is no proper recognition of the different cultures, histories, traditions and communities of practice that co-exist in schools. The education and preparation of teachers, now of a variety of kinds, and the changing role and constitution of professional discourses and professional expertise are also left out of account. There is little attention given to the material context of the policy process, neither the buildings within which policy is done, nor the resources available (see Chapter 2), nor are the students with whom policy is enacted often accounted for. The emphasis on sense-making literally de-materialises policy. Nor do these studies usually convey any sense of the way in which policies fit into the overall texture and rhythms of teachers' work – the different times of year in schools and the deadening tiredness with which teachers often grapple. This is an overbearingly rational and emotionless world. The clash of personalities, the dedication and commitment, the ambition and burn-out, the humour and the moments of cynicism and frustration are all erased.

> It doesn't matter how many [policies] there are or what they might be or whether we personally agree with them or can't see the logic of them... the whole idea of there being a debate of any kind or any sense of the teacher's opinion, even though they're the people that actually deal with it every day, it's completely ignored. Totally ignored!
>
> (Neil, English, 2nd in department, Union rep., Wesley)

> The external pressures on the school to meet certain targets is always going to override anything a school wants to do that's individual about personalised learning. And since most schools are stretched to the limit, with staff working over the number of hours, they're not going to be able to introduce anything substantially new.
>
> (Joe, head of Sociology, Atwood)

There is also an ontological issue here, or rather two. First, what kinds of teacher are conjured up in these accounts and analyses? Too often, they are cardboard cut-out sense-makers, just too linear and too rational, too focused and logical, too neat and asocial. Second, what is the relation between the teacher and policy? Do teachers simply make sense of policy, re-iterate, re-fract, implement it? Or does policy also make sense of teachers, make them what and who they are in the school and the classroom, make them up, produce them, articulate them. There is a complex web of interpretations, translations, 'active readership' and 'writerly' work round policy (Lendvai and Stubbs 2006) and the effectivity of policy discourse, that produces particular kinds of teacher subjects.

Teaching is set within policy regimes and policy discourses which speak teachers as practitioners – at least to an extent – through the language of curriculum and pedagogy and through the subjective possibilities that the relation to knowledge and to learning in policies makes possible. What we refer to as policy is most usually what is most recent and most immediate but there is a history of other policies, other languages and other subjectivities, a discursive archive on which, at least sometimes, teachers can draw, over and against contemporary policy. These other possibilities seem to be miss-ing from stories of implementation – teaching is de-politicised. In practice, schools are made up of different types of, and different generations of, teachers with different dispositions towards teaching and learning, set within different waves of innovation and change.

> Those people who have more recently joined the profession, it's some-thing that they've always known (change), it's something they always do… we do have a split between those who will be looking for new ways to do something and those who will, sort of, plod on as before.
>
> (Robert, AST Art, Wesley)

Above all, policy is also only ever part of what teachers do. There is more to teaching and school life than policy. There are 'discretionary spaces' (Fenwick and Edwards 2010: 126) in and beyond policy, corners of the school where policy does not reach, bits of practice that are made up of teachers' good ideas or chance or crisis – but this space for action is also produced or delimited by policy, as we shall see.

And policy enactment?

In this book, drawing on our data, we explore the ways in which different types of policy become interpreted and translated and reconstructed and remade in different but similar settings, where local resources, material and human, and diffuse sets of discourses and values are deployed in a complex and hybrid process of enactment. As indicated above, many of the studies that explore how policies are put into practice talk of 'implementation' which is generally seen either as a 'top down' or 'bottom up' process of making policy work, and these studies 'stress the demarcation between policy and imple-mentation' (Grantham 2001: 854). In contrast, we see policy enactments as a dynamic and non-linear aspect of the whole complex that makes up the policy process, of which policy in school is just one part. Policies 'begin' at different points and they have different trajectories and life spans, some are mandated, others strongly recommended or suggested (Wallace 1991). Some policies are formulated 'above' and others are produced in schools or by local authorities, or just simply become 'fashionable' approaches in practice with no clear beginning.

At any moment in time, schools have hundreds of policies in circulation, albeit of different status and reach (Braun *et. al.* 2010). Our attempt at a 'policy audit' identified more than 170 policies in play across the four case study schools; by now, some of these will have been discarded or reworked and others will have appeared. They range from safeguarding and CCTV policies, to health and safety, to community cohesion, to uniforms and school trips. Most of these never make an appearance in education policy research and yet in different ways they frame, constrain and enable the possibilities of teaching and learning, of order and organisation, of social relations and the management of problems and crises. They 'speak' differently to specific in-school groups and specialists, subject disciplines, or age-related cohorts and are (sometimes) differently enacted within the same school by different policy actors – for example, within different subject departments or in back offices or technical areas. Some policies also cluster, to form policy ensembles, inter-related and mutually reinforcing policy sets which can in some instances 'over-determine' enactment – as is the case with 'standards' and 'behaviour' (see Chapters 4 and 5). Some collide or overlap, producing contradictions or incoherence or confusion. Lyn, an assistant head teacher in George Eliot, talks of tensions between 'soft' policies, such as emotional support for students, 'harder' edged policies and the role of key policy actors like herself.

> They're so important, you know, they are soft but they do represent the emotional life, if you like, of the other bits of education, that we're in danger of losing in this drive towards raising standards. And what does concern me is that when I leave there will not be anybody who will bring that perspective into the school, because there isn't anyone who will be senior enough to voice those concerns.

All of our schools pay attention to the need for student voice and creativity in their policy documentation (Fielding 2004; Craft 2005); yet the imperatives of raising performance as measured by examination grades can interrupt these different and potentially progressive learning and teaching intentions.

> Well, I think in this school we really sometimes kill creativity. We're so – it's so directed. Like we have to do *this*, we have to do *this*, we have to do *this*!
>
> (Rachael, head of PE, George Eliot)

We have also begun to map the ways in which policy enactments are peopled and the roles played by different enactors within policy work (see Chapter 3). These roles include, policy *entrepreneurs* (Mintron 1997) and authoritative *interpreters* who drive the way in which policies are selected and understood; *transactors* and *translators*, those middle level implementers (Coburn 2005) who work to make texts into action and render actions into outcomes – those that Colebatch (2002: 117) calls the 'maintenance staff of the policy process'. There are also *critics* and *refusers* (Sanguinetti 1999: 19) who speak back to policy (like Neil below) and bring 'other' rationalities to bear; and the *copers* and *defenders* who are at the receiving end of policy in classrooms and corridors.

> I know the government policy is for setting classes ('ability' grouping) but we don't do that in English because we don't believe in it... the head's tried to put pressure on Paul, our head of department, before to do it because it's kind of recommended, and we don't – we won't do it.
>
> (Neil, English, 2nd in department, Union rep., Wesley)

In schools there are interactions and accommodations between mandated policies and institutional histories and commitments – this is part of the work of *interpretation* and *translation*. However, few polices arrive fully formed and the processes of policy enactment also involve ad-hockery, borrowing, re-ordering, displacing, making do and re-invention. Policies are sometimes poorly thought-out and/or poorly written and become 'rewritten' or 'retro-fitted' as government objectives change or ministers move on (Spillane 2004; Maguire 2007). Interpretation is sometimes at a premium, the onus is on schools to 'make' sense of policy where (sometimes) none is self evident. Policy work is often a piecemeal process of 'fixing' problems but, over time and through a process of complex iterations between policies and across policy ensembles, institutional transformation and regeneration can be effected. The cumulative effects of clusters of policies can sometimes act to produce second order effects and change schools as places to work in and learn in. As Skocpol (1992: 58) puts it: 'Too often social scientists... forget that policies, once enacted, restructure subsequent political processes.' They both act upon and encounter institutional micro-politics and become the focus of struggles over resources, posts and curriculum time. They empower some and displace others.

Our use of the concept of enactment is based on the related premises that 'Policies do not normally tell you what to do, they create circumstances in which the range of options available in deciding what to do are narrowed or changed, or particular goals or outcomes are set' (Ball 1994: 19) and that putting policies into practice is a creative and sophisticated and complex process. Policy work has its pleasures, satisfactions and seductions and for some it has personal benefits. Policies are suffused with emotions and with psychosocial tensions. They can threaten or disrupt self-worth, purpose and identity. They can enthuse or depress or anger. To reiterate a point made earlier, there is a lot of agency or 'interpretation' in our analysis and our conceptualisation of the policy process but also there is a good deal of discourse and power. Policy is very much 'a certain economy of discourses of truth' (Foucault 1980: 93) which becomes invested in the day-to-day existence of schools, the bodies of teachers and students and in forms of social relationship. Policies are permeated by relations of power, and 'To ignore issues of power is to ensure our own powerlessness' (Taylor *et al.* 1997: 20) but they are also 'a field of possibilities' (Foucault 1983: 93). Rather than taking power as a top-down and linear phenomenon, we see power in a relational and situated way. Usher and Edwards (1994: 89) see greater possibilities, and greater complexities, in understandings of power as 'manifested as relationships in a social network… Power, through knowledge, brings forth active "subjects" who better "understand" their own subjectivity yet who in this very process subject themselves to forms of power.' Rizvi and Lingard (2010: 12) refer to the ways in which the state 'uses its authority' to justify and legitimate the public policy process – but they add that in so doing, the state 'plays a major part in producing "self governing individuals"' or what Foucault calls 'governmentality', all points that we shall be returning to in many of the following chapters.

Scoping the project

Over the last twenty years or so, education reform has become an 'epidemic' of global proportions (Levin 1998). Reform has been attempted, to a great extent, via a proliferation of policies. In the process much education policy making has been appropriated by the central state in the determination to control, manage and transform education and, in particular, to 'modernise' education and 'raise standards', even if this sometimes involves the appearance of giving away control and enhancing autonomy (see Ball 2008). To a great extent, in the UK and in England in particular, the role of the individual school, and indeed the local education authority, has been subordinated to and by these national policy imperatives (Fullan 2003; Fielding 2007). The role and the work of schools and teachers have been increasingly prescribed by central government. Policy technologies – management, market and performativity – steer practice in the direction of what Barker (2010: 100) calls 'the relentless pursuit of the unattainable'; that is, constant improvement in examination results and other performances. What is being demanded of schools, their contribution to national economic competitiveness and cultural cohesion, is encoded in a litany of policy statements, documents and legislation; in short, a form of 'initiativitis' inscribed in a series of 'fast policies' designed to make the education system 'open, diverse, flexible, able to adjust and adapt to the changing world' (Blair 2005). Schools and teachers are expected to be familiar with, and able to enact, multiple (and sometimes contradictory) policies that are planned for them by others and they are held accountable for this task. However, as noted already, individual policies and policy makers do not normally take account of the complexity of institutional policy enactment environments. It is simply assumed that schools can and will respond, and respond quickly, to multiple policy demands and other expectations. Policy is easy, enactments are not. Indeed, most policy analysis research concentrates on single policies in isolation (Malin 2007; Vander Schee 2009) as though their processes and effects can be separated from everything else. Our study takes a multi-policy approach in order to chart and understand contemporary policy enactments in a more realistic/holistic manner.

As signalled already, what happens inside a school in terms of how policies are interpreted and enacted will be mediated by institutional factors. 'Schools in different contexts will have different capacities, potentials and limits' (Lauder *et al*. 1998: 62). These constitute a material context of interpretation and create different practical possibilities and constraints for policy enactment (as we discuss more fully in Chapter 2) and frameworks of expectation within which responses to policy are constructed. Enactments will also depend to some extent on the degree to which particular policies will 'fit' or can be fitted within the existing ethos and culture of the school or can change ethos and culture. It will involve what Riseborough (1992) has termed 'secondary adjustments'. By this, he meant that policies can be either 'contained' or 'disruptive' in schools. Policies can be fitted in without precipitating any major (or real) changes and/or they can produce radical and sometimes unintended changes. They may also be subject to what Ball (1994: 20) has termed 'creative non-implementation' or what might be called performative implementation. That is, schools may pay some attention to a policy and 'fabricate' a response that is incorporated into school documentation for purposes of accountability and audit, rather than to effect pedagogic or organisational change (Ball 2001). Indeed, some policies encourage this sort of response. Policy enactment in schools may concentrate on what superficially maps on to current practices with the result that any innovatory potential is simply ignored or avoided (Spillane 2004).

Schools have to make careful, and sometimes painful, decisions about where their policy priorities lie. Policy enactment is inflected by competing sets of values and ethics, but perhaps surprisingly, certainly surprisingly to us, there is a dearth of values-talk in our data. Social values and principles of social justice are less than obvious components of the policy process. Rather, they are glimpsed fleetingly as asides in the interview transcripts and referred to outside of, or beyond, policy. This is in part, of course, because of their implicitness within contemporary policy itself and is indicative of the displacement of values by other more instrumental priorities invested in policy thinking – although Every Child Matters might be viewed as a notable, if problematic, exception to this displacement. In this sense, a great deal of policy work in schools is reactive; interpretations and translations take place on the grounds set by 'bigger' educational discourses, as already noted. The scarcity of the articulation of principles may also be indicative of 'new' teachers at work, who have what Bottery (2000: 191) characterises as a focus on 'the individual, personal and the here-and-now'. It may be indicative of generational differences in teacher education and the construction of what it means to teach (see Chapter 3). It may also stem partly from the contemporary turn towards an outcomes-related notion of what counts as effectiveness in schools (Bottery 2000). This version of effectiveness works within a disciplinary infrastructure of targets, benchmarks, league tables, averages and inspections that work to overwhelm or displace values and principles, and to subvert social relations.

> Until our (current) head took over, we spent our whole time at this school responding to policy. If the government said jump, we asked how high every time and just did it without question. And I don't think we're doing that now... But, I think we've looked at what's out there and we are genuinely doing it with the best intentions here... But, you know, from the head's point of view... he has that top-down pressure, this is how you'll be judged and this is what will be published. And the same with the league tables and all those kind of things. I mean, he said quite openly to me, after giving me my results and differentials last year, he said 'Oh, but you know, as a head teacher, of course I want you here because you get the results and that's what I'm measured on'... there's always going to be tensions.
>
> (Laura, Teaching and Learning Coordinator, AST Social Sciences, George Eliot)

All this is not meant to suggest that teachers or head teachers are unprincipled or uncommitted, far from it. The overwhelming majority are concerned with the educational best interests of their students, and 'their' school, and, if somewhat narrowly defined at times, with good learning outcomes, and with creating a broad and positive school experience for the young people in their charge. Nonetheless, it is often the case that ethical–democratic concerns come into play only weakly over and against and within the interpretation and enactment of policy.

Intentions and designs

This book draws on an ESRC funded project, 'Policy enactments in the secondary school: theory and practice' (RES-062-23-1484), which was conducted between October 2008 and April 2011, and was designed to 'test' out and develop our ideas about policy enactments. The study had two main objectives, one theoretical (to develop a theory of policy enactment) and one empirical (a critical exploration of the enactment of three policies in 'similar but different' contexts). It focused on the following questions:

- How do different individuals and groups of actors interpret and enact policy in specific contexts of multiple policy demands given the resources available to them?
- How and in what ways do socio-cultural, historical and contextual factors affect the ways in which schools enact policies? And thus,
- How can differences between schools in the enactment of policies be explained?

These questions were addressed through case studies of four state secondary schools and a particular, but not exclusive, focus on three substantive policies. Such a design seemed manageable, doable and analytically effective. The policies selected for particular attention were: 1) personalised learning (PL); 2) performance demands or *standards* (specifically A–C targets in English and Mathematics GCSEs); and 3) behaviour management policies. None of these policies are simple and discrete; they are made up of sometimes convoluted sets of texts, regulations, exhortations, technologies and guidelines which have accumulated over a period of time. These three policies were chosen to represent specific kinds of policy differences such as: their national high profile; their specificity (particularly in terms of being target-related); their whole school or departmental focus; and their social, achievement or equity goals. We also sought to map these policies onto a more general audit of all those policies that were active in each of the case study schools, as noted above (Braun *et al.* 2010).

When we initially designed the project, personalised learning was a key piece of contemporary policy (Hartley 2007; Fielding 2008). It consisted of five components: assessment; teaching and learning; curriculum entitlement and choice; school organisation; and partnerships 'beyond the classroom' (DCSF 2010) but was also harnessed to the standards agenda. The intention was to raise standards by 'focusing teaching and learning on the aptitudes and interests of pupils and by removing any barriers to learning' (DCSF 2010). PL was thus a polyphonic, multiple policy agenda, or a 'big idea' for school reform. In some ways 'in practice', and subject to interpretation, PL in our schools was subsumed in and displaced by a more general policy thrust toward 'learning' and 'pupils learning and thinking skills' (PLTS). At the same time, and much more narrowly, performance-focused policies required schools to raise standards in literacy and numeracy and meet specified targets of five GCSE good passes including English and Mathematics as two of the five subjects (DfES 2005). In contrast again, our third policy focus, behaviour management (DfES 2005a; DCSF 2007) was a composite of texts and ideas addressed to and enacted by pastoral teachers and specialist assistants and other education workers in school (Bach *et al.* 2006). In selecting this as our third policy, we wanted to be able to explore the perspectives and actions of significant, but sometimes forgotten, groups of non-teacher policy enactors who work, often out of sight, in and out of school. Again we were interested in the way behaviour and standards were inter-related and inter-dependent in initiatives like 'Behaviour for Learning' (see Chapter 5). Our starting position was that across the three sets of policies, local authority personnel, advisors, consultants, head teachers and middle managers as well as teachers, learning mentors and teaching assistants and financial, technical and office staff as well as edu-business, would all play their part in the interpretation and enactment of policy in schools.

The case study schools and the data set: 'ordinary schools'

The decision to do case studies, and to do case studies in four English secondary schools, was carefully considered. We wondered whether we should interview a large number and wide range of teachers (a shorthand for adults working in schools) across a variety of types of schools, or ask our research questions in one large diverse school. Or should we explore our questions and interests in a wide range of contrasting schools? In the event, we decided that we could only satisfactorily and sensibly address our research questions by getting inside a small number of schools, and getting close to the policy process, over a long period of time (two years). Therefore, we needed an optimum and manageable number of schools and needed to establish a basis of comparison between schools by balancing similarities with differences. We felt that a set of very different schools occupying very different positions in the current policy environment (and to use the language of policy, 'outstanding', 'failing', 'coasting', etc.) would perhaps only throw up extremes of difference and peculiarities of circumstance. We felt that including schools with special characteristics – special schools, academies, faith or single sex schools – would throw primary emphasis on the mediating effects of those characteristics – something that remains to be seen in further work. We decided to opt for similarity and the middle ground, that is to work in four co-educational, non-denominational and non-selective secondary schools.

The underlying principle behind the selection of the schools was to find 'ordinary' schools which were not subject to any 'external' interventions as a result of 'under-performance' or, being 'star' schools, that may have enjoyed more than normal autonomy. The schools had to be moderately successful schools with a sound track record of academic achievement, performing at around the national average. They needed to have experienced and stable leadership during the period of the study. However, we did want a variety of locations (and different local authorities) which could be included as factors in policy work. Thus, the sample included Atwood School, a comprehensive school in central London; two schools in suburban education authorities, George Eliot School and Wesley School; and a fourth, Campion School, located in a smaller county town (see Appendix). Our intention was to work in schools that at least superficially seemed to be similar in many respects in order to explore, theoretically and empirically, our contention that policy responses are localised and may well become worked out differently even in schools that seem to have much in common (Maguire *et al.* 2011) although we were alert to patterns across and convergences between the schools – and there was plenty of this, especially in relation to 'standards' policy work (see Chapter 4).

Our data

Over the two-and-a-half-year period of the project we collected a wide range of contextualising data from each school. This included demographic information about: student intake; performance profiles; background and changes in the school over time; budgets; buildings and material resources; staffing demographics; staff turnover, etc. As we have already explained, we also 'audited' the range of policies in play in each school. Much of this information was collated from sources such as: Ofsted reports; school brochures; and in-depth interviews with head teachers and experienced members of the staff in each school. Documents were collected and analysed in relation to the specific policies that we were interested in, and we had access to the school intranets where many in-house policy documents were lodged. Other national policy documentation, outputs from local authorities and the case study schools including school documentation for internal use (teachers and support staff) and external use (parents, governors, inspectors, LEA staff) were also collected, although we were able to do much less analytical work on these than we had initially hoped. We also attended meetings where the targeted policies (and other emergent policies) were discussed and planned. We observed training and/or evaluation sessions in each school and attended staff briefings which occurred at the beginning and end of each school year and each term. Both provided further opportunities to speak with participants. We also collected planners, diaries and other ephemera and took photographs of the buildings and wall displays and posters in each school (see Chapter 6).

In addition, we conducted a series of semi-structured interviews with the head teachers; other senior managers, including the bursars or school managers; a range of classroom teachers (more and less experienced); union representatives; and support staff. In total, we conducted 95 interviews: 86 with in-school personnel and nine with 'outsiders' such as LA support partners and consultants. In previous policy studies, we have interviewed parents and students; they are significant policy actors. However, in this study, the focus was deliberately with those with some responsibility for and who were/ are legally accountable for enacting the specific policies that we identified for study. The interviews explored the ways in which policies were selected, interpreted and translated and 'how' they moved from the senior leadership team (SLT) (and elsewhere) into lesson planning and classroom activities and other aspects of school life. It could be argued that the study should have also attended to the classroom enactments of policy, and we did observe some classes. However, we chose to design the study and deploy our resources in different ways for two reasons. First, we did not see enactment as a 'moment', but rather as part of a process of interpretation that would be framed by institutional factors involving a range of actors. Second, we believed that it would be difficult and a rather different exercise to trace the playing out of the specifics of policy through the complexity of classroom events. A different kind of 'trajectory' analysis could do that. Overall, we collected and elicited an enormous volume of data. It sometimes seemed overwhelming and in our analysis work there are some materials to which we have paid less attention – with more time and money we could have done a lot more with what we have. The interview texts were excellently transcribed by Paul Laluvein and we stored and organised them on NVivo and we used the search, sort and count facilities frequently but did not do our analysis in NVivo.

Analysing and interpreting our data

Our theorising of policy enactments interweaves three constituent facets of policy work and the policy process – *the material, the interpretive and the discursive*. None of these we believe is on its own sufficient to capture, understand and represent enactment; all are necessary. Heuristically, to some extent, we privilege and separate out these facets in the different chapters, but, over-all, we attempt to hold them together in some sort of constructive tension. Accordingly, in analysing and interpreting our data sets we have drawn on a range of theoretical resources, including Foucault's work on discourse and governmentality (Foucault 1979), a little of Barthes' literary theory (Barthes 1970; Hall 1997), some actor–network theory (ANT) (Law 2008; Fenwick and Edwards 2010), earlier writing on the 'policy cycle' (Ball 1997), the more substantive work of Spillane (2004) and Supovitz and Weinbaum (2008) and some critical discourse analysis (Fairclough 1989); we did not use the latter as a form of systematic analysis. While policy texts are normally written to be authoritative and persuasive and are accretative and intertextual, in enact-ing these texts, policy actors may draw upon a variety of resources in making their 'readings' and interpretations. Individuals bring their own experiences, scepticisms and critiques to bear on what they see/read/are exposed to and will read policies from positions of their identities and subjectivities (Hall 1997); thus, enactments will be inflected by these different readings and are likely to diverge. Phillips *et al.* (2004: 637) argue in relation to policy texts that 'a substantial space exists within which agents can act self-interestedly and work toward discursive change in ways that privilege their interests and goals' but that may be too simple and too agentic. Some texts offer limited possibilities for interpretation. That is, they are 'readerly' in Barthes' terms. Others allow themselves to be subject to more active readings and reworkings, that involve a 'completion' or co-production of the text. These are 'writerly' texts, accord-ing to Barthes. In our approach, as will become evident, we were looking for and attending to examples of each sort of engagement with, and relation to, texts, both primary texts and secondary or recontextualising texts. We were also seeking to chart any discrepancies that might have arisen between 'readings' of texts by different policy actors as well as attending to the role of authoritative actors in producing pre-emptive 'readings'.

Critical discourse analysis, and specifically the work of Fairclough (1989; 2003), views 'language as a form of social practice' (1989: 20) and focuses on the ways social and political domination is reproduced by text and talk. In this book, we attend, very superficially, to some aspects of the language of policy actors, their grammars and lexicons and their structures of argumentation as deployed within policy enactments. We also focus on the 'techniques and resources that are employed to create versions of reality' and policy presentation (Atkinson and Coffey 2004: 57) – in particular we explore the narrational work of head teachers as they seek to make disparate policy expectations coherent and render policies sensible, palatable and doable for their colleagues.

We also detail and describe some of the discursive artefacts and activities that make up, reflect and 'carry' within them key policy discourses that are currently in circulation in English schools, and in our four case study schools. This work draws on Foucault, who writes that discourses are 'the set of conditions in accordance with which a practice is exercised, in accordance with which that practice gives rise to partially or totally new statements, and in accordance with which it can be modified' (Foucault 1986: 208–209). We explore policies as discursive strategies; for example, sets of texts, events, artefacts and practices that speak to wider social processes of schooling such as the production of 'the student', the 'purpose of schooling' and the construction of 'the teacher'. That is, what counts as school is made up of 'groups of statements' (Foucault 1986: 125) that constitute the discursive formation of the 'school'. However, this is not a totalising phenomenon, there is a fragility in all this; discursive formations are characterised by 'gaps, voids, absences, limits and divisions' (Foucault 1986: 119). We also use Foucault's work on disciplinary power to explore both the ways in which teachers and students are subject to the rigours of visibility and how they are constituted as productive subjects within the mundane and polymorphous techniques and apparatuses of policy and the logics of 'improvement'. Actor–network theory (ANT) has also been useful with its emphasis on 'translation' and 'accomplishment' (Timmermans and Berg 1997), and its attention to 'discretionary' practice and the place and role of objects within networks of practice. Law's (2008) admonition that there are no orders, but always 'ordering' and therefore always precariousness has also proved important – but we are not full subscribers to ANT by any means.

Reading this book

We began this chapter by acknowledging the difficulties and challenges of a collaborative writing project. In the process of 'doing' this book, our plans and planning and 'thinking' are changing, and will be changed further. Writing is part of the process of analysis in qualitative research. Writing began early around the process of coding, and the production of research memos and code-notes, but remained open to change right up the typing of the last word of the manuscript. Both the analysis work and the writing are the outcome of negotiations, argument and compromises within the team, indeed these words are being 'over-written' by us all on the original text of another, which was subject to several previous revisions, a process that will continue with each chapter – both analysis and writing, we think, are better as a result but are always a compromise and always constrained by lack of time and space. Nonetheless, perhaps 'the most important part of a story is the piece of it you don't know' (Kingsolver 2009: 652). There is much more to the research process than ever gets onto the pages of articles and books. Our work has been full of loose ends, omissions and false trails. It has been punctuated by buts and maybes, by avoidance and considerable perplexity. It has been untidy and sometimes frustrating and we have not always managed to write what it was we were trying to think.

The chapters that follow do not have to be read in a particular sequence – although we are going to try to draw our main points together in the final chapter. To describe each chapter in more detail: Chapter 1 provides some start at explaining the major themes of this book, our intentions, our approach to understanding policy enactments and our empirical work. Following on from some discussion of the *contextualisation* of policy enactments and contextual dependency, Chapter 2 deals with this in a more detailed and grounded manner. Chapter 3 looks at how policy work is understood, how meanings are extracted from policy texts and worked on in the school by a range of policy actors. Chapter 4 details and explores the ways in which the four schools construct, produce and even purchase various technologies of assessment in their drive to 'deliver' the standards agenda. Chapter 5 examines the ways in which schools attend to behaviour management in all its various formations. In Chapter 6 we describe policies as discursive strategies; for example, sets of texts, events and practices that speak to wider social processes of schooling such as the production of 'the student', the 'purpose of schooling' and the construction of 'the teacher'. Through exploring some of the schools' artefacts, we consider how processes of policy enactments are visually constructed and circulated in the everyday world of the school. In Chapter 7 we relate together the main elements of our analysis into a very tentative synthesis or model and we place the contemporary policy context into a general framework of schooling discourses. We also specify the limitations of our analysis. In these chapters, while there is an explication of policy and a focus on a small number of substantive policies, our major concern is with understanding the 'how' and 'what' of policy enactment, not the policies themselves. Our analysis traces and examines 'interpretations of interpretations of interpretations', that is, what different policy actors, with differential power/knowledges/allegiances and commitments actually 'do' in schools with different strands of, and pieces of, education policy, in circumstances often not of their own choosing. We are interested in all of those elements that 'make up' policy enactments.

As writers, we are involved in an iterative process of interrogating 'meanings' and symbols, and their ongoing modification, and interpreting interpretations. While we will be attempting this through a meld of reflexive ethnography, theory-testing and mindfulness for those we have worked with (in schools and in our own team), nevertheless, and always, 'we need continually to interrogate and find strange the process of representation as we engage in it' (Woolgar 1988: 28–29 cited in Grenfell and James *et al.* 1998: 124). Despite our sense that we have achieved something useful here we are also left with feelings of dissatisfaction – that we could have elicited more data, that we could have done more coding and recoding of data, that there were other themes and issues we did not have the time or space to explore properly, that other forms of analysis and interpretative resources could have been deployed. Perhaps we can say that what we have is good enough, so far, and that there is plenty here to serve as a basis for further work. We hope the book will be read, if we can use Foucault's term, as an 'open site', that is, as posing questions and problems, the clearing away of a new space for investigation, rather than as a set of definitive statements.

2   Taking context seriously

In this chapter we want to take context seriously. That contextual dimensions are important in education policy enactment is a truism in government as well as in academic circles. Nevertheless, in much policy making and research the fact that policies are intimately shaped and influenced by school-specific factors which act as constraints, pressures and enablers of policy enactments tends to be neglected. Policies enter different resource environments; schools have particular histories, buildings and infrastructures, staffing profiles, leadership experiences, budgetary situations and teaching and learning challenges (e.g. proportions of children with special educational needs (SEN), English as an additional language (EAL), behavioural difficulties, 'disabilities' and social and economic 'deprivations') and the demands of context interact. Schools differ in their student intake, school ethos and culture, they engage with local authorities and experience pressures from league tables and judgements made by national bodies such as Ofsted. In outlining a theory of policy enactment we want to take these factors seriously and in this chapter we are offering a typology derived from our data analysis that systematically collates and maps different aspects of context. Under the headings of situated contexts, professional cultures, material and external contexts we will examine the role of context in shaping policy enactments. In this way, we attempt to offer a framework through which to incorporate these contextual concerns into educational policy analysis, not as a comprehensive model, but as a heuristic device to encourage investigation and questioning and to illuminate frequently sidelined aspects of policy enactment.

Locating policy processes

Policy creates context, but context also precedes policy. Even in superficially 'similar' schools, as with our sample, the 'nuances of local context [can] cumulatively make a considerable difference to school processes and student achievement' (Thrupp and Lupton 2006: 309). Lupton (2004), in a study of four 'disadvantaged' schools in England which considered variables of student intake, school and area characteristics, calls for 'contextualised policy responses' that avoid generic measures and are not just adapted for all so-called disadvantaged areas, but are also sensitive to differences between and within these areas. Studies that foreground contexts in this way are surprisingly rare in education and policy studies. Whilst a concern with context is central to, for example, social anthropology (Dilley 1999), in educational research 'context has often appeared, if at all, as a general background which functions to set the scene so that the real drama can unfold in the subsequent account of particular people and events' (Gilbert 1992: 39). Research texts in education policy rarely convey any sense of the built environment from which the 'data' are elicited or the financial or human resources available – policy is dematerialised.

Some school improvement and school effectiveness research has always been concerned with some aspect of the wider community and family contexts of schools (for example, Rutter *et al.*'s 1979 study 'Fifteen Thousand Hours') but the focus of this literature is predominantly on outcomes. Only recently has there been a greater concern with examining the interplay of organisational practices with contextual variables. For example, Gillies *et al.* (2010: 21) in a study on learner engagement describe how, during the course of their research, they felt an increasing need to comprehend and analyse particular local contexts and thus move away from a 'static focus on learners' individual character traits to a more dynamic formulation which took account of context, environment and social interactions'. In the case study school discussed in their article, they identified a clash between the students' home/community culture and that of the school/schooling. The researchers examined the school's response in dealing with this, which was to build up students' cultural capital so that they could cope with and succeed in an education and economic system that differed markedly from their community culture. The school's attempts to transform rather than engage with the cultural assets their students bring were at the centre of the paper by Gillies *et al.* (2010). Their findings underline Thrupp and Lupton's (2006) observation that there still tends to be much more focus on differences between schools in terms of organisation and practice (aspects such as leadership and pedagogy), than on diverse 'external' contexts and indeed context is conceived of as solely made up of socio-cultural factors. Acknowledging the significance of context demands greater social complexity of analysis and the need to recognise that 'effective management and teaching in one context is not the same as effective management and teaching in another' (Thrupp and Lupton 2006: 312).

Thrupp and Lupton (2011) are unusual in considering contextual aspects in their analysis. On the whole, even nuanced studies such as Lupton's (2004) rarely mention some of the most 'material' of contexts – the buildings and budgets, available technologies and local infrastructures. Addressing these concerns, in this chapter we mean to provide a grounded account of the diverse variables and factors (the 'what'), as well as the dynamics of context (the 'how') that shape policy enactments and thus relate together and theorise interpretative, material and contextual dimensions of the policy process.

The importance of context

As argued earlier, policies are enacted in material conditions, with varying resources, in relation to particular 'problems'. Policies – new and old – are set against and alongside existing commitments, values and forms of experience. In other words, a framework for policy enactments will need to consider a set of objective conditions in relation to a set of subjective 'interpretational' dynamics. Thus, the material, structural and relational need to be incorporated into policy analysis in order to make better sense of policy enactments at the institutional level. In what follows, we will be using data from our case study research in the four schools to explore these dynamics of context and their inter-relationships. We are conceptualising and grouping these as *situated contexts, professional cultures, material* and *external* contexts (see Box 2.1 below) but these aspects can overlap and are inter-connected. For example, school intake is presented as 'situated', but intake in turn can shape professional factors such as values, teacher commitments and experiences, as well as 'policy management'.

Contextual dimensions:

- **situated contexts** (e.g. locale, school histories and intakes)
- **professional cultures** (e.g. values, teacher commitments and experiences, and 'policy management' in schools)
- **material contexts** (e.g. staffing, budget, buildings, technology and infrastructure)
- **external contexts** (e.g. degree and quality of LA support; pressures and expectations from broader policy context, such as Ofsted ratings, league table positions, legal requirements and responsibilities).

Box 2.1 Contextual dimensions of policy enactment

Situated contexts

Situated factors refer to those aspects of context that are historically and locationally linked to the school, such as a school's setting, its history and intake. Location and intake are of course inter-related. Our inner city case study school (Atwood), for example, has a multi-ethnic, socially mixed student body that reflects the diversity of its catchment area. One of the outer London schools (George Eliot) is located in an area where students of 'South Asian' heritage make up the majority of the school's student population. The other suburban school (Wesley) is ethnically more diverse, but in this case locality shapes intake in relation to other nearby schools that are perceived to be academically 'stronger', casting our school as a destination for the 'less academic' children in the area. The school in the county town (Campion) is located in a mainly white, lower middle and 'respectable' working class (Vincent *et al.* 2008) neighbourhood and this is reflected in its student intake. The four schools are all in some way 'typical' for their locality with regards to poverty levels. Taking the proportions of students on free school meals (FSM) as a proxy for poverty, the FSM percentages in the two suburban schools (George Eliot and Wesley) are broadly in line with the national average.[1] In Campion, the county school, FSM is lower than average and in Atwood, the inner city case study school, the percentage of FSM students is roughly twice the national average.

Throughout the fieldwork, in both interviews and during observations, there was a frequent voicing of sentiments that referred to 'students like ours'. Schools can become defined by their intake, but they also define themselves by it. Members of school communities, including teachers, construct stories about their school that are based on their own experiences but also on some broader generalisations. For George Eliot, the story of a predominantly 'South Asian' intake has been linked to its specialism (business and enterprise), with the senior leadership team (SLT) arguing that this 'tailors the curriculum offer to what the parents and students of this community want' (Justin, deputy head teacher, SLT, George Eliot). They also offered specific English GCSE interventions for second-generation EAL students:

> I think there are some English as an Additional Language issues, which is not because a lot of – most students are second generation [...] It's more in the way they write, particularly if they're speaking at home other languages, it's maybe the style of their writing or some of the ways the grammar and the ways things are expressed, I think there are issues there that we need to – we are tailoring our interventions to and our literacy lessons.
>
> (Justin, deputy head teacher, SLT, George Eliot)

There were other activities that took account of perceived student preferences or needs but also stereotyped the student body ('[O]ur kids love sport [...] they're cricket crazy, rounders, which is a reflection of the intake' (Rachael, head of PE, George Eliot). In addition, these 'internal' perceptions were reinforced by messages from the 'outside'. Following an Ofsted inspection which commented that female students – and given the predominant composition of the school, 'Asian' female students – did not participate enough in class activities, the school was looking into measures to raise levels of what they (and Ofsted) would see as 'active' involvement:

> I'm looking at group work within schools and how to... how to improve group work [...] because in our school, one of the things that Ofsted raised was the fact that we've got – some of our female students they don't involve themselves in lessons as much. So they're like ghosts or shadows, they're there but they're not necessarily actually actively involved in discussions, group work and so on.
>
> (Aabid, joint head teacher, Social Sciences, George Eliot)

I'm really glad that Ofsted picked up on this although probably a high proportion of our girls are Gifted and Talented [...] they just need some balls because they live in, I would argue a male dominated society.

(Laura, Teaching and Learning Coordinator, AST Social Sciences, George Eliot)

Feminist academics have expressed concerns about a recent, apparently uncontested, re-emergence of gender stereotyping as an accepted aspect of pedagogy (Youdell 2006; Skelton and Francis 2009) and there have been other criticisms of the representation of 'Asian' students as timid (Connolly 1998; Skelton and Francis 2003). More broadly, there is a problem with collapsing and essentialising ethnic identity categories in this way (e.g. Bonnett and Carrington 2000; Gewirtz and Cribb 2008). At the same time, George Eliot's response described above is understandable; it is hard to see how schools could distance themselves from the imperatives of powerful audit systems like Ofsted.

Another of our case study schools – Campion – has developed an institutional narrative that centres around its intake being comprised of white, working class students from relatively well-off family backgrounds who are not academically motivated:

I think it's a funny school. [...] I don't think we have the, sort of, extremes of poverty that you get in even other schools in [the town]. I think [other nearby schools] would tell you that they have much poorer kids, much more ethnically diverse [...]. But I think we have a strange sort of middle class affluence that's actually largely not based around academic success. And I think culturally that's created quite an interesting sort of melting pot, that we have, you know, plumbers' sons, for example, and things like that, builders' sons. Pretty affluent, they don't lack for anything these kids, they've all got mobile phones, they've all got iPods, they've all got PSPs [portable play stations] [...] they don't want for much these kids, I don't think, the majority of them. There's some definite exceptions to that rule but on the whole I think we're a, sort of, pretty lower middle class comprehensive. But, like I say, I don't think most of their parents' success has been built around academic success so I don't think there's a culture of needing – seeing the necessity to succeed at school to be successful.

(Gareth, deputy head of sixth form, History, Campion)

One of the assistant heads, Fiona, echoes this understanding of the school's students and their parents:

[T]here's a lot more students would like to go out and do some sort of vocational qualification. Again, that's the area that we're in, you know, our parents want their children to learn a trade. That's where they see the money, you know, you're skilled, you can go out, you can get a trade and that's it. So all of our parents are pushing for the students to go to college.

What I'm actually saying to them now is it's a lesser qualification than you can get at school. You can go on to the next level straightaway and then… The simplest way I put it to our students is: the more qualifications, the more money you demand. Take that certificate to your employer and they'll pay you these sort of pennies. So, that's how our kids communicate.

(Fiona, assistant head teacher, PE, Campion)

Campion is perhaps the school in our sample that is struggling hardest to keep within national averages for its GCSE results and it is investing enormous amounts of effort and resources into policy interventions and innovations aimed at boosting performance (see Braun *et al.* 2010). These efforts notwithstanding, results remain stubbornly modest. Teachers' disappointment at this lack of progress is palpable ('I mean, we're working our socks off, we're one of the hardest working schools around the area, but how is it that other schools are doing far better results-wise than we are?' – Anjali, Key Stage 4 manager, Campion). One way of coping with such frustrations is to seek explanations that are external to the school – the characteristics of the intake – and so Anjali concludes that even though there is a culture within the school that strongly emphasises helping students to succeed, 'It's just we don't have enough [students] coming to us [asking for help].' The social demographic here is both a 'real' factor in relation to performance outcomes *and* a way of accounting for these outcomes.

These examples drawn from two of the case study schools are not intended to be critical of the schools for stereotyping their students; rather, we intend to illustrate that context is an 'active' force, it is not just a backdrop against which schools have to operate. Context initiates and activates policy processes and choices which are continuously constructed and developed, both from within and without, in relation to policy imperatives and expectations. It leads to certain patterns of emphasis and de-emphasis, in the simple sense of choice of specialisms, for example – business at George Eliot and sport at Campion – but also the particular attention, for different reasons, given to girls at George Eliot and Atwood.

School intake 'drives' results (Gibson and Asthana 1998) and, as such, the 'policy eye' of schools is inevitably trained on the challenges – and opportunities – their student intakes pose. Within schools, there is much talk of the practical challenges that come with their location and subsequent intake. Below, one of the local authority advisors for Wesley relays a conversation she has had with the head teacher, Philip, on numerous occasions. The school is geographically close to another local authority whose schools are perceived as less 'good' than schools in Wesley's borough. Statutory admissions policies require local authorities and schools to give students with special educational needs priority consideration when allocating school places and as a consequence, Wesley has a high number of out-of-borough students with SEN applying for a place:

Annette: Would you still say there are particular problems that the school is facing, something you can talk about?

Diane: They would always perceive as the challenges of their intake, so I know Philip speaks to me sometimes about the fact that the number of statemented children they take, particularly because they're on the edge of [neighbouring borough]. So, a lot of [out-of-borough] parents will choose Wesley because it's a good school compared with [their local] schools. So, he'll then say, 'But look what I get!' I understand, you know, I think that's a legitimate point. You can't duck it. And some of their special needs children and parents need some very high maintenance support.

(Diane, LA advisor, behaviour, Wesley)

On the other hand, geographic location can be seen to offer opportunities and advantages to a school. Atwood, our inner city case study school, has a socially mixed catchment area and a specific student intake which holds centre stage within the school's story of itself:

And that's the great thing about this school is that you do get a proper mix and you get, to a greater or lesser degree, proper acceptance of huge chunks of different demographics. Like we have middle class, lefty parents who send their children to the one comprehensive in the area that doesn't make them wear uniform. And we have, you know, proper very deprived estate kids, and everyone in between.

(Beth, HoY 7, English, Atwood)

However, over and against this 'comprehensive' story, in this situated context, attracting and retaining middle class students has become one of the informal policy drivers at Atwood and something members of the SLT are keenly aware of:

It's the management that are, kind of more concerned about what the figure says and they worry about, you know, what kind of... There's a real drive in our school to attract middle class parents. [...] You know, obviously linked to the league tables. And therefore they do worry about the image of the school.

(Joe, head of Sociology, Atwood)

Managing the school's intake, so that it continues to be seen as an asset by the 'lefty' middle class parents mentioned by Beth (above) shapes a whole variety of policy activities within the school. The maintenance of middle class density is a complex, ongoing pressure for schools like Atwood (Reay *et al*. 2011). For example, when a breakdown of the school's exam results showed girls from more middle class backgrounds were 'underachieving' compared to their predicted grades, a girls' group was set up specifically targeting this set of students. The aim was to foster self-esteem and raise enjoyment of school for the participants and efforts were made to get teachers to be more aware of the participation of these girls in their lessons: efforts which also signal to (middle class) parents that they have made the 'right' decision to send their children to the school and that girls are expected by the school to do well academically.

School histories, and bound up in this their reputations, are aspects of context that are 'alive' within the collective consciousness of schools. In Wesley, a 'blip' in behaviour standards among some students around ten years ago has had serious effects on the way the school has been perceived within the local community ever since. The school is still fighting against this negative and by now outdated reputation:

> Now then, standing in the community, I mean, sadly that's worse now than it was. So I think, you know, in many ways our kids are more focused, the quality of staff is better, statistically speaking, you know, the results are [better] [...]. But, in spite of that, the standing in the local community, it's not as high now as it was twenty years ago. [...] We hit a bit of a rough patch, between about six and ten years ago, the school lost its way a bit. And the behaviour, whilst it was never bad, it did deteriorate. And in those days, we let our kids go out at lunchtime and there was a few incidents on the high street. And I think, yeah, you know, that helped to lessen our standing in the local community.
>
> (James, assistant head teacher, Social Science, Politics, Wesley)

Wesley's policy response was to forbid students to leave the school during the lunch hour. They have also introduced increasingly strict uniform requirements, for example, sixth form students are required to wear 'business suits'.

From the discussion so far, we can already observe inter-relationships and movement between different aspects of context. There are intersections of external policy drivers (schools' reputations and competition with other schools) with internal factors and institutional policy dynamics and foci, and between policy 'values' and the 'valuing' of and attention given to different sorts of students.

Professional cultures

Professional cultures refers to somewhat less tangible variables than those described above. We are interested here in examining ethos, teachers' values and commitments within schools, asking whether and how they shape policy enactments. We should point out that within this chapter, we will not be looking at leadership and leaders within the school but aspects of these dynamics will be picked up in later chapters. Other policy theorists often emphasise the role of leadership (e.g. Spillane 2004) and we write, for example, about the role of 'policy entrepreneurs' in shaping schools' policy responses in Chapter 3. However, in this section we are attempting to cast a wider net in emphasising professional cultures more broadly.

Most schools have distinct sets of professional cultures, outlooks and attitudes that have evolved over time and that inflect policy responses in particular ways. Atwood is a good example of a school with a particular self-understanding that sets it apart from other, outwardly 'similar', secondary schools in our study. In the interview extract below, a Future Leader[2] with a residency at the school explains her perception of the school's ethos and culture and how this influences uniform and behaviour policy:

> And I think [Atwood] really prides itself [inaudible] the governors and parents on this freedom of expression that it has as a school. So linking into the arts college but also parents, governors, really proud of the fact that, you know, kids do wear non-uniform, they do have the chance to express themselves, they don't see it as a traditional school and they – and people seem quite resistant to the idea of it ever becoming more of a uniformed establishment. It's – but I think with that, again from an outsider's point of view, sometimes I think there's an element of too much freedom in that, where do you draw the line then when it comes to behaviour and where are your boundaries? And I think that's where sometimes the policies seem to fall down a little bit.
>
> (Heather, Future Leader (English), Atwood)

As we can see, again there are relationships here between educational values and philosophy, intake and what and how policies are pursued. These relations are not always smooth. There can be potential dissonances between embedded institutional values and national policy trends, such as the recent emphasis by government on uniform in schools (DCSF 2007a; DfE 2010). However, the extract also illustrates that professional cultures are not necessarily coherent nor do they go uncontested within schools. For example, Heather (above), in contrast to many of her colleagues, would welcome uniform and greater emphasis on discipline over freedom of expression at Atwood. In another example, Paul, a head of department at Wesley, was critical of his head teacher's alleged failure to acknowledge the increased diversity of the student body and he wished for a policy response that emphasised cultural diversity and inclusion:

> The other issue is about things like bringing in and building an identity of the school. And also recognising the different identities within the school. So, for example, the head will get hung up about black boys' achievement but he won't necessarily focus on things like the multicultural aspect of the school or recognising that there are students who are from different cultures and different faiths, and so on and whatever, and actually highlight that and make a more inclusive school in that way.
>
> (Paul, head of English, Wesley)

Policy actors are always positioned; how policies are seen and understood is dependent on 'where' we are figuratively and literally. An obvious contrast would be to compare a member of the leadership team with a newly qualified teacher (NQT). Few policies have relevance to everyone and it was striking – although not unexpected – that the NQTs in our case study schools generally reported department-centred understanding of policy (see also Chapter 3). As newly qualified teachers, Trevor and Molly (below) work towards implementing policies by following procedures whose contexts, origins or trajectories they might be unaware of. When referring to context, one may assume that this refers to the whole school, yet departments can operate, at least some of the time, as fairly autonomous units. New teachers or teachers in large departments may work with reference mainly to their immediate colleagues, departmental contexts and local policies and may have little or no sense of the 'bigger' policy picture, 'I mean, the Maths department has quite good policies [around behaviour] but they are departmental rather than school-wide' (Trevor, NQT Mathematics, Atwood).

> [*Talking about the school's curriculum changes*] We've not done anything in INSET day, although what they've done prior to me coming I'm not quite sure. I know [the] Key Stage 3 leader, she's, sort of, more heavily involved in implementing that. I've not really had much training myself but these new, sort of, we do these core outcomes at the end of each scheme of work.
>
> (Molly, GTP English, Campion)

Sometimes frames of reference can be even more pragmatic (and arbitrary). In the case of part-time teachers, for example, which days of the week a teacher is working may determine whether they get hold of policy information or not. Naomi, who teaches part time at Atwood, reckons that the fact that she is working the earlier part of the week means she knows more about new policies and policy changes than her part-time colleagues working on other days:

> I think if Monday wasn't my day in school, I probably wouldn't, because, actually, because Monday tends to be INSET day [...] and then later on Monday briefing – we have a staff briefing every Monday. [...] I think a couple of other part-time teachers who do later in the week, Wednesdays and Fridays, say that they find out less because it's the head of department's responsibility to pass it all on. [...] And, obviously, heads of department are under a lot of pressure, time, so...
>
> (Naomi, RE, Atwood)

Policy information is passed on via departmental reporting lines and, as Naomi observes, given the impact of time pressure and competing priorities on middle managers and heads of departments in schools, such information can get truncated or simply forgotten about. Teachers make sense of their practice in institutional, departmental and year team contexts, all of which refract policy and offer readings of policy, sometimes differently, towards different ends. New teachers also bring their training experiences to bear and experienced teachers bring their history of work in previous schools. Professional contexts are multi-faceted and muddled. Such tangible yet random factors lead to our next area of context exploration, material factors and their impact and influence in shaping policy enactments.

Material contexts

Material context refers to the 'physical' aspects of a school: buildings and budgets, but also to levels of staffing, information technologies and infrastructure. Buildings, their layout, quality and spaciousness (or not) can have considerable impact on policy enactments. One of the messages from the preceding section is that schools are not of a piece; equally, the actual 'pieces' of a school can function, look and be equipped very differently. Schools operating across two sites, for example, may well have different capacities for enactment in each setting. Campion teaches its sixth-formers at a separate site around the corner from the main school building and the physical distance means that many policy programmes that the school pursues can become neglected in the second campus location:

> [W]e don't have a very strong SLT presence down here [at the sixth form centre]. In fact we barely have one at all, and so all the things that are being focused on the main site, you know, so there's one member of SLT who's chasing up who's doing their homework, there's another one who's chasing up, you know, teaching and learning, Assessment for Learning. We don't have those pressures down here. And, of course, you know, what that means is I think people are feeling under a lot of pressure to do the right things up there and they come down here and it's a bit of a kind of, 'Right, I don't have to put my learning objectives up because I'm down the sixth form and no one's going to come in and see that they're not up there' or, 'I don't need to worry about setting that homework', you know.
>
> (Gareth, deputy head of sixth form, History, Campion)

When it comes to buildings, our four case study schools operate in very different physical contexts. George Eliot has been recently rebuilt under the Building Schools for the Future[3] (BSF) program with PFI[4] (Private Finance Initiative) funding, with all the advantages and drawbacks that come with a new design and build. The other three schools operate with an eclectic mix of older and newer buildings.

As a newly built school, George Eliot has very good internet and computer access throughout and it is the school in our sample which perhaps makes the most extensive use of VLEs (virtual learning environments) in supporting both teachers' and students' work. (As classroom practice was not a focus of the study, our information on the use of technology in teaching and learning and as an aspect of pedagogy is limited and we have to rely on teachers' accounts in these matters.) George Eliot is arranged in several separate buildings over a generous area. Whilst this allows, for example, the art block to put their distinctive stamp on 'their' building, it also means that there is less interaction with colleagues from other departments. Central features, such as a shared staff room, are used less often. There are extensive security, surveillance and electronic access arrangements throughout:

> We're probably more concerned with making sure that this site is fit for purpose and building our all-weather canopy and making sure we've got security gates and... that the environment is safe and is conducive to learning for the students.
>
> (Owen, deputy head teacher, George Eliot)

These features are designed to increase students' safety – the statutory responsibility of schools and other public agencies working with children to keep them from harm and protect them from neglect (www.safeguardingchildren. org.uk) – but can also create an overall impression of a very controlled, even policed, environment. Management of the PFI contract is a material policy context that schools under the BSF scheme have to deal with, as Owen, the school's SLT member in charge of managing and liaising with the contractor explains:

> [I]t's a big mistake, I think, for schools to think they can manage a PFI without devoting considerable resources to it. You can't suddenly think, well, that's not my problem any more, facilities management is now down to them, because, you know, we spend just as much time as we used to, I think.
>
> (Owen, deputy head teacher, George Eliot)

The contract under which the school leases the building means that the leadership team has lost some decision-making capacity and this can have knock-on effects on policy decisions when, for example, the school can no longer decide to make or delay an investment:

> Yeah, it's a bit like renting a hotel room, you know, we now rent the school from somebody else, we don't own it as such. [...] So, for instance, if they decide that this carpet in this office is worn before they've life-cycled it, they will say that maybe we've misused it and we need to pay to have it replaced. But we don't have a decision to say, well, actually, we quite – we're going to have to live with that awful carpet for another couple of years because we can't afford to replace it. They can make us.
>
> (Owen, deputy head teacher, George Eliot)

Whilst the tying up of a senior leadership member like Owen in handling the ongoing procedures of the PFI contract is a hidden cost of the arrangement, building management in the other case study schools is not cost or time free either. Campion's 1960s buildings require constant vigilance and time-investment by the bursar and the head teacher and present serious problems of wear and tear with its associated repair and energy costs. These have to be offset against spending on staff or classroom material or ICT:

> We had a health and safety report and all the hinges on the windows had gone, which in themselves isn't a problem but you need scaffolding and it cost 180K to do it all. We did the main block and we painted it all. We did the painting and did all the panels, cleaned them up, and that took all our reserves, otherwise we would have plenty of reserves.
>
> (Terry, bursar, Campion)

> I mean, we haven't got enough money to maintain the buildings as we'd like, particularly the interiors. The classrooms are all now coming to the end of their life, like the carpets and tables and chairs all need replacing. And that's quite expensive, by the time you do carpets and whatever. Also the driveway, I don't know if you've noticed, it's all potholed. And… that will cost the best part of 100K they reckon.
>
> (Terry, bursar, Campion)

Policy initiatives related to school funding can shape investment decisions in unexpected ways, so that, in particular, capital spending becomes less about priorities and more about opportunities. Staying with Campion, for example, a decision to build a new sports hall was made when the school was able to secure two tranches of substantial external/government money: funds from the specialist schools sports trust (amounting to almost 60 per cent of the overall cost) which at the time had a high profile due to the upcoming Olympic games, and a smaller tranche of funding from the local authority. In this way, the school only had to contribute around a quarter of the half a million pound project:

> We had reserves and the governor, chair of governors and the head decided to use the reserves to build the sports hall. We felt as a school that it was such a good opportunity, bearing in mind that the majority of it was being funded from outside sources to go ahead and do that even though it depleted our reserves to twenty/thirty thousand.
>
> (Terry, bursar, Campion)

These types of funding and spending decisions inevitably lead to uneven outcomes across individual schools, as the Campion bursar put it: 'And that's not gone down, necessarily, well with some of the faculties because they feel that sports are getting the money and money's not being spent on them' (Terry, bursar, Campion). Equally, some buildings at Atwood and Wesley pose problems with old fixtures and facilities, as well as overcrowding. Wesley, for example, has a science block that is outmoded and in poor repair, but it also has a newly built dance studio and a big theatre, so different areas of the school offer learning environments of widely different quality:

> Alisa: We've got particular problems in science though because the
>   whole building is falling down, so they're going to replace the
>   roof but we're not so certain they're going to replace what's
>   underneath it, which really needs to go as well, but, yeah…
>
> Stephen: Maybe they should get somebody to blow it up.
>
> Alisa: We, yeah, we have joked about that.
>
> (Alisa, school business manager, Wesley)

Overall, Wesley has a capacity problem which has knock-on effects on teaching and learning. Whilst schools will always endeavour to provide their basic or standard offering, buildings and their limitations can seriously impede a school's capacity for innovation, as Alisa, the school business manager, explains:

> In terms of the fabric of the building [...] this part of the building was built in 1924 and then it goes around so it's kind of, you know, sixties/seventies, etc. But that is one of our biggest constraints. We are at maximum capacity, really. We are looking at the moment, depending on if we have any money left over, if we could actually get another mobile classroom. We've got two – well, I call them mobiles, they're not mobile, they're permanent now – classrooms there [*points out direction*] so, I mean, that certainly does limit in terms of generally the timetable. In terms of teaching and learning activities, money determines so much of that in terms of any additional activities that are over and above the, kind of, normal departmental requirements.
>
> (Alisa, school business manager, Wesley)

Sometimes, low tech, small investments can make a considerable difference to learning environments. Alisa gives the example of Wesley having started to put up curtains in some of the classrooms, which has greatly improved students' ability to follow work on electronic whiteboards, a problem which is also encountered in some of the classrooms at Campion:

> [J]ust something very simple that has a big impact is curtains. So, for example, the last two to three years we've actually looked at replacing curtains and actually having curtains in some classrooms. And it's amazing because it makes such a difference because the children can now actually see the board.
>
> (Alisa, school business manager, Wesley)

In Atwood, narrow staircases and corridors present problems for students entering and moving around the school, which, in turn, can have knock-on effects on behaviour management. The head teacher even described his building as not fit for purpose:

> [T]he building is basically almost a health and safety hazard because it's drastically overcrowded in terms of movement. You wouldn't think so looking here but in terms of movement around the building it's just not fit for purpose.
>
> (Ken, head teacher, Atwood)

Atwood was due to be rebuilt under the Building Schools for the Future programme with building work set to begin in the academic year 2010–11. Consequently, during our fieldwork period, there was frequent talk about the planning, design and development of the new building. Thinking about building design and school organisation also brought with it reflection about policy implications and the physical spaces for pursuing (or not pursuing) certain policies:

> [The BSF plan is] in two key areas it's moving us forward. It's driving a discussion on vertical school organisation and the notion of stage not age and what the implication of that is [...] it complements a more Personalised Learning and Thinking Skills emphasis. Or whether, in fact, it's going to pull things [...] apart if you go too radically with it, with the cross-curriculum skills agenda. So, those debates really have moved forward within the school. BSF in some ways has been a very useful driver of that.
>
> (Ken, head teacher, Atwood)

As it happened, Atwood was one of the 700 schools already signed up to the BFI scheme whose planned building projects did not go ahead when the new Coalition government announced the discontinuation of the programme in July 2010 (*Guardian* 2010) and the school will have to work with (and within) its present buildings for some time to come. In general, schools and teachers have to work within the constraints that buildings impose on them. Atwood has introduced a 'one-way-system' for some of the staircases, for example, and teachers adapt and improvise, as Gillian (NQT Science, Atwood) comments, 'Well, generally I think they're meant to line up outside [classrooms] but, because my corridor's really thin and it goes round the corner, I bring them in, and that's fine.' In these different ways buildings and infrastructure join with human agents to 'do policy'. In the language of actor–network theory, 'they mediate, they translate and get other entities to take action' (Koyama 2010: 11) as 'human actor-mediators do not act alone' (Koyama 2010: 41).

Apart from the fabric and layout of the buildings, the ways schools are equipped internally impacts on teaching and learning activities and thus on policy enactments; these days, this is especially the case in relation to ICT provision. Computer and internet access may by now be a taken-for-granted aspect of schooling, but it is also a major, ongoing expense which is only partly offset by special funding:

> I think we've got about five hundred computers. [...] We do get funding in the Standards Fund every year, through Partners in Technology, but I think that's only about sixteen thousand pounds, which in terms of ICT expenditure is not a huge amount. [...] We're looking to replace our core network, it's going to cost us probably thirty thousand pounds in itself, without all the cabling. So, it doesn't really cover it. And obviously when you're buying whiteboards for classrooms, putting whiteboards in there, that's three thousand pounds a time, so sixteen thousand pounds doesn't really go very far.
>
> (Greg, bursar, Atwood)

School budgets are perhaps the most 'material' of all the contextual factors. While school funding is primarily calculated by student numbers, differences in school size, local authority subsidies and location (e.g. inner city versus county funding formulas) can produce considerable differences in overall budgets. As one of the SLT members at Wesley pointed out: 'If the school was a mile or two in that direction we would be on a totally different scale of finance because, you know, the inner London boroughs get so much more than we do' (Hazel, deputy head teacher, Science, Wesley). Across our case study schools, total annual incomes vary widely. George Eliot, for example, receives roughly twice the amount of money Campion does (£10 million versus £5 million). Whilst George Eliot has to provide for around 500 more students, economies of scale, as well as the decision to employ more non-teaching staff in roles that are held by teachers in other schools, mean that the school spends a significantly smaller proportion of its income on staff costs compared to Campion (78 per cent versus 83 per cent), which translates into an excess of around £500K a year. Schools' reserves also differed considerably across the four schools, with George Eliot holding by far the largest savings. Being able to draw on savings, as well as larger budget amounts not tied up in staff costs, has consequences related to the policy process. George Eliot, for example, regularly hires external facilitators from private education service companies for their INSET days and has been able to financially support a 'Thinking Skills' intervention programme in the school to a generous extent. The school freed up time for some of their most experienced and dedicated teachers to work on the programme and customise materials, posters and other artefacts with a particular take on 'Thinking Skills'. As Justin, one of the deputy heads put it: 'you have to brand things' to instil a common language in students and staff for a policy to embed itself in teaching and learning practices. These expenditures created a strategic and material focus for enactment which was not matched in any of the other schools.

There are also differences between schools in terms of their capacity to generate income. George Eliot, as a PFI school, is no longer able to benefit financially from any lettings. Atwood, on the other hand, benefits from a central location and is able to make a reasonable amount of money from its facilities:

> We take about a 100K a year in lettings. [...] The Astroturf, sports hall, dance studio, assembly hall, some of the classrooms. [...] And by the time we've took in provisions for the repairs and maintenance and utilities and overtime for our staff, it does come out to about 30K profit.
>
> (Greg, bursar, Atwood)

As we have already discussed, the key issue in budgetary terms is fixed costs and particularly staff salaries. Changes to the ways staff are deployed in schools have financial consequences and our case study schools have started experimenting with some changes. George Eliot, for example, has non-teachers in senior pastoral roles such as head of year positions. Such decisions might be justified from a certain pedagogical and pastoral perspective, but they are also a cheaper option than appointing a qualified, experienced teacher to the role. Atwood has only just started thinking of such innovations:

> I mean, we're in early stages of what we're doing with the staffing because we only really started looking at it now, but we're looking at various options, whether we can get [...] Higher Level Teaching Assistants, whether we can, sort of, develop them more and bring them into the classroom a bit more as well.
>
> (Greg, bursar, Atwood)

Staffing is of course not just a cost; the staff are, in the first – and last – instance, a school's main asset, as one of the deputies at George Eliot points out:

> And fifty – I mean, I keep saying – fifty interventions from the SLT, the leadership team, count for having one decent head of department. [...] And we've found that as soon as we appointed a good person in one area you can almost, sort of, you know, let it – it'll run itself.
>
> (Justin, deputy head teacher, SLT, George Eliot)

Attracting and keeping 'good' teachers and other staff was a main concern for all of the schools and a particular challenge in some subject areas. The head of mathematics at Wesley, for example, described how in spite of receiving over 50 applications for a position and having interviewed six initially promising candidates, she ended up not filling the post. She emphasised that in the past she felt pressure to appoint and this meant that she ended up with teachers who 'struggled and it's, you know, it's caused so many problems [...] it has actually been a hindrance rather than a help' (Raaida, head of Mathematics,

Wesley). Maths is a shortage subject in England and many schools have difficulties recruiting good teachers in this subject area, but other contextual factors such as geographic location, cost of housing for teachers and transport infrastructure can also impact on staffing and the calibre of applicants. One of our suburban case study schools, for instance, was poorly served by public transport but was still in an area affected by London rush hour traffic, making it a difficult school to get to – and thus harder to staff.

External contexts

The last contextual dimension we want to discuss in this chapter is what we have termed *external* contexts. Here we are thinking of aspects such as pressures and expectations generated by *wider* local and national policy frameworks such as Ofsted ratings, league table positions and legal requirements and responsibilities, as well as the degree and quality of local authority support and relationships with other schools. Ken, head teacher at Atwood, sums up the changes that external structures have brought to the teaching profession as follows: 'The combination of the national curriculum and an inspection structure to hold you accountable, and publication of league tables of course, has completely changed the way people think about their work.'

The pressures of Ofsted and exam results were mentioned by many interviewees throughout the fieldwork, this preoccupation reflecting the centrality of such performative and audit mechanisms in initiating and shaping particular enactments of policy (Perryman *et al.* 2011). Below, a Wesley SLT member recounts how a by now 'old' Ofsted report profoundly changed the school's practices and its self-perception:

> When I joined the school it was very clearly a 'coasting' school and it was very difficult to turn things around. We'd got a lot of established staff who were of the opinion that we were a good school. [...] We then had an Ofsted in [2002] [...] which came as an absolute shock to a lot of staff. [...] They couldn't believe that we weren't a good school, that we were [...] an underachieving school. And that was a, you know, it was a really good thing that we had that Ofsted report because it did challenge those perceptions, it did enable us to really start moving things forward.
> (Hazel, deputy head teacher, Science, Wesley)

League table positions, both locally and nationally, form a constant backdrop to policy accounts within the schools. Wesley, for example is located in a very high achieving local authority and there is constant comparison with surrounding schools. The reputation and performance of schools are 'made' locally; they are relational rather than absolute. Both have implications for the recruitment of students and staff, which in turn has income and cost implications. Again, 'non-human actants', such as reputation and performance, form part of the network of policy enactments:

The league tables: even though our results are by national standards above average they're below average for [the LA]. [The LA] over the past fifteen years or so has become a very high performing LA. [...] So, a very high performing borough. Our position in the borough, you know, it's bottom half of the league table, so I think that's had an adverse impact on us.

(James, assistant head teacher, Social Science, Politics, Wesley)

In policy terms, league table positions and local comparisons generate an extraordinary amount of activity (and anxiety) (see also Chapter 4), as this interview extract with an assistant head at Campion illustrates:

INSET days, twilight INSET, staff meetings. [...] The deputy head did a very good staff meeting last night talking about use of data, you know, AfL, APP, what's the difference, how do they merge, how are we going to take it forward as a school and so on. And he basically was just setting the scene about, you know, this is what we do, we're doing all of these things but within [the local authority] actually we're going down in the league tables rather than going up. Why is it, what are we doing? We're collecting this data, what are we doing with it?

(Fiona, assistant head teacher, PE, Campion)

In this circular calculation where exam results, local league table positions and national policies promoting parental choice combine to impact on intake, it is not surprising that schools and head teachers are operating with a constant look over their shoulders as to what and how their neighbours are doing. Frank, an experienced teacher at George Eliot, describes their head teacher as 'petrified' of the prospect of neighbouring schools 'moving ahead' of George Eliot in terms of exam results:

And the head teacher is absolutely petrified that, now that a number of other secondary schools have overtaken us in the league tables, that it will keep nose-diving as the middle class parents send their kids to that secondary school rather than ours. And he's said himself that the cohorts coming in and the make-up of each Year 7 that comes through is changing and their academic ability is getting weaker.

(Frank, AST Science, Union rep., George Eliot)

These political and emotional responses to external pressures and changes become part of the way in which head teachers and SLTs 'read' and interpret new policy and reinterpret old policy. They also feed into the organisational narratives the head teachers construct (see Chapter 3). Local authority contexts, and in particular the centralised support they offer, can be another factor in policy enactment which gets overlooked in many accounts. For instance, the head teachers at both Campion and Wesley were disappointed by the lack of financial support from their authorities to improve their buildings and to address what they felt were urgent issues with the fabric and facilities of their schools. Graeme, Campion's head teacher, also notes a lack of administrative and organisational support:

> I wish they'd do more in terms of, I mean, human resources: I have to do a lot of work on it and then I have to ring them up for advice, then I do a bit more then... And, to be honest, I wish things like that they handled, you know, and just kept me advised what they were doing. And perhaps even asked me, 'Do you mind if this happens?' [...] Round here we [head teachers] share policies, which is just as well, but otherwise, you know, you'd be inventing things. And the county could do a lot of that. But on the other hand they're also – I've found the advisory staff, when we've used them, in the main have been very good. And I find them very supportive. So, it's not the education people who actually suddenly come up with demands, it's been people like the finance people who've come up with enormous demands and, 'Can you fill this in and make sure this, that and the other is done?'
>
> (Graeme, head teacher, Campion)

This positive endorsement of the LA's education consultants was echoed by teachers in Campion, Wesley and Atwood. Specialist subject or behaviour consultants were considered helpful and knowledgeable and teachers approached them for materials, advice and guidance:

> I think [*name of LA*] are a great authority, I really do, and there's some – I've always found them incredibly supportive. [...] I've picked up 'looked-after' children this year and I've been really impressed with the support I've had there on the safeguarding stuff.
>
> (Eric, assistant head teacher, Geography, BTEC Tourism, Atwood)

> The advisory service is good, they're good for giving us materials.
>
> (Adrian, head of Mathematics, Campion)

> The borough advisor's been very good. She's been in since September, actually, having interviews with students to try and get them to think about revision, what they can do to improve, you know, trying to get them to think about where their weaknesses are and identify that.
>
> (Raaida, head of Mathematics, Wesley)

These local authority advisors can be very influential in terms of policy information and dissemination. Heads of departments at Wesley and Atwood mentioned regular local meetings organised by their specialist advisors where policy was introduced and discussed and experiences and practices exchanged with colleagues from other schools. These meetings are thus key sites of interpretation and translation in the policy enactment process (see Chapter 3) and of policy exchange between institutions:

I meet up with the advisor, the borough advisor for EAL, and there's regular meetings, at which we get told about policies and so on. [...] There was a policy out on admitting new arrivals or mid-term arrivals and we [*as a school*] haven't really taken it on board, although, I've, sort of, been trying quite a lot. [...] I think it might have come to my attention originally through my – the advisor.

(Karen, head of language support, Wesley)

The relationships the four schools had with their local authorities differed considerably. At George Eliot, local authority influence seemed fairly minimal and, at a more strategic level, hands off. George Eliot is a foundation school, which means that historically it has a slightly more remote relationship with the LA (it is its own admissions authority, as opposed to community schools where admission is controlled by the local authority) and this might also find expression in current policy relations. Laura, George Eliot's teaching and learning coordinator, was part of a professional learning community organised by the borough, but otherwise, we did not come across much evidence of LA involvement in the course of our fieldwork in this school. Madhari's comment below captures the school's relationship with the LA well; George Eliot has 'earned autonomy' through its relatively good exam results and is mainly left to its own devices:

I mean, the local authority would just say to us, 'This is your target based on last year', but they don't come in. And, from what I've spoken to [Martin, head of Mathematics] about [the LA] Maths consultant, he actually said to Martin, and this is actually quite a compliment, he said, 'Well, I can leave you lot alone because I don't need to come in', because he has to focus on schools that aren't doing so well. So he did say to Martin, 'You are on your own. Just get on with it. If you've got any questions let me know'.

(Madhari, deputy head of Mathematics, George Eliot)

Campion has a closer but more ambiguous relationship with its local authority: they cooperated directly on some policy developments such as PLTS (Personal Learning and Thinking Skills, see Braun *et al.* 2010), but as a school that struggled to achieve its targeted exam results, it also often felt the punitive and auditorial side of the LA:

Graham: [W]ithin the last two years since we had the extra support [...] we would have termly meetings with the [authority] to go through what you've done so far and where you feel the impact of your changes and what the next step is.

Meg: Was that helpful in terms of developing the school, do you think? Or did it feel like a...?

> Graham: I think it was a bit of a… it wasn't a real deep support, it was, you know, a meeting where you'd have to write another report and present it.
>
> (Graham, head of sixth form, PE, Campion)

'Earned autonomy' mentioned above does not just apply to schools, it applies equally to whole local authorities. Crudely, apart from policies that are mandated or statutory, schools and LAs that are performing well in national tests and Ofsted inspections will have considerably more freedom to decide which policy initiatives to get involved with and to what extent:

> We're a light-touch authority so for me, and my colleagues, the other consultants, […] it's essentially down to you how you actually mediate things. I think, historically, my boss, who's now retired, that was almost the way I was trained into this job that, you know, the schools in [this authority] are successful generally, they're not perfect, there's still work to be done, but when you're in negotiation with them it's not a case of 'you have to do this' […] [The National Strategy[5]] talks about tailoring to your, you know, your local environment. But my experience is that in some authorities that aren't doing so well, they don't allow them to tailor as much as they say.
>
> (Jean, LA advisor, English, Wesley)

> I think [*the LA*] has always been in quite a strong position [*in relation to the government education department*] because of its… the schools are achieving schools, we don't have a school, a secondary school, that's in a sort of notice to improve or anything like that.
>
> (Roy, LA advisor, Atwood)

As we can see, external dimensions, such as the LA's own policy management, constitute different 'contexts of interpretation' which impact on the potential latitude of interpretation available to schools. They can even influence the extent of focus on particular mandated policies, as well as setting other institutional priorities.

Enacting policy in 'real' schools – summing up

Context is a mediating factor in the policy enactment work done in schools – and it is unique to each school, however similar they may initially seem to be. In the course of the fieldwork, we have become alerted to the prominence of context in many of the case study schools' policy decisions and activities, but we have also been struck by the absence of some contextual aspects we were expecting. Schools' specialisms, for example, played a negligible role in interviewees' accounts of the schools. Context is of course always specific. It is also dynamic and shifting, both within and outside of schools. A school may undergo changes in its teaching body and/or capacity, attitude and make-up of its staff group. Student intake may also shift, although this is perhaps more likely in urban environments where there is higher student mobility and the catchment area's social composition can change (Dorling *et al.* 2005).

The motivation behind this chapter has been to take context seriously in order to extend our 'model' of policy enactment, and whilst we have tried to capture a full range of contextual factors, such a list can never be exhaustive. We have not provided a complete or 'finished' analysis, nor comprehensive 'coverage' of the four schools, even if this were possible, but rather offer a heuristic device that is intended to stimulate interest and to provoke questions about the circumstances that influence policy enactments in 'real' schools. There is one dimension of school context in particular that we have not pursued in this chapter, which is related to the ethos and emotional capital of a school. Schools have different capacities to buffer junior staff and one another from stress, including policy-related stress – there are emotional differences between schools (and departments) in terms of trust, bullying, overt managerialism, transparency, capacity for dialogue, etc. (Bibby 2010). Often teachers (and other adults) work in a school (and stay working in it) because of the friendships they have built, the commitment to their colleagues and the energising ethos of the school. These affective dimensions can cushion the strains of everyday school life and enable staff to 'weather' the policy storm (Moore 2006). Teaching, like most of the education and care professions, is often conceptualised as 'good' people doing 'good' work and however problematic this external and self-perception can be (see Britzman 2003; Moore 2004), it can go some way in encouraging people to carry on working and innovating, even in stressful circumstances. A school that can cultivate and draw on this kind of emotional capital will have a different capacity for policy enactment than an institution which does not inspire loyalty or commitment in its staff. We are looking here at an affective dimension of context that goes beyond the perhaps more normative approach to context that we have presented in this chapter, to an extended version of context as a multi-dimensional process, and whilst we have not included these psychosocial aspects in this more 'material' chapter, we will return to these ideas in Chapter 7.

In attempting to outline a grounded theory of policy enactments in schools, we have focused in this chapter on the 'materiality' of policy. Schools enact policies in circumstances not always of their own choosing; policies literally move through different spaces, such as the narrow staircases of Atwood. Contexts, when they are evoked in policy analyses to 'hold' actors in place, frequently remain 'much too abstract as long as they have not instantiated, mobilized, realized, or incarnated into some sort of local and lived interaction' (Latour 2005: 169). Attempts to understand how and why policies get enacted, rarely, if ever, include details of budgets or buildings in their purviews. Contexts are magically dematerialised in the way that schools are represented in much policy analysis. Thus, policy making and policy makers tend to assume 'best possible' environments for 'implementation': ideal buildings, students and teachers and even resources. In contrast, we have attempted to disrupt this version of schooling by introducing the 'reality' of our case study schools, with their situated and material contexts, their specific professional cultures and challenges, and their different external pressures and supports.

3 Doing enactment

People, meanings and policy work

In this chapter, the primary emphasis is on the interpretive or 'the problem of meaning' (Fullan 2001: 8) – the hermeneutics of policy, although, as you will see, as the chapter progresses the role of the discursive becomes more prominent. These facets of policy cannot be separated out. As we have sought to make clear already, our conceptualisation of policy enactments draws upon and relates together three constituent aspects of the messy reality of school life. These aspects – material, interpretive and discursive – taken together make up a version of 'material semiotics', which as Law (2007: 2) puts it 'are better understood as a toolkit for telling interesting stories about, and interfering in' the webs of social relations and relations of power that produce and circumscribe policy and practices in schools. None of these aspects is, on its own, sufficient as a description of policy and practices: all three are necessary. Each opens up possibilities and introduces limits to possibility in conceptualising the policy process. Taken together these aspects, and the relevant theoretical resources in each case, can provide an account of *how* policy and practice get done in schools.

We tackle 'meaning' in two ways. First, by developing a heuristic distinction between *interpretation* and *translation* – these are key parts of the policy process and of the articulation of policy with practice, which are suffused by relations of power.[1] Second, by outlining a typology of 'policy actors' and the forms of 'policy work' in which they are involved. Again, this typology is heuristic and indicative rather than exhaustive. The limits of space make it impossible to explore all of the complexities and nuances involved in policy enactments in schools. These are starting points which rest upon the interplay between theory and data and which adumbrate an agenda for further research.

Interpretation and translation

Interpretation is an initial reading, a making sense of policy – what does this text mean to us? What do we have to do? Do we have to do anything? It is a political and substantive reading – a 'decoding' which is both retrospective and prospective (Ball 1993). This decoding is done in relation to the culture and history of the institution and the policy biographies of the key actors. It is a process of meaning-making which relates the smaller to the bigger picture (Fullan 2001: 8); that is, institutional priorities and possibilities to political necessities. These situated interpretations are set over and against what else is in play, what consequences might ensue from responding or not responding. Interpretations are set within the schools' *position* in relation to policy (performance levels, league table position, Ofsted rating) and the degree and type of imperative attached to any policy and the contextual limitations of budget, staff, etc. (see Chapter 2). These authoritative and authorial interpretations are presented to staff in events and meetings or through texts as frames within which practice is to be thought about and constructed or objectives to which practice is to be oriented – they 'focus' institutional activity. These presentations often take the form of sophisticated *(invisible) policy pedagogies*[2] which engage staff in discussion and seek to encourage their 'ownership' of new policy ideas (see Chapter 6).

> One of my colleagues who is in the senior leadership team, he talked about, you know, what has come up and what we need to focus on. And some of that got mentioned at our middle leaders meeting [some did not].
> (Alice, Teaching and Learning Coordinator, Technology, Campion)

> We're kind of, told these are the new initiatives and these are the things we are going to be introducing.
> (Aabid, joint head teacher, Social Sciences, George Eliot)

> In briefings [the head] talked about what's come up and what we need to focus on... things that we need to try to do.
> (Alice, Teaching and Learning Coordinator, Technology, Campion)

> We wanted to stand up in front of the staff and say, 'this is a national change to policy, but look chaps don't worry because we are already there, we may have to tinker. You have a chance now to have your say.'
> (Lesley, deputy head teacher, Psychology, Campion)

Interpretations are instantiated and elaborated in SLT meetings, staff briefings, working groups, and by identifying responsible persons *(peopling policy)*. In some cases making someone responsible for a policy *is the enactment of policy and its embodiment*.[3]

> They're the ones which I am currently working on quite hard: raising achievement, raising standards, raising punctuality. Child protection is ongoing.
> (Duncan, assistant head teacher, Geography, Wesley)

These are all moments of recontextualisation, different points of articulation and authorisation that make something into a priority, assign it a value, high or low. Interpretation is an institutional political process, a strategy, a 'genre chain', a process of explanation, elucidation and creation of an institutional agenda, 'often contradictory and always socially embedded' (Hodder 2003: 156). It involves 'selling policy to staff' (Alice, Teaching and Learning Coordinator, Technology, Campion) on the work of organisational *narration*.

> Part of the 'filtering' effect as we move along genre chains is on discourses: discourses which are drawn upon in one genre (e.g. meetings) may be 'filtered out' in the movement to another (e.g. report), so that the genre chain works as a regulative device for selecting and privileging some discourses and excluding others.
>
> (Fairclough 2003: 34)

Interpretation is an engagement with the languages of policy, whereas translation is closer to the languages of practice. *Translation* is a sort of third space between policy and practice. It is an iterative process of making institutional texts and putting those texts into action, literally 'enacting' policy using tactics which include talk, meetings, plans, events, 'learning walks', as well as producing artefacts and borrowing ideas and practices from other schools, purchasing and drawing on commercial materials and official websites, and being supported by LA advisors. These translations also give symbolic value to policy: 'Every classroom has a poster explaining what WWW/EBI [What went well/Even better if] is' (Kristi, student teacher, George Eliot). Making policy into materials, practices, concepts, procedures and orientations is a *'recoding'* (Buckles 2010: 18) of policy in relation to specific contexts, recipients and subject cultures (Spillane *et al.* 2002) and the 'logics of practice' of the classroom (Hardy and Lingard 2008: 66). Translation goes on in relation to both imperatives and exhortations with different kinds of creativity and spaces for invention and 'production' in each case. 'In department meetings and talk about what you've really done well, and when we have lunch and all the teachers are sitting together, you say "Today I tried this. It worked really well"'. (Mai, NQT Mathematics, George Eliot).

Translation can occur in staged events and processes – whole school and department meetings being very important – as well as in mundane exchanges, and through the work of 'enthusiasts' and 'models' – and importantly and increasingly, it takes place through the medium of lesson 'observations'. These observations are an example of banal policy 'enforcement', intimate moments of direct interplay between policy and practice, which sit alongside the reporting of student 'progress' and lesson plan writing. The observer may be a peer or the head teacher.

> I don't know if you've heard about the open classroom policy that we have here? There's open/closed signs in windows of classrooms and the idea is that if you're on a free [period], you'd like to, you know, see a class that you teach in a different context. Or you're interested in, you

know, developing aspects of literacy, behaviour management, whatever that may be, then there'll be an open classroom across the school where you can go and officially observe those lessons, either for a full hour or just part of it. And we just ask that you come in, take notes and perhaps be prepared to offer a little bit of constructive feedback at the end.

(Robert, AST Art, Wesley)

You get down to the nitty-gritty of ideas, we'll have a sort of observation week, peer observation was here when I came and I think it was very much part of the school culture.

(Ken, head teacher, Atwood)

You can go to different subject teachers and then also you can invite people to observe your lesson, observe something you want to improve. So that you are actually improving every week.

(Mai, NQT Mathematics, George Eliot)

Such visibility can be formative or summative, it can be about sharing and improving practice, a learning process, an opportunity to be 'outstanding' or it can be reductive, the reduction of the teacher to a grade. 'I don't want to sound like a bighead but myself and others, lots of others, sort of got "outstanding" lesson observations for the quality of our Assessment for Learning' (Gareth, deputy head of sixth form, History, Campion).

Observation is a tactic of policy translation, an opening up of practice to change, a technique of power enacted by teachers one upon the other – 'a marvellous machine' (Foucault 1979: 202) – and a source of evidence of policy activity. It may be that teachers have come 'to inhabit and live and think in terms of this discourse of a surveilled universe and accept it as non-problematic, until it becomes difficult to think in any other terms' (Bottery 2000a: 53).

Nonetheless, policy translations also engage with other sorts of classroom priorities and values and compete for attention (like at the institutional level). These multiple tactics policies 'drip', 'seep' and 'trickle down' into classroom practice to become part of the bricolage of teaching and learning activities, sedimented upon or displacing previous translation effects.

I suppose it's two-fold, it's being able to create activities and lesson ideas yourself, which support effective learning or creative thinking and so on, but I think we need to give staff a basis of ideas for each thing. I mean, borrowing role-plays for speaking and performing or delivering a PowerPoint; don'ts: not staring at it or not using notes or whatever. Just a kind of a list of activities that they can do [Campion has just such a list in their staff handbook].

(Laura, Teaching and Learning Coordinator, AST Social Sciences, George Eliot)

However, classroom and corridor practices (behaviour) are also sustained and constantly adapted in response to students and as Elmore (1996) asserts, we should not assume that policy is the only influence on the behaviour of teachers. Students are also policy actors. Responses are also mediated by subject and expert cultures of various kinds (see Chapter 5). Nonetheless, the stronger and clearer the policy imperative, the less 'leakage' in and through the processes of enactment.

> I think Justin [SLT] has learnt that if you brought this to the whole staff it would fall flat because it's too vague if you haven't been involved in any of the planning. 'What the hell is PLTS?' It's different because I've been involved in the planning and now I'm teaching it but, like, if you're the teacher, especially maybe I'm not saying an older teacher but certain teachers who aren't as open to new ideas, who, you know, have taught in a certain way, then you're like, 'Oh my God'. But they are bringing it in, they are filtering it in, like we're all rewriting schemes of work, every department, for PLTS.
>
> (Rachael, head of PE, George Eliot)

Interpretations and translations are usually enactments of policy in different arenas. These are different parts of the policy process and have different relations to practice but they also interface at points which relate practices to priorities more directly: 'the whole of his senior management team would regularly inspect, walk around the school, checking on these policies on a day-to-day basis' (Kristi, student teacher, George Eliot). Interpretation is about strategy and translation is about tactics but they are also at times closely interwoven and overlapping. They work together to enrol or hail subjects and inscribe discourse into practices. As noted already, they involve the production of institutional texts, doing training/professional development, changing structures, roles and relationships, and very importantly the identification and allocation of posts of responsibility and the allocation of resources. Two examples illustrate the complexity and sophistication of translation work:

> Mel and myself and some others in the group tried to go through this pack. We had a big box given to us by our line manager and she briefed me in a meeting about this new initiative. We're trying to get the students to think more creatively and how to launch that with staff. Mel went away and read the pack very closely. It was my job to try and put that into a staff conference day, to get faculties to think about it. Another thing we do is on Thursday mornings we have a teaching and learning briefing. And the idea being there's a rota for all members of staff to feedback… And getting faculties to share their good practice, that's the idea, so people can pick up ideas.
>
> (Alice, Teaching and Learning Coordinator, Technology, Campion)

Justin [deputy head teacher] has come up with a five-part lesson cycle so we're moving away from the traditional three-part lessons and so on; that it is about active learning... And talking to students, I think it's most interesting, it's very difficult at the moment because we don't have a language for learning, so they tend to equate being quiet or copying things neatly or something with good learning. And it's also quite interesting, Milton [head teacher] he's decided to observe every teacher in the school... So we need – you see, this is where the staff development comes in because you need masses of training because the implications are huge, there's a huge cultural shift. So there's training nearly very week on a Wednesday after school. We started by researching what's going on in other schools. We've had lots of sessions where we have looked at each other's materials. We've also got a coaching programme. We had the Learning Review where people from the LA and other schools came in to review where we were. We've kind of drilled down on more than the government's version of it.

(Laura, Teaching and Learning Coordinator, AST Social Sciences, George Eliot)

In the first example, the translator is directly briefed by a deputy head, while a colleague reads the official materials (the pack). These starting points are reworked into activities for a staff conference and a staff briefing where sharing is encouraged – policy materials are turned into practical 'ideas'. In the second example, classroom change and the development of a new language for classroom activities are mediated by observations and 'training'. Here there is a composite of texts, artefacts, support, training, observation, motivation, modelling, coaching, collaboration and exhortation involved in the work of policy translation. The language of policy is translated into the language of practice, words into action, abstractions into interactive processes. Translation is a form of 'active readership' (Lendvai and Stubbs 2006: 4), 'a process of re-representation, re-ordering and re-grounding through various discursive and material practices... a process of displacement and dislocation [Callon 1986]' (Lendvai and Stubbs 2006: 6). In all of this, the distance between the original policy texts and practice can be significant. It is a productive and creative process but at the same time a set of techniques; 'tiny, everyday, physical mechanisms' (Foucault 1979: 222) and 'petty machinations' (p.194) that 'constitute the individual as effect and object of power, as effect and object of knowledge' (p.192). Translation is simultaneously a process of invention and compliance. As teachers engage with policy and bring their creativity to bear on its enactment, they are also captured by it. They change it, in some ways, and it changes them. The degree of 'play' involved in this interface varies between policies. This is what Riseborough (1992: 37) calls the 'empirically rich under-life to policy intention'. The double-edged character of translation processes is indicated by Lesley, deputy head teacher at Campion:

Our teachers arrive here with a whole set of skills and experiences. And some of them are very, very junior and some of them are quite experienced.

And I suppose it underpins the whole CPD here, which is we will try our very best to give you the training and development that enables – I don't like the word training, I'm quite uncomfortable with the word training – but the development opportunities that enable you to shape yourself into the teacher you want to become.

Whose meanings? Which actors?

It may be stating the obvious but in work which gives primacy to 'the problem of meaning' in policy analysis, in which 'participants are both receivers and agents of policy' (Saunders (1986) cited in Trowler (2003: 129), cited in Buckles (2010: 19)), participants and institutions, and agency and interpretation, are all typically undifferentiated. (We return to this point in Chapter 7.) Much of the policy interpretation genre tends to take all actors in the policy process to be equal, with the exception of school leaders who are given particular attention, and seen to be working on and with policy in similar ways – as receivers and agents (e.g. Spillane *et al.* 2002). A great deal of the complex and differentiated activity that goes into the 'responses' of schools *to* and their work *with* policy is thus obscured and distorted. Our data indicates very clearly that actors in schools are positioned differently and take up different positions in relation to policy (see Table 3.1 below), including positions of indifference or avoidance.

In an attempt to explore and identify the different sorts of roles, actions and engagements embedded in the processes of interpretation and translation, and despite some wariness of the seductive neatness of typologies, we discuss the 'policy work' of eight types of policy actor or *policy positions* which are involved in making meaning of and constructing responses to policy through the processes of interpretation and translation (see Table 3.1). The actors/positions are listed on the left and the work they do on the right.

These 'actor' categories or positions are not necessarily attached to specific individuals, nor are they fixed, unified and mutually exclusive 'types' of teacher/adult in every case. Some people may move between these roles in

Table 3.1 Policy actors and 'policy work'

Policy actors	Policy work
Narrators	Interpretation, selection and enforcement of meanings
Entrepreneurs	Advocacy, creativity and integration
Outsiders	Entrepreneurship, partnership and monitoring
Transactors	Accounting, reporting, monitoring/supporting, facilitating
Enthusiasts	Investment, creativity, satisfaction and career
Translators	Production of texts, artifacts and events
Critics	Union representatives (reps): monitoring of management, maintaining counter-discourses
Receivers	Coping, defending and dependency

different aspects of their work or may combine different aspects of policy work in their interactions with colleagues. For example, SLT members may be *trans-actors* and *entrepreneurs* as well as *narrators*; *enthusiasts* are often *translators* but will also be *receivers*, etc. Some roles may be more prominent or significant in some schools. The actors/positions are introduced rather schematically below.

Selection, narration and interpretation

As noted already, the filtering out and selective focusing done by heads and their SLTs is a crucial aspect of policy interpretation – 'explaining' policy to colleagues, deciding and then announcing what must be done, what can be done and what cannot. There is often a fine balance between making policy palatable and making it happen. Head teachers were sometimes aware that they had to work hard to convince their staff of the worthwhileness of policy ideas and indeed were sometimes unconvinced themselves.

> If you stand back and think about it for too long you'll think: 'I can't ask the staff to do all this.' So where you ask you always try and give a bit back as well. But, yes, when you look at the curriculum drive at Key Stage 3, the changes in GCSEs and the significant changes in the GCSE syllabi and then the significant change at AS-level, and diplomas are coming in this year. All at the same time, you know, along with, I mean, behaviour management and rewards that's almost ongoing, you know, you're always looking at refining that. But we are also continually putting additional demands on middle leaders for monitoring all this stuff as well. So we expect a lot of them.
>
> (Ken, head teacher, Atwood)

> What I said was, 'Look, we've got to do something about making it possible for all staff to think about learning', and they've gone off and come up with the teaching and learning development process.
>
> (Philip, head teacher, Wesley)

> It's our time and energy you know. Certain things the [Local Authority] say have to be done, because someone's on their back insisting, but it's also looking at the time and energy of your own staff because if you implemented everything that's flying through…
>
> (Graeme, head teacher, Campion)

A whole range of constraining and enabling factors are brought into play in the work of interpretation, including the contextual factors discussed in Chapter 2. Interpretations are constructed in relation to the resources at hand, including those of energy and time. As Graeme indicates, some policy is, of necessity, selected out. However, it is at this stage that things can begin to 'go wrong' if authoritative interpretations are botched or misjudged. Head teachers and institutional policy entrepreneurs play a key role in interpretation and meaning-making and are themselves key sites in the discursive articulation of policy. That is, part of the role of heads and the work of entrepreneurs is to join up disparate policies into an institutional narrative, a story about how the school works and what it does – ideally articulated through an 'improvement' plot of some kind (see Philip below), often very inventive, even fantastical (given that parts of a school maybe written out of the story or parts of the story are 'over-written').[4] One aspect of this effort of narration is what leadership writers call 'vision'. This includes an articulation of collective endeavour around the idea of what sort of school 'we' want to be. It is about harnessing commitment and energy and cultivating enthusiasm. Boje calls this kind of policy work storytelling. There is now a considerable body of work on organisations as storytelling systems (Boje 1991; Currie and Brown 2003; Brown *et al*. 2008). Narrative or story is one rhetorical mode of discourse, and is part of the work of *knowledge management*[5] in organisations. For example:

> I think any half-decent head teacher or whatever knows that you take the bits that you want, but you've got a strong enough vision. I think we know what we want to do with our school, we know exactly what's needed, because of our own self-reflection and whatever, and we're taking the school in this direction. Policy comes at us and we'll, sort of, harness it to continue going in that direction.
>
> (Justin, deputy head teacher, SLT, George Eliot)

> During that period, I've re-evaluated the vision of the school. As a school, we were in a position where we were obviously looking at different groups and their achievement and so on and so forth and raising achievement. And we got to the point last year where our exam results were pretty good in terms of five As to Cs with the English and Maths and extremely good on RAISEonline,[6] significantly above similar schools and so on in value-added terms. And so, we've re-evaluated our vision and direction where we've got a very solid base now and it's about being more sophisticated with certain groups. So, in those terms, that sort of emphasis was already coming into play prior to Every Child Matters, in some ways like health, Healthy Schools and all those sorts of things, and the welfare. It provided a framework for thinking, which has helped. And last year in particular, certain things have become clearer and it's helped us to develop as a school [...]. I mean, our improvement plan [inaudible], but within that comes a whole welter of things, like how do we guide and support the children, for example. I think it's providing a framework for our thinking and that, of course, impacts on the decision making and where we're going. The third thing is actually about the curriculum because we have the new national curriculum, obviously, coming into play and that's been helpful in the sense that it's allowed us to concentrate on the things we

really want to concentrate on, which is learning, and develop the quality of our learning and the whole issue of cross-curricular things and the PLTS, which has helped us to move pedagogy on, on the basis of what we're already doing.

(Philip, head teacher, Wesley)

These sophisticated stories or narratives are both retrospective and prospective and work to 'hold things together' and 'move things on' and construct historical continuities or dramatic breaks with the past, as appropriate. At Campion, for example, considerable effort was made to distance the present school from its traumatic past when it had four different head teachers in quick succession and a narrative of recovery was constructed in relation to this. Several of the head teacher's accounts of the school began with the phrase: 'When I first came here…'. Hazel, the deputy head at Wesley, explained the current position of her school in relation to a poor Ofsted report in 2002. 'A lot of the staff', she explained:

> … could not believe that we weren't a good school, that we were what was then Ofsted category five, which meant that we were an underachieving school. And that was a really good thing that we had that Ofsted report because it did challenge those perceptions, it did enable us to really start moving things forward.

Narratives can be made to work through some 'principle of integration', which coheres policy and the school itself, but this integration is not always successful, sometimes teachers do not see themselves as characters in the 'official' school story (see Braun *et al.* 2010). Narratives are aimed both at staff (and students), as a focus of organisational commitment and cohesion, and for consumption by various publics (parents, Ofsted, LA, etc.). Boje (1995: 1000) says: 'At one extreme, the story-telling organization can oppress by subordinating everyone and collapsing everything into one "grand narrative"'. On the other hand, there can be both narrative failure and a lack of willingness or confidence on the part of key interpreters to maintain narrative coherence in relation to policy – as least in the eyes of some critics in some schools.

> This sort of scattergun approach to policy is just not working. Why don't we try taking our foot off the gas and focus on the ones we really think are valuable and really going to have an impact on this school, and get them right. It seems to me pretty elementary management and leadership.
>
> (Gareth, deputy head of sixth form, History, Campion)

> There's a lot of good practice in the school that contributes to that agenda [Every Child Matters] but I don't think we've answered the question fully of how to look at it as a whole.
>
> (Nick, deputy head teacher, Atwood)

There's not enough of a reflective process to say how are these things really going, what's expendable, what's really valuable to us.

(Gareth, deputy head of sixth form, History, Campion)

Effective narratives speak in and combine different logics and languages – what in actor–network theory is called 'multi-discursive ordering', or is referred to as 'bilingualism' (Gewirtz *et al.* 1995) – creating different conditions of possibility and recruiting different kinds of support, both moral and practical from teachers, students and others. Narration is also part of the work of *policy entrepreneurs* (see below).

We need to tread a fine line here. The recent focus on the role of head teachers as *leaders* has led to a neglect of the analysis of other policy roles and policy work, which we hope to redress. Nonetheless, it would be a mistake to under-emphasise the role of heads within policy and the extent to which, as Thomson (2009) puts it, their 'heads are on the block'. As she goes on to say, 'being a head is now a risky business' (p.3) and headship is 'an extreme sport'. Those 'whose schools "perform" get increased financial rewards... Those who deliver the reality of the fictional "hero head" get feted...' (p.121) but 'for some there is a heavy personal cost from the new accountabilities' (p.122) and most just 'grit their teeth and cope...' (p.122). The head teachers in our study were very different and had different leadership styles. They were also at different stages in their careers. By the end of the study, two had left their school and left teaching. None bore the pressures of policy lightly, none were paragons but all were in their different ways effective and all managed what Thomson calls the predictable and unpredictable risks of the job. They were each in their different ways key to maintaining direction and stability in the schools. In other words, their interpretational work was mostly affective and their narratives were mostly convincing.

Entrepreneurs

One of the most intriguing but uncommon policy roles is that of entrepreneurship – that is, the work of policy advocacy within schools. These are actors who originate or champion and represent particular policies or principles of integration. They are exceptional but significant. They are charismatic people and 'persuasive personalities' and forceful agents of change, who are personally invested in and identified with policy ideas and their enactment. They seek to recruit others to their cause (see *policy enthusiasts*) to build a critical mass for change and to bring off policy enactments. They rework and recombine aspects of different policies, draw on disparate ideas, examples of 'good practice' and other resources to produce something original, and crucially they are able to translate this into a set of positions and roles and organisational relationships which 'enact' policy. An example:

My number one bit of my role is building up capacity because learning and teaching often didn't have enough people working on it. I've got now quite an elaborate diagram [referring to diagram]. You've got assistant heads, quality of learning and teaching, with different coaches underneath them. This assistant head also deals with literacy and we've got different intervention teams. Student Voice is very important now. Gifted and Talented, where we're not doing enough. This is the head of our training school, and we do a lot of training for teachers. Curriculum, we're doing a lot of curriculum innovation at the moment. Thinking Skills we've talked about. Creative Partnerships, we've got someone leading on that; we've got different people coming in. E-learning, we're trying to get e-portfolios and have more e-learning online. We're improving our data and tracking at the moment and then we're doing a lot of GCSE intervention. But a lot of these posts didn't really exist before and so we're really trying to build up. [...] In theory this isn't scattergun and all of it should be combining to improve the quality of lessons. So measuring from lesson observations, is the quality of learning and teaching improving? So they all should be combining and they are, sort of, matrixed to make that happen.

(Justin, deputy head teacher, SLT, George Eliot)

The interesting point about this entrepreneur is that he is a late entrant to teaching, who draws on his previous career to 'think' about education 'differently'. The entrepreneur produces original texts, reads widely to inform thinking and challenges ingrained assumptions about practice.

I'm a change agent and I know that. I'm the kind of person who can come in, take a situation that's not working and focus on where we should be and get us there.

(Lesley, deputy head teacher, Psychology, Campion)

This thinking about teaching and learning, drawing on a variety of discursive sources (e.g. multiple intelligences, Philosophy for Kids), is then *translated* into and through structures and roles and tactics and techniques. This is a particular kind of, and very sophisticated form of, policy enactment that involves creativity (within limits), energy and commitment (as available). This is also a dynamic and unstable process. Policies in our schools always seemed to be not quite finished, or about to be changed. That is, there was a 'complex interplay between discourses and ground-level practices, conflicting choices and pressures, between the "political" (standards/learning) and the "technical" [coping at the chalk face], and indeed the metamorphosis of flexi-actors, criss-crossing sites, scales and spaces' (Lendvai and Stubbs 2006: 28). Entrepreneurs seek to join up these sites, scales and spaces, but to reiterate, they are not to be found in every school.

Outsiders: business, partners and monitors

Not all of the significant actors in the policy process are based inside schools. In some instances, LA advisors, consultants or edu-businesses play a key or supporting role, introducing or interpreting policies and initiating or supporting translation work or brokering visits to other schools that are experimenting with policy ideas or are models of 'good policy'.[7]

> One of the staff said: 'Well this is something that I've been talking to [the Local Authority] about. What do you think?' And we said: 'Hold it! Great idea but if we get into that as well we'll start to crumble at the edges.'
>
> (Graeme, head teacher, Campion)

We made the point in a previous paper (Ball *et al.* 2011a) that some policies in schools can only be 'brought off' by including outsiders in the policy process. However, many existing accounts of policy in schools omit these players from the policy process.

> I think Cawforth are a great authority, I've always found them incredibly supportive... when I used to do a lot of stuff on citizenship, Janice Smith she was superb. I've picked up looked-after children this year and I've been really impressed with the support I've had there on the safeguarding stuff. You know, they're a pain in one way, on safeguarding they've been really, really good.
>
> (Eric, assistant head teacher, Geography, BTEC Tourism, Atwood)

> Dylan Wiliam[8] came in [to run an INSET day] he said that he doesn't really like the way that learning objectives are used for AfL, that wasn't quite what he meant and there were various things weren't quite what he meant. But he gave us a lot of strategies that also went into the planner and things like that. I think people were keen. When he came in, he was an inspiring speaker, people were very keen on the activities he suggested for learning in the classroom.
>
> (Naomi, RE, Atwood)

The work of LA SIPS advisers (school improvement partners) also fits here, as they work with heads to 'raise standards' and clarify their priorities.[9] Two of our schools made considerable use of consultants and education businesses to run CPD and events and work with staff. They were 'bought in' as both 'interpreters' of policy, offering what Rizvi and Kemmis (1987) call 'interpretations of interpretations', and as translators, in the process of accommodating policy to practice. Over the past 15 years such businesses have become increasingly active in these aspects of policy work (see Ball 2009). Osiris Educational is one such company whose 'products' were bought by our schools (see Box 3.1).[10]

Osiris Educational are passionate about providing pioneering, challenging and effective training solutions in teaching. At the forefront of innovation in education, we use around 200 of the best and most renowned trainers in Britain. INSET training days provided by Osiris are held in schools throughout the UK. Thousands of teachers have attended our courses and have altered their ways of thinking, approaches to teaching and even saved teaching careers. Our products are of the highest calibre and are under constant review to ensure they are as pertinent and relevant as possible.

(http://osiriseducational.co.uk/about-osiris-educational, accessed 7 January 2011)

Box 3.1 Osiris Educational

Policy transactors: transaction accounting and policy monitoring/supporting and facilitating

Here we refer to two sorts of *transactors*. One of the peculiar features of current education policy in England is the extent to which some types of policy must be seen to be done, that is, reported as done and accounted for. There is a low trust policy environment in which accountability work and the reporting of performances can take up increasing amounts of time and divert time and effort away from that which is reported on (see Ball 2003). This is a form of transaction work and many senior staff and others have significant parts of their roles defined by this work.

> There's too few of our leaders who are willing to dedicate that kind of time and support. I think they're quite happy in their offices typing up their forms, they're not out in the school enough.
>
> (Gareth, deputy head of sixth form, History, Campion)

> Far too often, the lower down the totem pole you are, your time and your workload are increased because other people have boxes to tick.
>
> (Tanveer, AST Science, Atwood)

> The school tends to be organised around the needs of the administration department rather than the teachers, which totally goes against what the point of a school is, as far as we can tell. The only way academically or spiritually, or any kind of way that school is going to improve, is if teachers are helped, because that's where the actual education goes on. It doesn't go on in a collection of data in an office somewhere.
>
> (Neil, English, 2nd in department, Union rep., Wesley)

There are several other references like these in the transcripts that point to the increase in the number of senior teachers and administrators who are appointed to generate, work on and work with data. This involves both policy monitoring and enforcement (see Ball *et al.* 2011). Policy responses are made calculable and teachers become continually accountable for their 'effectiveness'. In this sense also, the policies that count most are those that are counted, although *transactors* can also be creative accountants and fabricators of policy responses. Their work makes policy 'visible' by 'evidencing' policy activity and effects. All of this has direct and indirect costs. It inflates staff costs and diverts time and effort from first-hand work with students.

There is a second very diverse group of *transactors* whose relationships to policy are supportive and facilitatory, but who also in some ways interpret policy. Their role within policy in schools is sorely neglected by research. These range, on the one hand, from bursars/business managers and various office staff to, on the other, specialist support staff like parent support officers, behaviour support officers, student welfare administration officers, community liaison officers. Behaviour policy in particular, is constructed, managed and developed across school boundaries, inside and out, and within local policy networks involving a wide variety of *transactors*. Some of these roles are well established but have evolved considerably as more budgetary and administrative responsibilities have been devolved from local authorities to schools. Others are new and either have taken over work done previously by teachers or are tactical inventions as responses to new policies or policy intensification, particularly in relation to pastoral work, behaviour and special educational needs. Our schools varied in the number of these 'support' staff employed (see Chapter 2). These people are part of the collective effort that enacts policy in schools, enactments of various kinds depend upon them, but they bring different kinds of experience and training and expert knowledge and perspectives to bear (see Maguire *et al.* 2010). They are also often outside of the mainstream processes of policy interpretation and translation. Indeed, in many cases they operate literally out of sight working in what Goffman (1971) calls backstage or the back *regions*.

Business managers and office staff also operate in the back regions of schools but are very significant actors in the policy process. As the Campion bursar explained: 'I'm part of the SLT. I'm responsible for finance, premises, personnel, exams, the support of staff in the admin office and the reception areas and the caretakers' (Terry, bursar, Campion). In addition to these areas of responsibility, bursars and managers are key stakeholders in the decision-making processes around the curriculum and teaching and learning, and the appointment of frontline and support staffing which effect or constrain school responses to policy (see Chapter 2). The bursar or school manager is also often faced with having to find 'flexibility' in and across budget allocations which will fund new initiatives and unanticipated difficulties. They 'interpret' policy in relation to resources and set limits or open up possibilities for translation work. 'Money is always key and curriculum staff always forget about money... I'm probably the other way, I think in terms of money and then what can actually be achieved' (Alisa, school business manager, Wesley). The budget is one of the interpretive frames through which policy is viewed and translation activities need to be funded and staffed. There is an ongoing interplay between 'policy restructuring', as schools adapt to changing responsibilities or shifts in national policy emphases, and staffing and staffing costs.

> My personal strategy is to say, we don't want to go above 80 per cent [staff costs] otherwise other areas of the schools will suffer. So when it comes to the appointment of staff I will say that to the head teacher.
>
> (Owen, deputy head teacher, George Eliot)

In a similar vein Alisa at Wesley commented:

> We were talking about this, this morning, the head and I, if it really became difficult in terms of staffing. And his view is that you do need a teacher in every classroom... one of the interesting things obviously is that non-teaching staff cost an awful lot less than teaching staff.
>
> (Alisa, school business manager, Wesley)

There is a nascent tension here between a budgetary perspective which would suggest that more non-qualified staff are employed, as against a performance or quality perspective which stresses the need for experienced and well-qualified teaching staff, in order to do policies 'properly'. Thus, different rationalities are involved in the policy process and have to be resolved. Greg, the Atwood bursar, explained:

> Currently we're doing a curriculum costing process where we look at need and resources within the curriculum sectors, to see where there is over-staffing and understaffing... You could probably do the process through natural wastage, so people retiring, do you need to replace them? Can you redistribute the work?

There are important issues signalled here about the way that we research and conceptualise policy in schools, both in the sense of who comes into the gaze and analytics of research but also substantively how one set of policies which are concerned with school funding and school's budgetary responsibilities and autonomies relate to issues about who does the work of policy, who is employed to do what and, as indicated in Chapter 1, the overall balance between teachers and 'other adults' in the business of schooling.

Policy enthusiasts and translators

The teachers in our four case study schools relate to and engage with different policies in different ways. For some, their general lack of enthusiasm for 'standards' work[11] can be contrasted with particular enthusiasm for other policies which they felt enabled them to do 'proper' teaching, to engage with students in exciting ways, and to grow and develop themselves through creative and productive policy work.

> They [students] are given total control of their own project and it's my job to guide them and make sure that they learn the skills appropriately to manage in a project. But what project they do is down to them, really, as long as it's appropriate. And it's been great seeing what some of the things… it's the first time the students, they're coming in, they're not being chased, they want to do it.
>
> (Joe, head of Sociology, Atwood)

> I'm a big Assessment for Learning freak, you know, that's one of the policies that I've really, ever since I started teaching, just threw myself into. And I thought, yeah, this is definitely the future, I wish somebody had sat me down when I was doing my A-levels and said: 'This is a marking scheme.'
>
> (Gareth, deputy head of sixth form, History, Campion)

> I loved Thinking Skills, I was begging to get on to this. I had to do all that in my free time; not everyone's going to do that. I don't have any children, you know, so I can afford to give up this time.
>
> (Rachael, head of PE, George Eliot)

> I like AfL [Assessment for Learning] I was an *In the Black Box*[12] PGCE student… that's what my training was all about. And I use it all the time. I mean, we just had Dylan Wiliam in our INSET at the start of the year and he enthused everybody. I'm big on peer marking; I'm big on peer assessment. AfL is kind of there and formative assessment is much more important to me than summative assessment.
>
> (Beth, HoY 7, English, Atwood)

Enthusiasts can also be *policy models* or what are called 'influentials' (Cole and Weiss 2009) – those who embody policy in their practice and are examples to others; policy paragons. Policies are simultaneously translated and enacted through their practice. For example, at George Eliot, model lessons were observed and videoed as part of systematic CPD work around particular policies. Visits to other schools are also a source of exemplars and models. Enthusiasts are also often *translators* – who plan and produce the events, processes and institutional texts of policy for others who are thus actively inducted into the 'discursive patterns' of policy. They constitute a core of 'policy activists' in any school. Translation is a process of animation; teachers are drawn into a positive and active relation to policy as enactors. It is a point of the intersection of discourse, incentive and social action. Alice, Robert and Laura are *translators*.

My role is to work with all the faculties, try to share policies, practices, when they come in. We've got an Improving Learning group, which involves all the coordinators; so there's the Gifted and Talented coordinator, who's the numeracy coordinator; Jill, who teaches science but she's the literacy coordinator; we've got an Advanced Skills teacher, Hugh, he works with us; and then there's an INSET coordinator called Ben. So, we're a team of six. We sometimes involve the PSHE coordinator as well… And I think management prefer us to do it because none of us are senior managers, we're all classroom teachers, we're not leaders of anything, we're coordinators, so I think they like it to come from us, our ideas. So we will be planning the next staff conference, which will be very much the two targets for marking, that's a big thing, and Assessment for Learning, challenging our children a lot more.

> (Alice, Teaching and Learning Coordinator, Technology, Campion)

The TLC (Teaching and Learning Community) have been feeding back to staff and encouraging them to take on new strategies, new ways of doing things, new thinking.

> (Robert, AST Art, Wesley)

This year there's been about twelve teaching staff who've volunteered to be part of a working group, we've called it Thinking Skills. We started by researching what's going on in other schools because it was soon apparent we're quite behind because we're doing nothing and most other schools are the third or fourth year into the journey.

> (Laura, Teaching and Learning Coordinator, AST Social Sciences,
> George Eliot)

Enthusiasts and translators recruit others to the possibilities of policy, they 'speak' policy directly to practice, and join up between specialist roles and responsibilities, to make enactment into a collective process. The extent of cooperation and collaboration is very evident from the examples above. The abstracts or ideals of policy exhortations or dry texts are translated into actions; things to do in 'real' situations. That is, they are made meaningful and doable, a dual process. In some schools ASTs (Advanced Skills Teachers),[13] when they can be afforded, have a particular role in translation work.

I know some schools have a bunch of ASTs who drive the, sort of, teaching and learning agenda, we haven't been able to do that in the past, you know, we didn't have the funding. [But now] we've got a group of people who are attending to the different aspects of learning and are promoting it through our group of team leaders and with members of staff. Alongside that we've created – we've instituted what we call the learning development groups. Now, every member of staff belongs to that and they pick up a particular aspect of achievement.

> (Philip, head teacher, Wesley)

The interactive network of shifting and changing relations among and between teachers, groups, teams and departments and the events, activities, meetings, observations and reviews which are occurring involve overlapping, intersecting and mutual reinforcing and productive relations of power. These are immanent within institutional, professional and personal relationships and mundane social interactions.

Critics: marginal and muted

Over and against enthusiasm there is criticism. Certainly there are plenty of 'murmurings' in our data, that is, 'discomforts' that were expressed about policy (see Chapter 4), mundane criticisms that are part of everyday life in almost all organisations. Principled and political critique was less apparent. So it is important not to overestimate the role of policy critics like union reps and union activists but they do contribute to policy work and policy interpretation and can become significant in the policy process at particular moments; that is, moments when policies or policy translations threaten the interests of members – related, for example, to the boycott of SATs. Generally, however, their relationship to policy is marginal and muted. Union reps were not mentioned in any of our interviews by other teachers as significant or influential in the policy process. Nonetheless, there are two particular aspects of their 'policy work' which are important aspects of and contributions to *interpretation*. First is the monitoring of policy translations in relation to the conditions of work and service and well-being of teachers, locally and nationally.

> We wanted to do a little questionnaire about workload within the school… they [SLT] thought I was going to try and stir up trouble and create, you know, sort of rebellion or something… In fact, we've just done a motion on workload, it was passed at the meeting. They never tried to interfere with the strike too much because there has been lots of awkwardness about it in terms of the head demanding a list of people who are in the union.
>
> (Neil, English, 2nd in department, Union rep., Wesley)

> We're not doing Learning Conversations. I just put a questionnaire to everyone and said, do you understand what they're about, do you have enough time, when do you do them? And people said, generally they thought they were a good idea but that they didn't have the time. And that it was one of these things that had been put on top of your normal everyday lessons. So, it was one of many initiatives. People think it's a good thing to do but it's about being given the resources to do it properly.
>
> (Stewart, Science, NUT rep., Atwood)

The interpretative work in these examples involves looking at the second order implications of policy or policy translation for the work–life balance of the teachers. These union activists also draw upon the policy interpretation work done and policy texts produced by their unions locally and nationally. Taking these issues up often leads to union reps having meetings with head teachers, which can in theory also be part of the general process of interpretation of policy.

> And it's much better than it was; to start off with it was quite heavy weather. You'd regularly seem to make progress on lots of issues and then we end up with exactly the same thing happening the year after and promises that he'd [the head] made, nothing had been done about them. But some things are beginning to improve now and I think he's listening more.
>
> (Neil, English, 2nd in department, Union rep., Wesley)

> Generally what I tend to get is there'll be an announcement out at a staff meeting or something in the bulletin and it'll say something about consultation. And then, basically, it's up to me to ring him [the head] up and arrange a meeting to go and talk to him about it.
>
> (Stewart, Science, NUT rep., Atwood)

> Ken does a lot of negotiating with Stewart, who's our NUT rep., behind the scenes that no one ever knows about.
>
> (Debbie, deputy head teacher, History, Atwood)

Second, critics are involved in the maintenance of counter-discourses; some of these are drawn from the historic archive of teaching discourse – 'the field of memory' (Foucault 1972) – that is, the field of statements which have lost their general validity within the diversity of statements which presently enunciate the teacher, but which are nonetheless a source of potential challenges to and critique of new policy.

> Everything about the system encourages schools to pour every penny they've got into the C/D borderline students. Everything about the system points them in that direction and then we're meant to go Every Child Matters. It's an absolute farce because clearly every child doesn't matter to the school in the same way, at the same level, because what matters to the school is, can we meet our target and everyone in the school's life will be made a misery by constantly having to do more and more administration and conform more to a robotic sense of what's good teaching until whoever's investigating us thinks that they're satisfied with it.
>
> (Neil, English, 2nd in department, Union rep., Wesley)

These critics keep these counter-discourses alive in sites like union meetings and their 'statements' in some kind of circulation in staff room and departmental interactions, providing a different way of talking and thinking about policy. These critics are carriers of a collective history and are sometimes irritants to policy, making 'official' interpretations or narratives more difficult to sustain or just slightly less credible. However, these archival counters to policy were articulated only very loosely with the more mundane discomforts and ambiguities that teachers expressed when values and policies were misaligned. Even what Sanguinetti (1999) calls the 'micropractices of resistance' were hard to find in our data. What Sanguinetti refers to, quoting (Foucault 1980: 190), as a 'positive economy of the body and pleasure', the passion, enthusiasms and excitement of the classroom, are almost all set within the incitements of policy. This does not mean that teachers are politically inactive in other parts of their lives, that they do not support their unions or go on national demonstrations or take industrial action – they do! However, there was little or no evidence of links being made between big political issues 'out there' and the more immediate demands of and processes of policy at school.

Receivers: junior teachers coping and defending[14]

Not surprisingly most junior and newly qualified teachers (NQTs) and many TAs (teaching assistants), and at times more experienced teachers, exhibit 'policy dependency' and high levels of compliance. They are looking for guidance and direction rather than attempting any creativity. Or rather, their creativity is strongly framed or articulated by the possibilities of policy. For NQTs policy bears very directly upon their classroom practice. It has to be 'done' even if it is not understood – they have, by definition, no sense of history or grasp of context on which to draw. The smaller picture dominates, the bigger picture is mostly blurred and distant, managing in the classroom is the prime reality. They rely heavily on 'interpretations of interpretations' and are attentive participants in and consumers of translation work. They are also to some extent 'shielded' from policy by more senior colleagues, although this is subject dependent, but nonetheless they tend to experience a lot of policy as reified and oppressive. The subject department is their primary reality and the conduit for their experience of policy. Some manage and are 'copers', others struggle and are 'defenders' – short-term survival is the main concern. Even more experienced teachers sometimes feel oppressed by policy.

> It's government policy they've got to, got to follow it, got to implement it.
> (Aabid, joint head teacher, Social Sciences, George Eliot)

> I think it can feel like we're hammered a lot… you're expected to do these things.
> (Alice, Teaching and Learning Coordinator, Technology, Campion)

> People feel it's top-down rather than bottom-up; there isn't a chance to feed back.
> (Naomi, RE, Atwood)

Policy usually seemed distant from the immediate concerns and perspectives of the new teachers. The first year of teaching in particular was described as a 'blur', a matter of getting by from day to day, and being very tired. As Morgan *et al.* (2010: 191) report: 'while remote structural factors may heavily influence teaching, it is the perception of events at micro-level that impinge most strongly on motivation'. From this position, policy is something that comes from 'them' – either the SLT or 'government' or both, and is mostly something to be 'followed', to be struggled with, to be 'made sense of' or not, in less time than is really needed. Policy work at this level is a matter of muddling through, although almost all of the newer teachers felt well supported by their colleagues and were determined and resilient. National, institutional and 'classroom' policies and priorities, mix and filter, clash and overlap in their practice; although in some respects some of the newly qualified teachers felt that they had a good grasp of new policy ideas such as AfL and APP schemes from their university training courses and these were built into their practice from the start.

The verbs employed by these teachers are interesting. Policy is 'enforced' and 'required' of you and 'foisted' on you and you have to 'adjust'; you are 'expected', 'pressurised', 'instructed', 'dictated' to, 'hammered', but also 'measured' and 'judged' by policy. There is little room for active engagement here, rather compliance predominates, although new teachers were keen to participate in in-service activities. This is a language of assault, a sense of being battered by policy and policy expectations which creates dependencies. Dependency means a reliance on senior colleagues, local texts, materials, guidelines, etc., generated by translators, which may also be the case in relation to some policies for more experienced teachers. You have to 'just keep going, keeping on top of new things *they* introduce' (Molly, GTP English, Campion).

> My challenge is to keep going and get through my NQT and then I guess, look toward the future… and it's not an easy department to work in at the moment. There's a lot of friction and it doesn't gel like I've seen other departments gel.
>
> (Molly, GTP English, Campion)

> In my experience, if you do an INSET training day it's got to be very, very practical for teachers. As soon as you do – I mean, we're going to try another one on neuroscience quite soon, which may completely bomb; we want to, sort of, elevate the debate a bit. And that'll be interesting how that goes on because in the past if you do something like that, half to three-quarters will come out saying, 'Well, you know, I can't apply any of that to my next lesson. You know, it's not a practical tip that I can take.' And, you know, I think that's a shame all that.
>
> (Justin, deputy head teacher, SLT, George Eliot)

On the one hand, there are attempts to recruit all teachers as active and creative participants in processes of translation, through in-service activities, meetings, observations and 'sharing'. On the other, there is the reliance by new teachers on local policy texts and artefacts and other forms of guidance which can lead to standardisation (e.g. the three- or five-part lesson) or what Buckles (2010) calls 'designed teaching and learning' – which is perhaps what is intended by policy!

> It's important to have schemes of work that people can follow.
> (Molly, GTP English, Campion)

> [People] weren't happy with INSET because they weren't being told what to do. They want a toolkit – dependency!
> (Robert, AST Art, Wesley)

> The school's been a lot better, you know, in terms of telling us what you should be doing, you know, on a day-to-day basis and these are the things that we need to prioritise and these are the things we need to focus on.
> (Aabid, joint head teacher, Social Sciences, George Eliot)

> You just kind of follow exactly what you're told to do.
> (Naomi, RE, Atwood)

> There seems to be a formula. I think a lot of teachers in this school can pull a good or an outstanding lesson out of the hat, just by following a formula. And then... and then you can tick the boxes but it's kind of an outstanding Ofsted lesson but in some ways it's not an outstanding lesson.
> (Eric, assistant head teacher, Geography, BTEC Tourism, Atwood)

Such standardisation is, again, not limited to the newer teachers. Translation tactics work to produce common responses to the incitements of policy. Sonja captures the tensions here between creativity and guidance, risk and support.

> Everyone teaches the same lessons now. It used to be more of a case of everyone, kind of, on their own, you know, 'Here's your plan for the year, do it in the way you see best.' And now it's very much everyone who's teaching the same set and the same year teaches the same lessons. I don't feel like there's as much creativity in your own lessons. No one's going to get cross with you or anything like that, but... And in another way it's fantastic for teachers who are new because they have something to actually follow, they don't have to make it up. I don't think I've got enough of a long-term view on that, to be honest with you, because, I suspect, you know, 40 years ago it was even more individualised, whereas now it's, you know, 'Here's the strategy, this is how you're going to teach it.'
> (Sonja, Mathemathics, Atwood)

There is little discrimination in all of this, which is very understandable. Most newer teachers are focused upon day-to-day survival and getting the classroom right, and responding to what they see as expected of them – what key *interpreters* prioritise. Furthermore, new teachers have themselves been educated and done teacher training within a particular regime of accountability and 'design', and may not be able to imagine a different way of being a teacher. They may have no 'field of memory' of 'different times' on which to draw, although the *TES*, the *Guardian*, union magazines – or families, in the case of the children of teachers – may be points of access and recovery of faded discourses for some new teachers.

The subject department plays a key role for the new teacher, although departments do vary in their coherence and supportiveness and centrality to policy. Also, departments vary in degrees of 'earned autonomy' and institutional confidence (see Chapter 2), often in relation to their 'output' performances, which can have implications for the junior teacher's experience of and engagement with policy. Some subjects, like English, 'carry' well-established subject cultures, and all departments are to an extent 'different worlds' (Siskin 1991: 156) and important organisational sub-structures in the socio-cultural terrain of secondary school. Nonetheless, over and against departmental differences there are the pressures towards standardisation, the pressure to 'perform' (see Chapter 4) and the inroads of 'principles of integration' like 'Thinking Skills'.

> We are using Thinking Skills, PLTS, to personalise learning, to make lessons more active, to overhaul Key Stage 3 and make it more enjoyable, to overhaul all the schemes of work, to ensure consistency across the school. And under this umbrella, a revised tutor programme starting in Year 7.
> (Laura, Teaching and Learning Coordinator, AST Social Sciences, George Eliot)

However, the infrastructural and translational 'support' given to and aimed at teachers may not be available in the same ways to teaching sssistants and learning support assistants, and indeed many appear to be outside of the main circuits of the policy process. Charlie, a Learning Support Assistant (LSA) at Atwood, commented in interview that he had not been to an INSET event for four years, which he said 'are mainly for the teachers to do stuff' and he described the Monday morning staff briefings as 'just teachers really' although 'some LSAs go'. Cheryl, a TA at Campion said that she attended 'most' INSET days 'But a lot of LSAs don't... we don't get paid for INSET days.' Here again, staffing, budget and curriculum policies intersect. Sheila (Atwood), one of the LSAs we interviewed, explained about working with individual children: 'I don't think there's any training involved, just sort of talking to the teacher.' Laura, a teacher at George Eliot, said: 'we try to [get them involved] but sometimes our learning assistants try and, kind of, remove themselves. So they'll be invited on whole staff things but they go off and do their own thing.' LSAs, as noted already, normally operate in the back regions of the school and work in groups which have a strong cultural specificity and develop systems of mutual support. Rather than being enrolled into the professional cultures of teaching, Molly (Campion), who began work as an LSA and moved into teaching through the GTP, said: 'We're lucky we've got a large SEN team, at least 15, so they are a sort of community on their own, but very supportive.' LSAs and other support workers are actors and subjects brought into being by policy, and in effect they embody shifts in the way policies, of a whole variety of kinds, work upon and rework what it means to be a teacher and who does what in the processes of schooling and who does policy work. They embody a new kind of policy career (see below), with different working conditions from those of teachers and are, in a practical sense, both on the periphery of policy *and* key players in the heterogeneous social networks of policy.

Policy careers

For some teachers policy can be a career opportunity. Identification with and expertise in a high profile area of policy and related posts of responsibility can be a route to promotion and further advancement. This can be the case for entrepreneurs and enthusiasts and translators. Enthusiasm gets you noticed. Nonetheless, the relation between policy and career was most evident among senior staff, some of whom were given specific responsibility for policies, and were required to bring enthusiasm to bear as part of their role. This was most directly the case for Future Leaders;[15] they embodied policy in a literal sense, and were thus also identified with ambition and fast-track promotion. Getting policy done 'successfully' was important to their career development. Their enrolment as 'future leaders' was also a very direct enrolment into policy enactment. Other teachers were sometimes cynical about these fast-track careers and their relation to policy, and as vehicles for getting policy done.

> I think there's a feeling among the heads of years and the heads of department, that kind of middle leaders range, that there's been an explosion of senior management. We've got more senior managers than we used to have, even in the three years that I've been here. And that they all tend to come with a policy attached, like so-and-so is responsible for that and so-and-so is responsible for implementing that. And that means that there's more policy happening. Now, whether that's because there's more policy coming down from the top, I don't know, it probably is, but I think in the staff room it gets blamed on the individual members of staff. Like we've got more policy because we've got more SLT.
>
> (Naomi, RE, Atwood)

> So what you get is they are all fairly ambitious, they've all got things they want to do, and the feeling from the heads of department last year was that all these initiatives were not about helping the kids, they're helping the school and it was all about putting something on their CV so that

they could go for a promotion. It's a game that everyone plays. But when it leads to lots of things being brought in, it doesn't lead people to buy into the initiative.

(Stewart, Science, NUT rep., Atwood)

There were many other teachers in the case study schools who had a strong personal investment in particular aspects of their work, like the enthusiasts above. In these cases policies became part of their professional selves and identities and commitments to practice but not in such obviously career-related ways.

Discussion: policy language and policy discourse

The policy roles and positions outlined above combine to make policies happen. The policy process is iterative and additive, made up of interpretations and translations, which are somewhat inflected by existing values and interests (teachers have a multiplicity of interests and values, personal and institutional), by context and history, and by necessity. In all of this, interpretation and translation can become disconnected. Institutional priorities articulated in staff events still have to be made into the stuff of lessons, in different settings and in relation to different subject and professional sub-cultures, within networks of heterogeneous policy actors.

> [We] are trying to implement whatever vision Ken [head teacher] has and whatever things they [SLT] want to do to show their own ambitions and so on, their own ideas that they think should be put into place. Therefore, we're at the mercy of all of those. I don't think that there is enough thought at either of the three levels, government, the head and senior management team, as to what it is actually like for the classroom teacher. Because neither the senior management team, nor the head, nor the government actually do our job.
>
> (Stewart, Science, NUT rep., Atwood)

The teachers and other adults here are not naïve actors, they are creative and sophisticated and they manage, but they are also tired and overloaded much of the time. They are coping with both what they see as meaningful and what seems meaningless, often self-mobilised around patterns of focus and neglect and jostling uneasily between discomfort and pragmatism, but almost all those we talked with are also very firmly embedded in the prevailing policies discourses.

In all of this there is a lack of space for 'other' discourses, the historic archive of 'democratic' or 'inclusive' teaching is always in danger of erasure, glimpsed in our case studies only in asides, and occasional discomforts and murmurings, or recovered fleetingly at moments of crisis – although if we had asked our questions differently...! This partial erasure is connected in part to a lack of sociality – a lack of time and space in the school day to meet and talk. There is also some evidence here of different discursive generations, trained or educated differently as teachers, with access to different discursive archives. As Mannheim (1952: 291) argues, generational locations point to 'certain definite modes of behaviour, meaning and thought'; generations may exhibit a distinctive consciousness and different situational responses. Here each tends to caricature the other.

> We do at times have a split between those who will be looking for new ways to do something and those who will, sort of, plod on as before. And, you know, if you were to take a graph or a survey of people who really enjoy it and had a passion for what they're doing and those who didn't, then that would correlate pretty much to those who are flexible and those who aren't.
>
> (Joe, head of Sociology, Atwood)

> At the end of the day, if you only teach nine lessons a week then reading a book about Gardner's[16] different styles of learning and trialing them in your classroom and having the time to plan the lessons to do it, is great, because it would be effective, there's no doubt about it. If you spend more time planning your lessons and introduce something new and it involves new strategies, it would be effective. But most people don't have the time to do that.
>
> (Robert, AST Art, Wesley)

Within all of this, teachers are positioned differently in relation to policy in a variety of senses. They are at different points in their careers, with different amounts of accumulated experience. They have different amounts and kinds of responsibility, different aspirations and competences. Some people advance, others are worn down, or tread water; experience can produce possibilities for and limits to fulfilment. The former are most clearly glimpsed through teacher enthusiasms and the institutionalisation of ambition in schemes like Future Leaders – and the production of new kinds of teacher subject, which need further research attention (see Chapter 7). There are also different psychosocial and value positions in relation to policy which relate to teachers' sense of self-worth, and of fulfilment, and their emotions and personal principles. Clearly, discourses and their technologies, and authoritative interpretations do not operate uniformly across schools, teachers are subjected differently and act differently. There may be different spaces or pressures in English and Maths, as opposed to Art and PE, or in the sixth form or in work with SENs. However, for these latter, being outside the direct gaze of policy is double-edged: it can mean being starved of resources or otherwise neglected, or having your curriculum time raided or redistributed to serve the needs of imperative policy (see Ball *et al.* 2011). The point is that the school is not always sensible as the unit of analysis for policy research, and what we mean by 'the school' in such research is typically partial and neglectful. Over and against that, there are few spaces of escape from policy; imperatives and exhortations are both taken very seriously by teachers and schools as they do policy work on themselves. The micro-pressures of survival, improvement and of performance are woven into the daily fabric of school life through 'the meticulous and often minute' (Foucault 1979: 139) apparatuses of policy work. Meetings, materials and models of 'good practice' operate subtly and innocently to make-up 'good' teachers within the discourses of policy.

Policy then cannot be reduced to an algorithm (iterations, community, learning, influence or whatever) but also the school cannot be reduced to policy. What comes across in our analysis is school as a creaky social assemblage, that is continually re-validated and underpinned and moved on by the various efforts of networks of social actors with disparate but more or less focused interests and commitments. It is necessary to recognise the place of incoherence in all of this; policies (and other things, particularly the vicissitudes of context) produce a tendency towards what actor–network theory would call 'precariousness'. The school is continually disrupted or faced with contradictory expectations, but this is an incoherence that can be made to work, most of the time.[17] This precariousness is partly produced by the specifics of policy but is also inherent in the incompatibilities embedded in the general functional demands on schooling (order, acculturation, certification).

Our data taken as a whole convey a sense of overload and contradiction being held together by fragile structures, more or less convincing narratives and a great deal of raw commitment (of some different sorts and degrees, to students and to schools) and much goodwill. Policy enactments trade on a sense of service and the promise of fulfilment and 'improvement' over and against moments of disillusion. These assemblages are strategic and tactical, relational and productive. Schools are classic, complex, single systems made up of multiple interacting parts and what Law[18] calls 'the messy practices of relationality and materiality of the world'. A great deal of what goes on in schools in terms of policy enactment is 'configuration' and 're-configuration' work. This aims to maintain the durability of the institution in the face of the de-stabilising effects of context, of change and of policy. There is a danger that as researchers we try to analyse away this incoherence as an effective complexity and represent 'school' as more stable and coherent than it really is. We are captured by the narratives we are told by school teachers.

> Most teachers' response to that [criticism of educational standards] is to think, 'I have to survive, I have to get through. I have to get through all my admin and get through the system in a week and everything else in a way that means that I have the least pressure on me from these various sources. So whatever I can do to get through the week I will do and then still try and make my lessons as engaging for me and the students as possible within the limits of what I've got to do.' Sometimes the policies are good policies but they don't all link together.
>
> (Neil, English, 2nd in department, Union rep., Wesley)

As we try to suggest, there are a variety of positions and roles within this nascent incoherence that are vital to its management in the face of, and in response to, multiple policy demands (Braun *et al.* 2010). The enactments of policy within all of this range from interpretation, to translation, to practice and performance. They take place at many moments, in various sites, in diverse forms, in many combinations and interplays. Enactments are collective, creative and constrained and are made up of unstable juggling between irreconcilable priorities, impossible workloads, satisficing[19] moves and personal enthusiasms. Enactments are always more than just implementation, they bring together contextual, historic and psychosocial dynamics into a relation with texts and imperatives to produce action and activities that are policy. Also, as we will see in the following chapter, and as already evident above, despite the complexity of enactment processes they do 'join up' classrooms with abstract political priorities.

4 Policy subjects

Constrained creativity and assessment technologies in schools

In this and the next chapter, we want to 'get down to cases'. That is to say, we want to pursue our analysis and conceptualisation of policies in schools and, in particular, the 'enactments' of policy by looking at some specific examples, although in doing this we want to re-emphasise the point made already that policies do not get enacted in isolation. As Latour puts it, local actions 'overflow with elements which are already in the situation coming from some other time, some other place, and generated by some other agency' (Latour 2005: 166). The main substantive focus of this chapter is on *standards* policy, although at the end of the chapter, as a caveat, we briefly contrast standards policy with a different type of policy – Pupils Learning and Thinking Skills (PLTS). This is done to make the point that different types of policy interpolate different kinds of policy subjects.

We will use some of the tools introduced in previous chapters and deploy ideas drawn from Foucault's *Discipline and Punish* to think about some of the ways in which policies are rendered into *practices* through a complex of techniques, procedures and artefacts – or '*force relations*'. Here teachers are both the enactors of techniques, which are intended to make students visible and productive, and are themselves enmeshed within a disciplinary programme of visibility and production, a 'dense network of vigilant and multi-directional gazes' (Hoffman 2010: 31) which is both simple and inconspicuous but, thank goodness, incomplete. Nonetheless, in contrast to other moments in the book, here the teacher is actor and object and subject, 'caught up' in a marvellous machinery of policy – specifically what has been termed by Michael Barber (2010) as *deliverology*.[1] The spaces of negotiation and contestation of policy are relatively narrowly defined here, overwhelmed for the most part by necessity and responsibility as teachers 'do their best'. The teachers are sometimes uncomfortable with some of this but are mostly 'willing selves' as they measure and compare their students and seek to extract 'productivity gains' from them and attempt to find a balance between the interests of students and the interests of 'the school'. Indeed, the ligaments of productivity are also extended laterally to include parents in the apparatus of *standards* and to hail them as policy subjects. Here then the teacher is enrolled into grand political narratives of policy which link their classroom work with students to the processes of globalisation and national economic competitiveness; as UK Coalition government leaders David Cameron and Nick Clegg assert in the second sentence of the preface to the 2010 Schools' White Paper *The Importance of Teaching* – 'What really matters is how we're doing compared with our international competitors. That is what will define our economic growth and our country's future' (DfE 2010: 3).

As part of these globalising concerns to 'fix' economic problems through producing a labour force that is 'fit for purpose' in the knowledge economy, all schools have to ensure that their standards are continually rising and that students are being provided with a platform of core skills, particularly in literacy and numeracy. The focus (see below) on standards is achieved through a very effective national mechanism of performance management which, in England, uses particular indicators, based on students' examination achievements, to generate league tables of school 'outputs' and to set national benchmarks. Schools which fail to achieve the benchmark are deemed to be 'failing schools'. The primary indicator is five or more A* to C grades at GCSE. However, this has now been reconfigured twice, first by New Labour, to include the requirement for students to achieve a mathematics and English qualification at grade C or above, and second by the 2010 Coalition government, who added science, a language and a humanity to the list of required subjects – creating what has come to be referred to as the E-Bac, the English Baccalaureate. Defending the E-Bac, in a speech to school and college leaders in March 2011, Michael Gove, Secretary of State for Education, said the choice of subjects was 'not arbitrary, nor nostalgic but based on countries that are often doing better than us' (see www.mikebakereducation.co.uk). The use and manipulation of standards benchmarks in England and elsewhere has proved to be a tempting and decisive mechanism by which governments can 'steer' schools 'at a distance'.

This chapter critically explores how this steering 'works' within schools and concrete examples will be provided that illustrate the tensions, struggles and resources that are involved in the resulting enactments of policy. In particular, we want demonstrate how the new science of 'deliverology' operates in schools through the discursive and interactive articulations of 'expectation', 'focus' and 'pressure' and indicate some of the policy discomforts and contradictions which are created as a result. By this, we mean the professional conflicts that teachers have to deal with in responding to the 'raising standards' agenda. We conclude with an account of teachers as *policy subjects*, set alongside the discussion of *policy actors* in the previous chapter.

'Deliverology' and the 'play of dominations'

[E]very child doesn't matter, what matters is getting A to C grades above a certain percentage.[2]

(Neil, English, 2nd in department, Union rep., Wesley)

One of the major education policy commitments and policy preoccupations of the New Labour government (1997–2010) was 'raising standards' of school performance, specifically those performances indicated by Standard Assessment Testing (SATs) and GCSE examination 'passes'. This version of 'standards' continues to hold centre stage in the politics of education in England and is a major concern of the present Conservative–Liberal coalition government. The issue of 'raising standards' has been a constant theme in ministerial speeches and official documents. The DfE press release announcing the publication of the 2011 Education Bill declared that: 'The Education Bill, published today, will help teachers raise standards in schools. It includes measures to root out bad behaviour, tackle underperformance and improve the way in which schools are held to account' (DfE 2011). Under New Labour, the DCSF website (Department for Children, Schools and Families) had an extensive dedicated *Standards Site* (www.standards.dfes.gov.uk) and the Coalition government lists 'improving standards in all schools' as one of its policy priorities on its Department for Education website (www.dfe. gov.uk). The 'standards discourse' of New Labour education policy was both complex and polyvalent; it inter-connected individual student outcomes to national economic competitiveness and to issues of social inclusion (so-called) and individual opportunity. As one example among many, there is the 2005 Education White Paper *Higher standards, better schools for all: More choice for parents and pupils*, which states that: 'The aim is to ensure that every school delivers an excellent education, that every child achieves to their potential [as indicated and represented by their performances in public examinations] – whatever their background and wherever they live' (DCSF 2005: 7). However, in relation to the enactment of the 'standards' agenda in schools we will suggest that things are not that simple!

The discourse of 'standards' works to articulate a particular version and vision of what schooling is and should be – more, higher, better! Such a discourse exists at an abstract level in the politics of education but it has the ability to arrange and rearrange, form and re-form, position and identify whatsoever and whomsoever exists within its field and it has a 'heavy and fearsome materiality' (Probyn 1993: 167), as we go on to demonstrate. This discourse is 'enacted' within institutions, departments and classrooms as: 'new relations between institutions, new procedures, and so forth; "inculcated" as new ways of being – new identities; and indeed "materialized" as new ways of organising space and time' (Fairclough 2003).

Here we are interested in the standards agenda in terms of a set of practical enactments both elicited and specified by policy, that is, a set of actions which are produced by and within interpretations and translations (see Chapter 3). As a policy, *standards* 'works' through a very simple but effective and very public technology of performance – made up of league tables, national averages, comparative and progress indicators, Ofsted inspections and benchmarks. These together are intended to instil into schools a 'performance culture'.[3] This technology creates a set of pressures which work 'downwards' through the education system from the Secretary of State to the classroom and into the home to create expectations of performance as 'delivery' (see Figure 4.1), that is, the delivery of improved systemic and institutional performances and the achievement of examination benchmarks by individual schools and individual students – all of which are part of a broader 'audit culture' (Power 1994) embedded in the public sector through the introduction of New Public Management (Cabinet Office 2006).

This is what Barber (2007) calls 'the delivery chain'; that is, hierarchies of 'expectation' that connect the 'front line' service delivery to the responsible minister by ensuring a 'sharp focus' on performance priorities (rather than purposes) and creating what Loveday (2008) calls a 'tyranny of conformity' or what Elmore (2009) calls 'tight-coupling'. That is, a conformity and a coupling that produces 'subjected and practiced bodies' (Foucault 1979: 138) and particular 'capacities'. In education, this constitutes what Jones (2003) calls

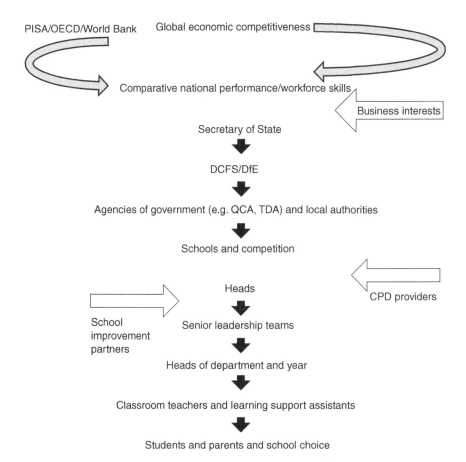

Figure 4.1 The 'delivery chain': passing on the pressures to perform[4]

'a regulatory system' which works by establishing strong links between 'the micro-world of classroom interactions and macro-level objectives of standards and achievements'. In Foucault's terms, the chain consists of specific and rather mundane techniques of government (some of which are presented below) which give rise to a general method of discipline, producing a general and essential transformation. It is a method of ongoing public sector reform that is applied to education, health, policing and almost all other fields of public service. It is *'deliverology'*, a science of delivery, a response to the 'productivity challenge' (Barber 2007). In 2001, Michael Barber was appointed as head of the Prime Minister's Delivery Unit (PMDU), to concentrate on specific targets, such as hospital casualty waiting times, school tests, league tables, street crime, transport, etc.

According to Barber, the key elements of deliverology are: the use of good data; setting targets and trajectories; consistent, regular and frequent stocktaking (reporting); figuring out the 'Delivery Chain'; and tracking progress on a regular basis, all of which are very evident below. These tactics produce day-to-day 'pressures' for and 'awareness' of and a 'focus' on 'standards', as a new meta-narrative of *schooling as performances*. Three examples from interviews with teachers will start us off:

> It's all about awareness of grades going up, awareness of parent pressure, awareness of government pressure which comes from some form of business statement about what kids are supposed to be like [this is what Foucault calls 'normalisation'[5]]... you are aware of a whole series of pressures.
>
> (Neil, English, 2nd in department, Union rep., Wesley)

> [E]verything should feed into standards.
>
> (Manuel, deputy head teacher, ICT, Campion)

> Standards, definitely! And there is a lot of – teachers talk about standards a lot more than any other school, well, not any other school I've been in before. But, you know, there is definitely a focus on standards.
>
> (Caroline, assistant head teacher, SLT, History, Atwood)

Within this meta-narrative of the 'obvious', there is little call for or space for thinking differently. Enactments are put together out of technologies and inventions that are readily available and closely specified.

Focusing on standards

In almost all of the interviews at all levels in all the schools, 'standards' are identified as the major priority, as the scientists of deliverology would expect in relation to schools like ours.[6] In schools occupying other positions in the hierarchy of performance, the pressures may be greater or less acute – but none can escape entirely. The word 'focus' is used repeatedly in interviews to describe the orientation of schools and staff to the question of standards at all levels. One assistant head at Atwood (Caroline) uses the word 32 times in one interview, almost always in reference to standards raising – as in:

> … keeping a really strong focus on you should be, you know, increasing two levels over three years, so two-thirds of a level this year and then reporting that to parents.

> … making teachers – traffic lighting the data so that the teachers are aware of the students that they need to focus on… (see 'educational tri-age' later in this chapter).

> … that is constantly the focus, how are these students doing, what are we doing to make sure, then that becomes everybody's priority.

> So there's all stuff like that, which is really, really good and it would just be much better to just focus, say, 'Okay, we're going to keep the focus up on Assessment for Learning. Assessment for Learning is really important.'

> … the focus on the data, the focus on who's underachieving, what are we going to do, learning from previous year groups.

> And part of what I like about the head is that he is very keeping things simple. Focus on students making progress; quite a tough discipline system. If they do something then they know what's going to happen to them.

> … the good thing will be about keeping the focus really straightforward and not always, kind of, changing initiative and… but just keeping a, really, a focus on the basics, really, to enable the students to make progress.

> … the focus can wholly be preparation for GCSE.

> … look at the schools that are doing really well, what are they focusing on? Well, you know, they're not focusing on every initiative that comes out of the DCSF.

Now, apart from its relation to the pressures to deliver outlined above, the word 'focus' is interesting in other ways. It suggests the idea of bringing a lens to bear, a close-up view, a point of concentration, bringing things into visibility. It also suggests precise, organised and efficient action. It is also used in relation to different subjects and objects. That is, teachers, students and schools, and pedagogies, procedures, performance, data and initiatives, all of these objects and subjects are to be 'focused' *on*, in order to raise standards. As Foucault (1979: 187) explains, 'disciplinary power' – and that in essence is what we are addressing here – 'imposes on those whom it subjects a principle of compulsory visibility… it is the fact of being constantly seen, of being always able to be seen, that maintains the disciplined subject in his subjections.' (We commented on visibility of a different sort in Chapter 3 and the ubiquity of 'observations'.) One of us has written previously about this and its implications for teachers generally as *performativity* (Ball 2003). The primary and ultimate point of focus here is on students as productive subjects or, as we shall see, on some students in particular, and one effect of their visibility is also their classification, that is 'the objectification of those who are subjected' (Foucault 1979) but teachers are also brought into the gaze of judgement in similar terms.

> [T]he deputy heads of year have been given a responsibility that they look at the data and they focus on which are the groups of students that we need to focus on, so that's – that's been built into the culture of the school.
>
> (Caroline, assistant head teacher, SLT, History, Atwood)

> I'm slightly dreading the summer because this is my first results summer as head of department so I can't tell you exactly how this will be. I know the heads of core subjects [English and Maths] have interviews with the head pretty much immediately at the beginning of term, which go on for a number of hours, where you go through all of the results and you will be asked a lot of questions… that's quite nerve wracking.
>
> (Nicola, head of English, Atwood)

> [W]e just know that we have to do well. We still have some teachers, individuals perhaps, who are not focused… it was blamed on the students, you know.
>
> (Daisy, NQT Mathematics, Campion)

Students are objectified as talented, borderline, underachieving, irredeemable, etc. As external policy changes focus on different metrics of performance, these changes are reflected in changes of emphasis within the schools to focus on different sorts of students.

> We're not allowed to focus on that any more [value added] which was really demoralising because maybe we're going to be picking out different kids now… there was C/D borderline intervention last year, more so than was done in the past and it looks like it is going to be stepped up.
>
> (Naomi, RE, Atwood)

So, while attention to a 'value-added' indicator may make the contribution of all students significant, the A–C grade indicator does not.

While the pressures of and focus on standards is not always well received by teachers, and various 'discomforts' were expressed (see further on), it is the case that the processes of delivery work most of the time. They 'necessitise' and naturalise 'results' as part of a policy obviousness, a 'necessarian logic' (Watson and

Hay 2003) that drives what schools need to be doing, 'obviously' and 'clearly' (see below for further examples of these terms in use). Most teachers in our study appear to be thoroughly 'enfolded' into and part of the calculated technologies of performance. Its 'obviousness' needs no explanation.

> The head's emphasis is always just on results, *clearly*.
> (Nicola, head of English, Atwood)

> The school's definitely very concerned about the GCSE results in Maths.
> (Daisy, NQT Mathematics, Campion)

> They're [SLT] very driven by this A* to C figure, it seems to me to be the number one thing.
> (Martin, head of Mathematics, George Eliot)

> The head wants a complete revision package starting in February.
> (Nicola, head of English, Atwood)

> We have a really special focus on the underachievers with a special focus on our, you know, our C/D borderliners with English and Maths because, *obviously*, you know how we are assessed as a school.
> (Anjali, KS4 manager, English, Campion)

> I understand why they [SLT] are doing it and they have to get all these results, I mean that's the bottom line, we have to do them.
> (Roger, Mathematics, Campion)

The rhetoric of necessity legitimates, generates and naturalises a varied and complex set of practices and values, which colonise a great deal of school activity and teacher–student interaction, particularly in relation to Year 10 and 11 students, particularly in Maths and English (Perryman *et al*. 2011), particularly in the second half of the school year, but to some extent at all times and increasingly in relation to all students in our sample of schools. The totalising and individualising of performance is disseminated and driven by an infrastructure of technical methods such as Assessment for Learning, which is being rolled out nationally, and which the QCA described on its website as 'a powerful way to improve learning and raise standards' (http://webarchive.nationalarchives.gov.uk/20100209101751/qcda.gov.uk/4338.aspx, accessed 10 June 2011). Nonetheless, this obviousness also rests upon a *form* or version of social inclusion, which is built on a commitment to getting qualifications and credentials for students who have not been well served historically in this way by schools. However, it could be argued that the forms of teaching and learning involved here are still not serving them well.

The passing down of pressures and construction of *focus* is evident in a complex matrix of emotions, anxieties and role changes and relationships which produce particular meanings for practice and values, and success and self-worth – for teachers and students (Reay and Wiliam 1999). This is one aspect of what, in the USA, is referred to as 'high stakes testing' (Thomas 2005).

> [Y]ou're constantly harassed for the names of kids that are improving… you are encouraged to concentrate on the students that you think are the ones you need to worry about.
>
> (Neil, English, 2nd in department, Union rep., Wesley)

> We've changed the pastoral system of the school. We've tried to shift the focus away from predominantly behavioural issues much more towards making heads of year have an overarching responsibility for the achievement of the year group.
>
> (Hazel, deputy head teacher, Science, Wesley)

> I had a C/D borderline GCSE group this year and that concentrates your mind, because it's quite a pressure group to teach, it's quite important that you get them their Cs… you just feel there's an expectation there.
>
> (Trevor, NQT Mathematics, Atwood)

> Maths and English are now *the* subjects.
>
> (Martin, head of Mathematics, George Eliot)

For some teachers (and perhaps some schools) pressure is offset by confidence. The *degree* of anxiety, especially as experienced in Maths and English departments[7] seemed related to the degree of coherence, mutual support and sense of confidence in colleagues' teaching skills.

> I don't feel pressure personally because I feel confident in the job that I do and I think most of us feel that way in the Maths department.
>
> (Daisy, NQT Mathematics, Campion)

As is evident here, the relationships, techniques and expectations of delivery work on and through teachers, heads of departments, senior leadership teams, parents and students to 'focus' them and their efforts in relation to this overriding institutional priority. For example, Campion has 'a countdown to GCSEs' on its webpage and publishes a revision timetable in its weekly e-zine for parents (see Chapter 6). 'Focus' renders the enactment of the standards agenda into a set of more or less sophisticated technologies and techniques, which are discussed below, within which 'the individual has to be trained or corrected, classified, normalised or excluded, etc.' (Foucault 1979: 191), with the aim of maximising the production of docile bodies but 'productive' minds (see also Chapter 6). As we discuss in the next chapter, even behaviour policies are now predominantly oriented to learning – Behaviour for Learning!

Working on the C/D boundary

The description and discussion of this machinery of standards and performance involves re-visiting, ten years on, Gillborn and Youdell's (2000) exemplary analysis of what they call 'the A–C economy'. However, the primary focus here is on the technologies (literal and metaphorical) that drive the machinery of delivery, as enactments of policy, rather than on its differential consequences for students who are 'objectified' by the technologies as in Gillborn and Youdell (2000). That is to say, what is of concern here is the 'multiplicity of often minor processes' (Foucault 1979: 138) by which policy 'pressures' – the 'delivery chain' – are *translated* into practices and articulate 'focus', for all of those concerned; that is, the enactments of performance and standards. However, the analysis also reiterates Gillborn and Youdell's point that a *focus* on some students, as strategically productive, means the relative but *systematic neglect of others* and patterns of uneven access to expenditures and efforts at school, with the effect of producing a structured distribution of identities and opportunities and exclusions based on ethnicity, social class and gender. However, currently the 'culture' of performance draws attention to the 'improvement' of almost all students, none can be neglected entirely, but some 'improvements' are more strategically important than others.

As explained earlier, the key point of focus is produced by the system of indicators by which performance is measured and, as indicated, the A–C metric in particular. As other researchers and commentators have noted, this is the point at which efforts and intervention can have most effect in terms of school performance. *Obviously*, this becomes the site of greatest activity and anxiety, and it is this which generates patterns of neglect. This is what Gillborn and Youdell (2000) call the 'A to C economy' which produces and drives practices of 'educational triage'. Put crudely, techniques of monitoring, labelling and selective attention identify those who can be left to succeed on their own, those who can be boosted across the C/D boundary with sufficient intervention and support, and the remaining 'hopeless cases'.

> The C/D kids got first choice of revision classes, the C/D kids get an expensive weekend away, where they're meant to bond... the C/D kids get mentors and motivators that are meant to harass and bully them into thinking about work all the time. A huge amount of budget goes on the C/D borderline.
>
> (Neil, English, 2nd in department, Union rep., Wesley)

> I'd like to think we target everybody, I'd certainly like to think that way. Maybe subconsciously all schools will target the C/D borderlines. And if I am to be honest we do have our most experienced teachers tending to teach those classes... I am not happy just focusing on these, but in Maths we do it all the time... we have after-school classes, lunchtime sessions with them, that seem quite popular.
>
> (Martin, head of Mathematics, George Eliot)

[T]hese kids that are on the borderline, taking them out of a subject they may be failing in and putting more time in English and Maths instead of continuing with that one subject they are not going to get a grade in.

(Molly, GTP English, Campion)

{O}*bviously*, as everybody else, C/D borderline is our first target group.

(Nicola, head of English, Atwood)

[M]ine were the bottom set so they weren't targeted in the same way… *obviously* the bottom set wasn't, if we got a couple of Cs that would be amazing… they're middle sets and obviously middle sets are the ones that could possibly get Cs, *obviously the top set will be OK*,… we did a lot of extra activities when we took them out of PE and things like that and we would work with them. We took days off the timetable when they did Maths and extra Maths.

(Daisy, NQT Mathematics, Campion)

The delivery chain, as intended, is enacted through an accretion of minutiae. All of this becomes part of the normal life of schools, it becomes ingrained in routines, patterns of work, assumptions and perspectives. Indeed, it is impossible to over-estimate the significance of this in the life of the school, as a complex of surveillance, monitoring, tracking, coordinating, reporting, recording, targeting, motivating. As Fairclough puts it, again using the chain metaphor:

Power is exercised not only in particular types of events but across chains of events which are shaped by relatively stabilized and institutionalized genre chains, and the balance between cooperation and conflict in nego-tiating differences of interest is conditional upon the chain of events and the genre chain, not just the particular event.

(Fairclough 2003: 10)

Across the four case study schools there was a bewildering array of activities, initiatives, programmes and interventions as responses to the pressures of pol-icy. These were mostly aimed at those students on whom it was judged they would have a short-term positive impact with the resulting effect of boosting the overall performance of the school in terms of national indicators, most specifically the percentage of students obtaining five-plus A* to C grades in GCSE examinations. Some of these initiatives were limited to one school, but most were used by all four schools, and anecdote and media coverage suggest these techniques are widespread:

Schools are increasingly focusing on average pupils in an attempt to 'flat-ter' official league tables, according to research by the Liberal Democrats.

(Paton 2009)

The list below shows a diverse range of often very imaginative techniques being applied in our case study schools which overlap and reinforce one another.

- 'Mike and Ben sat down with about 20 intervention strategies of how they were going to do it…' (Roger, Mathematics, Campion)
- Easter revision classes
- Saturday revision classes (extra pay for teachers)
- Buying in revision teachers and exam coaches
- Targeting marginal groups (C/D borderline)
- Targeted students meeting regularly with SLT
- 'Changing staff mindsets' (Duncan, assistant head teacher, Geography, Wesley)
- 'Challenging staff' (Hazel, deputy head teacher, Science, Wesley)
- Using data to identify underachieving students (see below)
- Course work clubs
- Gifted and Talented programmes
- Mentoring
- Enrichment activities
- Schools trips/residential weekends 'we went to Dorset with a group of kids who are gifted and talented' (Duncan, assistant head teacher, Geography, Wesley)
- Interviews of 'underachieving' students by SLT
- Photographs in the staff room of targeted students ('there are 35/36') – making teachers aware of who they are
- MTLs (motivational team leaders) (teams of five students per teacher)
- Cards/points – 'we give them a doughnut' – a prize for 'positives'
- After-school meetings
- Changing examination board
- 'Another group went to the Westbourne centre… and another group somewhere else' (Duncan, assistant head teacher, Geography, Wesley)
- School targets ('73 per cent A* to Cs this year')
- League approach, creating teams and competition between the boys
- Meeting for parents 'to get them on board and support their children' (Hazel, deputy head teacher, Science, Wesley)
- Planning meetings – setting down the year's strategy
- Maths club
- Software and website for revision (e.g. My Maths/SAM learning)
- Writing to parents
- Entering students early for exams/fast tracking/re-sits
- Moving students from their 'failing' subjects to more time on core subjects
- Interventions during tutor group registration time
- Use of software to track student performance/regular and repeated testing
- Timetabling for intensive revision classes (Maths to replace PE)
- One-to-one sessions with local authority advisors
- Getting students to monitor their own progress.

The pressure to perform is enacted through these interventions. All teachers, and especially those in the core disciplines (Perryman *et al.* 2011) are expected to mobilise a set of targeted activities that will maximise student performance in the A* to C range. Teaching and learning are 'adapted' to the processes of 'output' (see later). Nonetheless, to an extent, the experience of pressure and the extent of focus will ebb and flow across the school year.

> At the beginning of term, everyone's focused on their teaching and learning-type policies and by the end very much on their target setting, and panicking.
>
> (Naomi, RE, Atwood)

> [W]e are called in to have a meeting to say, when we sit down with our lists of target students, what are we doing for those individual students... so we are accountable directly to the head in terms of GCSE target groups.
>
> (Nicola, head of English, Atwood)

> [O]bviously, you do extra coaching and you're going to do Easter revision classes and things like that.
>
> (Martin, head of Mathematics, George Eliot)

> [S]omebody comes to find us with this grid [revision timetable] and we fill it in... it's every day that something is going on... it just looks grotesque... there are pages and pages of it... suddenly you realise things from the students' point of view, it's horrendous.
>
> (Nicola, head of English, Atwood)

This 'reduplicated insistence' (Foucault 1979: 180) is another tactic of discipline and its effect is to achieve intended outcomes, not punishment or deterrence for their own sake. We try to mirror this reduplication and insistence in our deployment of data in this chapter. Even so, we have only selectively quoted from the relevant data we have on this topic.

> [W]e started enrichment, which is after-school activities in Maths, right back in October... all the Maths department turn up for it every week... in the last month before the exams we worked out a timetable where they had Maths three hours a day some days and two hours a day on other days.
>
> (Daisy, NQT Mathematics, Campion)

> We've got revision materials made up for smartboards that we've all produced over the years.
>
> (Sonja, Mathemathics, Atwood)

> [W]e were talking the other day, why are we not intervening in Year 7, when they're a bit more malleable.
>
> (Roger, Mathematics, Campion)

With some exceptions, the emphasis of interventions is on a very *constrained creativity*. They involve a *predictable inventiveness* and almost always focus on 'strategic teaching' and 'strategic learning'[8] with little attempt at 'deep learning'. That is, an emphasis on forms of teaching and learning that are firmly oriented to the requirements of examination passing, that is, short-term knowledge and 'surface learning' (Marton and Säljö 1976).[9] Information rather than understanding!

> I don't like the idea of force-feeding information into people's heads so they pass the exam, I don't think any teacher does. But that's what you end up having to do.
>
> (Roger, Mathematics, Campion)

Grids: 'they can click on a child'

These techniques of 'repetition – reduplicated insistence' (Foucault 1979: 180) in turn rely increasingly heavily on the collection and analysis of data, in measurement and monitoring, often using software systems. These provide an array of 'small techniques of notation [which work by] arranging facts in columns and tables' (Foucault 1979: 190) to represent students. These then generate taxonomies – which 'makes possible the measurement of quantities and the analysis of movement' (p.149), that is 'improvement'. These policy artefacts and devices contribute to a new kind of technical professionalism and a process of enactment which is articulated within the procedures and manipulations of assessment.

> It's taken quite a long time to work with Middle Leaders to realise that the data is there for them to use, that they should be using data to identify underachievement… therefore how are they going to respond to it… they can dig deeper if they want, they can click on a child and find out more…
>
> (Hazel, deputy head teacher, Science, Wesley)

Taken together, these small details and 'acts of cunning' produce 'the coherence of a tactic' (Foucault 1979: 139). They work together to generate a general method for raising standards. They exemplify the form of 'discipline' that Foucault portrays as realised through meticulousness, fussiness and trifles. The monitoring technologies which are used are becoming ever more refined, ever more specific.

> [S]o this is our assessment that you're just seeing there. So, when they come, they come with Key Stage 2, which I've converted into a two decimal place by interpolation. Their Year 7 target will be 14 per cent on that… from the line of best fit, it looked like a 14 per cent increase was a decent sort of figure to work with… it's quite fine lines if you're doing percentages, it's not As, Bs and Cs.
>
> (Martin, head of Mathematics, George Eliot)

[T]here's been a lot closer monitoring of how students are progressing, there's much more emphasis on analysing the data. Any student who isn't making their three levels of progress over two key stages would be a focus for intervention.

(Nicola, head of English, Atwood)

Assessment Manager [commercial software], that's quite good because it can calculate for you whether they are on target and comes up colour-coded and pretty when you do a graph. It does help you to pick up people maybe you didn't notice. But it's very divisive, it is like a machine suddenly that is everything, you are in these categories and you're supposed to go to all of these slots.

(Naomi, RE, Atwood)

The measurement and monitoring software systems, which are deployed in all four case study schools, and different ones in different departments, are used to derive 'a distribution of individuals in space' (Foucault 1979: 141) – but these are not taken to be 'fixed position(s)', at least not in all cases, for progress is required. Through these techniques, the educational space is made into 'a learning machine' (Foucault 1979: 147), a machine for 'supervising, hierarchising and rewarding' (Foucault 1979: 147). The school becomes a 'centre of calculation' (Latour 1986: 235), a space in which information is used by professionals in an authoritative manner. Clearly, this is a refinement and hyper-intensification of what English state schools as institutions have always done.

We use SIMS [commercial software], so we do nine-weekly data collection where we give them attitude scores out of five; based around the new PLTS (Personal Learning and Thinking Skills) system and then you level them as well on national curriculum levels.

(Molly, GTP English, Campion)

There are profits to be made from these monitoring and recovery technologies. Commercial providers now offer a range of tracking software, virtual learning environments, revision software and other materials (see Figure 4.2).

However, the machine is not infallible. When things go wrong, the delivery chain acts upon those 'responsible', and renewed and still more tightly focused pressures are brought to bear.

[W]hen we had our awful results summer, the head and the deputy head came to talk to the whole department at great length, and basically we were pretty much roundly told off for the results, so I don't think she [head of department (HOD)] was able to shield anybody from anything… lot more emphasis this year on making the HOD accountable for their team… you will have been, sort of, monitored yourself in doing these

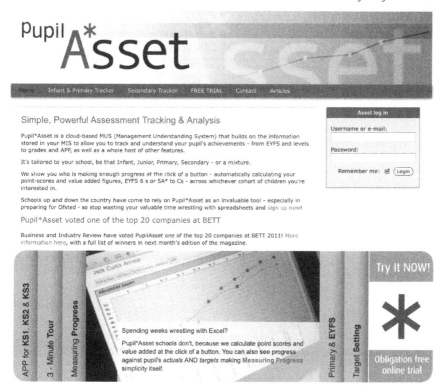

Figure 4.2 Commercial technologies of assessment

things… we've been supported a little more in the lead up to results: supported, obviously having more demands made of you.

(Nicola, head of English, Atwood)

Costs

There are costs of various kinds involved here in addition to the software. Specific funds are allocated to support these interventions, which might be used in other ways, including the buying in of agency teachers, away days, weekends and visits, paying teachers for overtime and tutoring, producing and buying revision materials, etc. Learning support assistants (LSAs) are also allocated to support specific targeted interventions. Schools were able to apply for, but did not always get, money from the 'intervention budget' which was part of the Standards Fund administered by the DCSF. Other monies were allocated specifically for interventions. There are also costs in terms of the distribution of teachers' time, effort and attention, which are also part of the rationing process outlined above, and there are opportunity costs in relation to other kinds of classroom work and other kinds of learning experiences which are not attended to. There are all sorts of issues involved here in the ways in which finite resources are allocated and performance and equity focuses can be deployed to support very different sorts of distributions.

> We got an outside agency in to do the Easter holiday sessions.
>
> (Nicola, head of English, Atwood)

> [I]t's amazing how much time you spend chasing up kids to attend these things.
>
> (Sonja, Mathemathics, Atwood)

> [W]e had examiners come in from the exam board. I don't think that worked that well… we can do it in-house in future rather than paying Edexel [Examination Board] quite a lot of money.
>
> (Martin, head of Mathematics, George Eliot)

> [I]t costs the school a lot of money to re-enter them [for exams].
>
> (Molly, GTP English, Campion)

> [Y]ou get more support, you get more budget… it balances out.
>
> (Daisy, NQT Mathematics, Campion)

> [Targeting] determines the allocation of LSAs.
>
> (Nicola, head of English, Atwood)

> And certainly they were talking about some extra after-school lessons, maybe paid, for kids that are on that C/D borderline.
>
> (Douglas, HoY, Mathematics, Wesley)

> This is this new government scheme that they're going to pay teachers extra money to do extra hours of tutoring on a one-to-one basis, £25 an hour. It's quite a difficult process, the deputies identify the students who are borderline, who would benefit from one-to-one. It's quite controversial because you're going to get parents saying 'this child's getting it, why isn't my child getting it?'
>
> (Molly, GTP English, Campion)

For the schools these costs are also investments. First, in the immediate returns they may generate in terms of boosting examination outputs, and second, as a result, in making the school more attractive to parents within the local performance economy (see Chapter 2).

Discomforts

There are also emotional costs which arise from the narrowness of 'focus' and the pressures to 'improve' which constrain the enactments of 'standards'. Not all teachers are convinced by the rhetorics of performance, and many teachers are not convinced all of the time. Some discomforts were expressed in interviews, but more public expressions of concern seemed to go unheeded in the face of the pressures to perform and the risks of underperformance. The technology does not respond to dismay or dissent, and it operates not by the success or sincerity of any one of its specifics but by the combinatory and relentless effects of its myriad constituents. Indeed, the responsibilities which are generated by the delivery chain mean that many teachers find it difficult to establish a clear ethical position in relation to the *techne* of performance.

> All of this pressure on the C/D borderline is obscene in lots of ways… it's incredibly divisive between kids that have got a hope and kids that have not got a hope. And as much as the lady that runs the SEN department will pipe up and say every year: 'What about the kids that are on F and want to get an E?' the school will say 'Yeah, no. It's a shame but this is government policy so we're putting every ounce of money we have, every ounce of effort we have, into kids on the C/D borderline.'
>
> (Neil, English, 2nd in department, Union rep., Wesley)

> [B]ut focus is genuinely on doing the best for our kids [but] I think we are more focused on the outcome, so we do have more of an eye on the assessment.
>
> (Nicola, head of English, Atwood)

> [N]o doubt the people who came up with these ideas would be able to justify it fully in terms of maximising the students' life chances.
>
> (Martin, head of Mathematics, George Eliot)

> Year 9 tutor groups are now disbanded and a tutor group will now receive intervention during registration times; now I feel myself that that's a bit too far.
>
> (Martin, head of Mathematics, George Eliot)

> It means that a lot more effort is put into kids who are on the C/D borderline than kids who are on D/E borderline. And you can question whether that is fair.
>
> (Sonja, Mathemathics, Atwood)

> We've opted to put our current Year 11s in for the language exam early… it was a controversial decision in terms of being able to justify why you're putting those children in early… how do they feel if they haven't passed,

our focus has been on the exam... and some want to re-sit to get higher grades which defeats the object. Some of us thought it was a good idea, some of us didn't.

(Molly, GTP English, Campion)

What is highlighted in these examples is the immanent tensions between the interests of the school and the interests of the students. It is not always clear whether students generally, or some students in particular, are well served by the strategies and methods for raising performance. In some examples, it is the overall A* to C percentage and the competitive interests of the school that are the focus of attention rather than individual students' needs or student well-being. The rhetorics and rationales which are deployed are not always convincing even to the main protagonists. Pragmatism and necessity trump wider responsibilities towards students.

I think sometimes SLT doesn't agree with the policies that are coming in, and do it anyway... [the head] started his presentation saying: 'Obviously this is a contentious issue but this is what we have to do for Ofsted.'

(Naomi, RE, Atwood)

In their daily practice, teachers move between very different emotional states in a context of overload and time poverty. Kelchtermans (2003: 995) argues that 'teachers' emotions have to be understood in relation to the vulnerability that constitutes a structural condition of the teaching job', which is very evident here, but also he says that 'emotions reflect the fact that deeply held beliefs on good education are part of teachers' self-understanding.' In these schools this vulnerability often works against or muffles such self-understanding.

I think in this school we really sometimes kill creativity. We're so – it's so directed, like we have to do *this*, we have to do *this*, we have to do *this*.

(Rachael, head of PE, George Eliot)

We don't talk about government policies and new initiatives... we're so busy we don't actually get to talk about things like that. I think that's a shame.

(Aabid, joint head teacher, Social Sciences, George Eliot)

As Mahony *et al.* (2004: 78) write, 'increasingly there are sets of regulations and requirements and expectations built around those teachers who are at the peak of their professional expertise and yet who don't have the autonomy to define how they work.' In another sense, what professionalism is and what autonomy is, and therefore what it means to be an 'expert' teacher, are all redefined within policy.

An infrastructure of 'malicious minutiae'

Alongside the 'work' of competition and benchmarking, which drive the focus on performance in and into schools and animate the performance delivery chain, there is also a set of programmes (state and commercial as indicated above) and some new 'disciplinary professionals' (transactors) that contribute in an infrastructure of performance, or an 'anatomy' or 'physics' of power as Foucault would put it. In particular, there was (until abolished by the Coalition government) a system of compulsory 'support' for schools – School Improvement Partners (SIPS) – to provide 'professional challenge and support to the school, helping its leadership to evaluate its performance, identify priorities for improvement, and plan effective change' (DCSF 2009: 3). The first of four guiding principles for the improvement partner's work was to 'focus on pupil progress and attainment across the ability range' (DCSF 2009: 3). Furthermore, the partners 'need[ed]' access to 'core data' in going about their task, including among many other things: 'performance management policy arrangements', 'schools data analysis from RAISEonline', 'Fischer Family Trust data analysis for the school' and data from the 'Learner Achievement Tracker' (DCSF 2009: 17–18). SIPS at the local level were run or 'brokered' by LA School Improvements Services (SIS) – they can still be 'bought' by schools if they so wish.

Furthermore, while we have sought to indicate that performance technologies lead to patterns of focus on certain students and the relative neglect of others, SIPS and other programmes like Assessing Pupil Performance (APP) do seek to address the whole ability range. 'APP is a structured approach to periodically assessing mathematics and reading and writing so teachers can: track pupils' progress from Year 1 through to the end of Year 6; use diagnostic information about pupils' strengths and weaknesses'.[10] APP materials set out a language for assessment which is intended for use in classrooms and which Ofsted inspectors expect to see in use; although APP is not compulsory in schools at present, many schools are using the materials as part of their repertoire of interventions. All of this further emphasises the materialities of enactment, the significance of non-human actants in networks of policy relations, and the relationalities of enactment, the diverse set of actors and entities that are mobilised around 'the problem' of standards.

For both student and teacher, this technical matrix of 'malicious minutiae' (Foucault 1979: 226) produces 'an indefinite discipline: an interrogation without end, an investigation that would be extended without limit to a meticulous and ever more analytical observation' (Foucault 1979: 227). This is a 'cellular' system that is inclusive and exclusive simultaneously through its constant use of divisions. Students are both 'branded' (as being outside or beyond redemption) and 'altered' (see APP above) (as subject to further intervention). One or other is to the fore at different points in students' school careers.

Different strokes for different folks

Our focus so far in this chapter has been on the disciplinary subjectifications of a particular policy and a particular kind of policy. It is important to acknowledge that different policies, or more precisely *kinds* of policy, position and produce teachers as different kinds of *policy subjects*. Different narratives of the teacher and teaching are discernible within different policies, which also shape what it means to be a teacher, a learner and what it means to be educated. In these respects policy makes sense of teachers, makes them what and who they are in the school and the classroom, makes them up, produces them, articulates them and what or who they can be. Teaching is set within policy regimes and policy discourses which speak them as practitioners – as least to an extent. Thus, we want to contrast what we call *imperative* policies, like 'standards', with those we call *exhortative* within which very different relations of power are realised (we pick up this point again in Chapter 5).

Imperative/disciplinary policies like those involved in the standards agenda produce a primarily passive policy subject, a 'technical professional' whose practice is heavily determined by the requirements of performance and delivery, particularly in the high-stakes disciplines (Ball *et al.* 2011; Maguire *et al.* 2011). Little reflexive judgement is required of this teacher; indeed, it could be argued that it is 'required' that judgment is suspended and ethical discomforts set aside. As MacBeath (2008) puts it, 'warrant' is given to teachers, that this is what their role is. Teachers are reactive and constrained in the form and modalities of their responses. Enactment and creativity here are narrowly defined and mostly unoriginal, although there is always room for invention within the terms of the formal structures of practice. However, the multiple 'interventions' which are developed to boost student performances are repeated almost exactly in all of our case study schools. We can think of these as *readerly policies*; teachers, particularly those of the subjects that 'count' directly for the key performance metrics, are put under pressure to submit to the disciplines of necessity; these necessities bear differently upon different parts of the school. They do not locate the teacher–reader as a site of the production of meaning, but only as the receiver of a fixed, pre-determined, reading. School policies and practices are *products* rather than *productions*, which are articulated within a 'linear logic' (Buckles 2010) – like the 'delivery chain'. Teachers (and students) are consumers of the policy texts, which are 'intransitive' and serious (Barthes 1970: 4), although it is possible to see forms of 'gaming' and 'fabrication' which go on around performance measures as a kind of creativity and resistance. Compliance is key – acceptance or rejection are the only options. The rationale for such policies is extrinsic – outcomes (test and examination attainments) as opposed to the 'intrinsic' rationale and legitimation of PLTS (Pupils Learning and Thinking Skills – see below). The problem of education here is defined by policy as one of standards and the need to raise standards, represented in quantitative outcomes and measures. In effect, a 'performativity discourse' is set over and against a 'humanist discourse' (Jeffrey 2002) and privileged by a set of 'correlations' and 'exclusions'.[11] The forms of teaching and learning involved are for the most part 'traditional' and superficial – they are forms of 'surface learning'.

> The external pressures on the school to meet certain targets is always going to override anything a school wants to do that's individual about personalised learning. And since most schools are stretched to the limit, with staff working over the number of hours, they're not going to be able to introduce anything substantially new that would fit that programme.
>
> (Joe, head of Sociology, Atwood)

The school here is represented as a cipher of government policy, policy that comes from outside, and which 'overrides' local particularities or priorities or principles and that enacts 'designed teaching and learning' (Buckles 2010: 7). In turn, overall, the needs of performance and the competitive interests of teachers, departments and schools are prioritised over and against those of students.

The interpretative/political work of the senior leadership team (SLT) is decisive and unequivocal in relation to 'standards' and sets narrow and well-defined conditions for the enactment of policy. Power relations are explicit. There is little or no space for 'alternative' interpretations of policy. The SLT acts as agents of policy, *policy enforcers*, or as 'suitably fitted leaders' (Wright 2001; Buckles 2010). Even if sometimes members distance themselves from the messages they convey and the pressures they bring to bear, others revel in the opportunities for exactitude.

> In our last INSET a couple of weeks back, the new Ofsted framework came in, particularly the focus on raw data rather than contextually value-added, which is going to have implications for who we focus on in terms of intervention and things. Ken [head teacher] was more diplomatic but other members of SLT, when they were presenting it to us, basically said, 'We don't like this but we're on the list for a no-notice inspection, we only got a "satisfactory" last time, we were "good" before, we're going to have to do it anyway.'
>
> (Naomi, RE, Atwood)

> The feeling that I get from senior management and heads generally is, whether they agree with the policy or not, it's totally nothing to do with them, whether they're educationally for it or not they feel that, I mean, I don't want to be crude, but they're literally balls in a vice kind of effect.
>
> (Neil, English, 2nd in department, Union rep., Wesley)

A caveat: different policy subjects

In contrast to and alongside the imperatives and pressures embedded in the standards agenda there are other *exhortative/developmental policies* in play in schools, like PLTS, that *can* enable an active policy subject, perhaps a more 'authentic' professional who is required to bring judgement, originality and 'passion', as some teachers put it, to bear upon the policy process, although this is tempered by the nature of the whole school response to PLTS and whether or not departments have a choice in implementing PLTS or not. On the whole, these are more *writerly* policies which offer a 'plurality of entrances' (Barthes 1970), they are productions rather than products, the teacher as producer has 'access to the magic of the signifier' (p.4) and the 'pleasures' of production – hence the possibilities of passion. A sense of *writerliness*, creativity and sense-making, is conveyed by Gareth (deputy head of sixth form, History, Campion):

> Personalised Learning is a kind of umbrella term for a lot of things that are already going on, you know... learning styles and things like that needs to come into it, and differentiation, all of that kind of ties in together, for me, to mean Personalised Learning. Now, I kind of hope that's what the government think it is as well, I don't know...

The uncertainties here and their opportunities, contrast with the absolute and clear certainties of performance policies. Policies such as these can also be ignored, or underplayed or sidelined, they can be spaces of delay or neglect or creative re-packaging.

> I looked at PLTS and I just thought, this is from my point of view – I am not convinced.
>
> (Nick, deputy head teacher, Atwood)

> We need to decide how far we're going to buy into secondary SEAL [Social and Emotional Aspects of Learning]. The local authority was also still deciding how much weight to give to this.
>
> (Bryan, assistant head, Wesley)

However, it is often the case that the selection of attention is done by some, the SLT or middle managers, for others, for example junior teachers (see Chapter 3). As Aabid (George Eliot) observes, 'It's more filtered, so they pick out the best bits, I suppose, and then implement them...'. Some of our respondents were enthused and excited by these sorts of developmental policies and their possibil-ities – reading, theory, CPD and visits to other schools to observe good practice of all sorts are brought to bear upon the 'co-production' of materials, organi-sation and practice. Practice often emerged as a bricolage of inventions and borrowings from diverse sources. Here the teachers are engaged in the produc-tion of original local texts, methods, artefacts and pedagogies which generate a sense of policy 'ownership'. The 'problem' of education defined by these policy discourses is that of *learning*. That is, as a process and a set of skills and dispositions, and a disposition of reflexivity on the part of students as against 'output' or performance. The forms of learning involved here might be described as 'deep', a kind of 'new' child-centred progressivism which is, when taken at face value, meaningful to the teachers, and related to principled views about student interests.[12] There is a different genre of 'delicate connexions' here.

The striking thing in our case studies is that teachers move between these different forms of policy, these different professionalisms and subjectivities and modalities, for the most part, with unreflexive ease. This is indicative perhaps of contemporary teaching as 'a liminal state of being' – that is a state of being on the 'threshold' of or between two different existential planes, being an essentially incoherent subject (see 'dissonance' below), both rational and passionate, compliant and inventive. As Rachael (George Eliot), says, 'I feel that I can change things... I put my case forward, he is extremely supportive... It's so directed, like we have to do *this*, we have to do *this*, we have to do *this*.'

The liminal state is normally characterised by ambiguity, openness and indeterminacy but there was no clear evidence of disorientation in our data. In part perhaps because there is neither time nor space for most teachers to reflect on the contradictions embedded here, they are 'working their socks off' (Anjali, Campion), although the possibilities of thinking about and 'doing policy' in different ways vary across the school year, 'April/May time it's just mad' (Anjali).[13]

> I think at the beginning of term, things like AfL [Assessment for Learning], everyone's quite excited about, then about halfway through the term everyone's worrying about things like, 'I haven't set a homework and I was meant to set two by the half term.' And then by the end of term everyone's, sort of, 'Oh my goodness, they're one quartile down on their thing'... I think at the beginning of term everyone's focused on their teaching and learning-type policies and by the end very much on their target setting and panicking.
>
> (Naomi, RE, Atwood)

There is a strong sense throughout the data of the dominance of 'coping' and 'keeping up' and of being tired and sometimes overwhelmed, which work against systematic consideration of contradictions, although these are sometimes noted in passing. To some extent, the problems that these contradictions pose are 'solved' by the impossibilities of the job. Some of the time it seems that teachers do not 'do policy' – policy 'does them'. This is the most recent iteration of the long-term and ongoing 'intensification' of teachers' work.

> There is the danger that it does feel like it's more paperwork, more bureaucracy. But in terms of the teaching and learning changes that are made, it's very clear why they are brought out and ultimately why every

policy change is made. But, you know, it's the old adage that it's just more work and less time.

(Robert, AST Art, Wesley)

We do get tired but, do you know what, I think as a school we just keep going. I don't think any of us just stop. We have a whinge and a moan about doing... I don't know, we just keep going, I think, and then by the end of it we're, kind of, like, we're on our knees.

(Anjali, KS4 manager, English, Campion)

There is a sense, I think, at the moment, of a lot of people there that they're quite worn down by the number of policies that are out there that are not [inaudible] allowing them to do their job.

(Joe, head of Sociology, Atwood)

The sheer number and diversity of policies in play, set in relation to the routine demands of the working day, work against, most of the time, what Hoyle (1974) calls 'extended professionality', within which the teacher acquires skills from the mediation between professional experience and educational theory; although we did glimpse some examples of such mediation embedded in the work of translation (discussed in Chapter 3). Rather, in many sites and much of the time, teaching is enacted as short term and pragmatic, a nonetheless complex and sophisticated juggling of pace, selection and order. 'You just ignore it, you forget about it and just teach lessons. It's much easier in the classroom' (Beth, HoY 7, English, Atwood).

This flexible (or unstable) teacher subject, with all its incoherence, has been produced over time through policy and the enactments of policy, and the inescapability of policy on many planes, in many forms and in many aspects of school life. This is a relatively superficial subject, defined more by responsiveness than principle, pragmatism rather than reflection, action rather than judgment, each of these aspects is present but unevenly so, again as noted in the previous chapter. Schools, Fullan (2001: 109) says, frequently struggle with a lack of coherence, 'the main problem is not one of the absence of innovations but the presence of too many disconnected, episodic, piecemeal, superficially adorned projects.'

Nonetheless, as we have tried to indicate, different kinds of policy foreground or 'call up' different kinds of teacher and different teacherly qualities and thus make different sorts of careers and different sorts of satisfactions more or less possible. These are policy paradoxes. They are versions of schooling and the teacher, which contradict and coexist at various levels of discourse. They enact different versions of teaching and learning, of the teacher and the learner, of what it means to be educated.[14] Schools privilege these different versions at different times (staff conferences and briefings, CPD and performance monitoring). However, for the most part, these remain unaddressed or are avoided.

Enactment within a 'logic of conformity'

We have been writing here of both policy and school as generalities. There may be no escape from some policy imperatives but while policies do engage and hail teachers differently, they also hail different teachers. Specialists of various sorts are subject to specific policies, but may be peripheral to other more general policies. There are spaces in schools where some kinds of policies do not reach or are relatively insignificant, but these spaces are also re-configured over time *by* policy. Different spaces within schools have their moments in the glare of policy but, in some cases, these moments are few and far between. To reiterate, schools are not *of a piece*, they are complexly structured and culturally diverse – in terms of geography, departments and subject cultures (Goodson 1983), support services, professional identities and the distribution of students. These diversities and distributions also produce spaces of avoidance and creativity and different ways of being a teacher and doing teaching – different possibilities of enactment. Policies also have their time as well as their place. The school year has rhythms and pressures which vary. 'Standards' and their attendant anxieties dominate a lot of the time and more so at particular times but there are periods like after exams and before Christmas when other priorities take over or within which teachers and students can think about those bits of school life which are not measured or tested at all.

In this chapter, we have mainly sought to map the ways in which a particular policy travels through the school system and is enacted in schools through the technology of delivery. There is, as demonstrated, and in contrast to other sorts of policies, little need/opportunity for sense-making in relation to the obviousness of this – standards. We have sought to indicate the ways in which the logic of performance enters and engages institutional policies and priorities, colonises the most immediate interactions between teachers and their students, and inflects the way in which teachers think about themselves and their work. It also discomforts and de-stabilises and re-conforms teacher values. It makes 'what to do for the best' unclear and difficult. The enactments we see here are not the teachers' own in any simple sense. They are creative and sophisticated but they are set within a logic of conformity and the imperatives of performance and competition. This example of enactments also highlights again the combinations 'in' policy between actors, texts and objects. In particular 'grids', tables and software systems are key elements in the enactments of policy (see also Chapter 6) and also starting points in 'the ceaseless transport of information' (Koyama 2010: 44) which join up classroom to department, to school, to local authority, to league tables, to national benchmarks, to international comparisons, as centres of calculation, always leaving 'traceable traces' and establishing continuities between teachers' actions and political goals – a delivery chain!

5 Policy into practice

Doing behaviour policy in schools

Schools have always had a pressing and pragmatic concern with managing student behaviour. In addition, behaviour is a 'problem' that governments – both left and right – utilise to demonstrate that they take education seriously. It is an arena that always attracts policy attention from within, as well as outside of the school and alongside the standards discourse we attended to in Chapter 4, behaviour is one of the dominant discourses of schooling. Compared with standards, however, behaviour and discipline and its management and organisation in institutions and by individuals are to a greater extent open to what Spillane (2004) termed 'sense-making'. Behaviour is an area of education infused with long-standing and agonistic discourses and sets of diverse professionals with attachments to different interpretations of the what and the why of behaviour management (e.g. Slee 1995, 2011). More than in many other policy areas, behaviour policy is thus a site where professional conflicts and different approaches to 'sense-making' can come to the fore – rich ground for our investigation of policy enactments. Amongst the key professionals 'doing' behaviour in schools – not just teachers and senior management, but also TAs and LSAs, learning mentors, behaviour and attendance officers, etc. – power dynamics and hierarchies remain, but practice and pragmatics can blur some distinctions. Behaviour and discipline is also clearly an area that is susceptible to different patterns of enactment throughout the school year, with the end of the academic year or term likely to be relatively lax, in contrast to the beginning. Different practices and rules may apply to the sixth form versus lower down the school and within different sets or teaching groups. Thus, it is a policy site that is very much mediated by time, place and policy actors (junior as well as senior) with different professional backgrounds, perspectives and practical tactics.

Like assessment and standards, behaviour policy is also a key arena for marketing opportunities. Schools are targeted by private as well as not-for-profit providers offering a range of tailored and off-the-shelf solutions designed to address behaviour issues. In enacting behaviour policy, there are fashions and distinct styles of behaviour management, techniques, technologies and procedures that are marketed and deployed by schools. The motivation for schools to engage with such marketing activities is obvious, behaviour is a key concern that everyone takes seriously – from the government, to teachers, to parents. In many ways, a school that can demonstrate a strong record of behaviour management, a unique approach or considerable improvement in this area, will be seen as a 'successful' school.

In this chapter, we will focus on three particular aspects of behaviour policy enactment. First, we examine behaviour as one of the major discourses of schooling; it is a policy arena that must be attended to and is an integral part of schools as institutions. As such, behaviour policy has undergone a series of reiterations in government and school discourses. Second, we will explore conflicts in philosophy and pedagogy that lead to different versions of 'doing' behaviour policy in schools. Here we are looking at the assemblages of people 'doing behaviour', their motivations, philosophies and practices, and the contestations and conflicts these can lead to within schools. Third, we will be considering the prescriptive regimes of doing behaviour policy, contrasted with its different interpretations and translations between policy and practice and the physical and emotional places in which behaviour policy is actually enacted in schools. When studying how behaviour policy is 'done' in 'real' schools, in many schools specialised provision around behaviour is often located in peripheral spaces – in 'inclusion units' on the lower ground floor or buildings across the playground – tucked away and out of sight. Yet, behaviour is simultaneously a major preoccupation, part of the public face and reputation of the school rendering it institutionally both marginal and central. We will be starting off the chapter by asking why disciplinary discourses are in circulation and what form these discourses take, before looking at the 'doing', the enacting, of behaviour policy in our case study schools.

Behaviour discourses: proliferating, revolving and reversing

Behaviour, classroom management and student 'control' have always been areas of concern and activity for 'policy-makers, schools and their teachers' (Powell and Tod 2004: 1). A search through the 95 interviews carried out for this project reveals that the term 'behaviour' has been mentioned 1,098 times overall[1] and there is no denying that dealing with constant, mostly low level behaviour issues is tiring and tiresome for teachers:

> I think the behaviour is quite poor. And I think – and I've been talk-ing about this recently – I think that's changed since I got here, even in just seven years. And I've been talking to teachers who've been here longer than me and they're agreeing with me. There's very much a sense of entitlement and, you know, students will quite happily listen to iPods in lessons without really seeing why there's anything wrong with it. Or answering back to teachers. You can deal with a lot of it with humour but there are – there is difficult behaviour here. It can get a bit wearing.
>
> (Sonja, Mathemathics, Atwood)

The preoccupation with behaviour and discipline in schools is highly visible even, or perhaps particularly, to those outside of schools; behaviour is one of the more prominent issues in media debates on schooling, as even a cursory scan across the English press will evidence (e.g. Richardson 2010; Fielding 2011; Roffey 2011). In schools, classroom and behaviour management become the formal systems, the technologies, through which the institution imposes and maintains its view of order. At the level of the individual, failure to manage this aspect of the professional repertoire of the teacher can signal either an inability to teach or that the school itself is 'failing'. Moreover, school behaviour has been a constant cause of social and moral 'panic' more broadly (Slee 1995). Some of the current concerns about behaviour and order are driven by wider social fears that characterise what Beck (1992) sees as the 'risk society', i.e. there are concerns about potential social fragmentation and the chaos that is sometimes taken to typify the modern world. There are fears about the 'dangers' of modern living, street crime and a perception that social order and civility are under threat (Putnam 2000). There are concerns about alleged increases in lawlessness and violence. Sometimes these 'cross over' into school life, e.g. drug use and knife crime. One response has been reflected in a significant increase in demands for schools to 'safeguard' their students as well as promote positive social attitudes and discipline. Simultaneously, schools placed in a market setting have had to attend to the pressures of parental choice. Parents want to select schools for their children that provide safe and orderly environments, as well as achieve good results in performance league tables (the emphasis on 'standards' discussed in Chapter 4). In consequence, the production, circulation and attention to clear codes of discipline and behaviour have been part of this marketising process – just as much as part of the everyday world of managing the school.

The New Labour governments (1997–2010) prioritised 'standards' in schools and, in the ceaseless attempts to optimise achievement levels, government policy attention also focused on the role of behaviour in shaping possibilities for learning. This iteration of policy was rendered as Behaviour for Learning (see for example www.behaviour4learning.ac.uk or the Sir Alan Steer reports on behaviour, Steer 2005, 2008, 2009) and refers to attempts by schools to raise achievement via a sustained effort to ensure a 'safe and secure' learning environment for all children (DCSF 2009). The dominance of behaviour for learning under New Labour does not mean that other competing views of 'behaviour', 'control' and 'discipline' did not exist, but rather that the overt policy focus at that time – which coincided with our fieldwork – was captured in a specific set of texts and policy practices which marginalised and de-legitimated alternatives to some extent. The change of government in May 2010 to a Conservative–Liberal Coalition brought with it a renewed emphasis on behaviour. The Conservative Party manifesto promised to give 'heads and teachers tough new powers of discipline' (Conservative Manifesto 2010: 51). This move to a 'tough' version of discipline, however, still operates under the umbrella of raising standards which are headlined in both the manifesto and the Coalition government's first Education Bill published in January 2011 (DfE 2011a). The bill introduced extensions to teachers' powers to search students for banned items, issue same-day detentions, protect teachers from false accusations by students and stop appeal panels from overturning schools' decisions on exclusions (DfE 2011a). Giving this an additional discursive spin, the press release accompanying the bill used some strong and emotive language to illustrate these points: 'The bill will give teachers powers to search for items that disrupt learning', 'give schools the final say in expelling violent pupils', 'protect teachers from pupils telling lies' and 'make it easier to impose detentions' (DfE 2011). The press notice contains the following response by James McAtear, head of Hartismere Secondary School:

> These reforms will help to redress the balance in favour of good discipline in schools. They send out a strong message that our society is not willing to tolerate poor behaviour and that we will provide a safe and supportive environment in which every child can learn.
>
> (DfE 2011)

The response of the head teacher above, with his aim to provide 'a safe and supportive learning environment in which every child can learn' would not be out of place in the New Labour Behaviour for Learning approach with its stated aim of improving standards by ensuring a 'safe and secure' learning environment for all children (DCSF 2009). Policy messages around behaviour change emphasis, but they revolve around a limited set of interpretations and preoccupations. As governments change leadership (or departments change ministers), parties and individual politicians are keen to make their mark on policy. Discipline, with its constant presence in the policy arena, can be ideal territory for just such an appropriation. Sets of behaviour discourses, like those focusing on standards, are in constant circulation in schools; shifts in policies and politics create different inflections, they do not transform the discourse overall. The final Steer Report (2009) found that in most English schools, student behaviour was acceptable and that schools were on the whole well managed with effective behaviour strategies in place. Yet, in the political arena, discipline is consistently presented as an urgent 'policy problem' (Ozga 2000), raising the question of who or what determines 'policy problems'. Most schools are concerned with behaviour as it affects learning and outcomes, rather than pursuing discipline for discipline's sake (although teachers also want to work in emotionally stable, secure and predictable classrooms).

Setting policy

Achieving the common sense goal of Behaviour for Learning has become a central and organising policy initiative in schools, informing approaches to classroom management, teaching and learning practices and school leadership structures and responsibilities. As four of our respondents (drawn from many examples), two deputy head teachers, one assistant head and one learning mentor, explained:

> We deal with behaviour if it's inappropriate or interfering with a student's achievement, but the focus is all about achievement. We don't want to turn out well-behaved individuals, we want to turn out individuals who have got the skills, qualifications to be able to go on and lead a successful life.
>
> (Hazel, deputy head teacher, Science, Wesley)

> The impact of behaviour on learning isn't something you can afford to take for granted.
>
> (Nick, deputy head teacher, Atwood)

> We work hard on behaviour here, and I think it is much improved. We have a behaviour support learning area downstairs – the Learning Zone.
>
> (Duncan, assistant head teacher, Geography, Wesley)

> I'd like to think that the work that we do [on behaviour] encourages and, sort of, opens gates and lowers barriers to, you know, higher attainment.
>
> (Nigel, learning mentor, George Eliot)

During our fieldwork period, schools were awash with policies, initiatives, procedures and strategies aimed at producing and sustaining positive behaviour for learning. Programmes and publications included the launch of 'The Behaviour Challenge' (DCSF 2009a) 'Safe to learn: Embedding anti-bullying work in schools' (DCSF 2007b) and 'Drug Education: An entitlement for all' (DCSF 2008). In this way, Behaviour for Learning has been linked with and articulated through various policy imperatives and programmes, acting upon and operating within schools: for example, uniform regulations, truancy and attendance, bullying, violence, substance misuse, knife crime, civic engagement and citizenship and the promotion of social and emotional aspects of learning (SEAL).

Within schools, Behaviour for Learning consists, as we shall see, of an ensemble of behaviour policies and initiatives and their related discourses. These are mediated through the enactments of groups of diverse social actors and school contexts (demography, staffing, resources, buildings and facilities, history, etc.), as discussed in Chapter 2. The figures below give a flavour of behaviour-related policies in our case study schools (Box 5.1) and the behaviour initiatives, interventions and strategies – the technologies – associated with them (Box 5.2).

Behaviour-related policies in the case study schools

Anti-bullying
Attendance and timekeeping
Child protection
Classroom rules
Deportment in school
Drugs education and prevention
Every Child Matters
Exclusions
Extended schools
Family holidays
Knife crime initiatives
Looked-after children
Nurture groups
Pastoral work
Students' well-being and safety
Uniform

Box 5.1 Behaviour-related policies in the case study schools

The main behaviour policy documents in each of the schools ranged across all or most of these issues, tying them together, more or less convincingly, into a single policy perspective. The documents utilised lexicons and ideas which drew from a range of supplementary texts related to these constituent parts of behaviour (see Box 5.2).

Behaviour policy is constructed, managed and developed across school boundaries and inside and outside of local policy networks. In the language of actor–network theory, these are contested and precarious multiplicities which order practices, bodies and identities through complex enactments (see Fenwick 2010). This means in our schools the involvement of the Youth Offending Service, local Pupil Referral Units, social services, education welfare officers, learning mentors and LSAs, SENCOs, youth disorder teams, mental health service teams, psychotherapists, behaviour consultants, LA behaviour advisors, community police liaison officers, Safer Schools police officers and Behaviour Partnerships (involving other schools, although interestingly these were not mentioned in our interviews). Internally, behaviour policy is enacted by everyone, but in particular heads of year, SLTs, SENCOs, peer mentors, LSAs, teachers with responsibility for ECM, Child Protection, PSAs (parent support advisers), BSO (behaviour support officers), drama teachers (theatre was used in three of the schools) and students (Atwood had a consultation group called Behaviour Improvement Group (BIG) with student representatives).

Behaviour technologies in the case study schools

Anger management training
Anti-Bullying Club (ABC)
Assertive mentoring
Behaviour Forum
Behaviour Improvement Group (BIG)
Boys' group/girls' group
Community cohesion meetings
Competitions for the best attending tutor group
Conflict resolution
Crime prevention/diversion programmes
Detentions
Emergency call-out
Home–school links
IBehave (software)
Internal exclusion
Peace Child (organisation) theatre around knife crime
Peer mentoring buddy group
Praise, warning and concern
Reward systems
SLT member attached to each year group
Training teachers in behaviour management
Transition groups
Truancy Call (professional phone system)
Yellow/red cards
Youth Against Bullying project
Zero tolerance on holidays in term time

Box 5.2 Behaviour technologies in the case study schools

Ken (head teacher of Atwood) explains his school's overall approach to behaviour like this:

> So, it's just a consistent policy for setting standards in the classroom... but also building in systems to support those students who are being picked up by this... It's an inclusion system [involving] the heads of year, the careers advisor was there, the educational psychologist was there, the SENCO was there... we've got an on-site family therapist. So, all the people that can conceivably have been working with students who have barriers to learning, emotional or behavioural ones were there... the ethos of the school is that you do things by consent in the school because it's the right thing to do. It's the right way to treat somebody.
>
> (Ken, head teacher, Atwood)

In this way, they too are policy actors, contributing to interpretation and translation work:

> [W]e have sat down with groups of students to discuss their views about behaviour in the school, we've taken students to visit other schools and look at their systems, we've had feedback from students... and we have had applications for memberships of the BIG (Behaviour Improvement Group) which will be an ongoing group to help run behaviour policy.
>
> (Nick, deputy head teacher, Atwood)

Senior teachers who have worked in more than one school bring with them an accumulation of personal and professional experiences which are brought to bear within the enactment process, often in the form of 'policy borrowing':

> By the time people reach my position and you've worked in four or five different schools, one is most likely making comparisons between the different schools and working out your own working hypothesis on why behaviour in some schools is better than in others.
>
> (Nick, deputy head teacher, Atwood)

> I think what I would do is [...] keeping it very simple, the school focus next year on three things: attainment, attendance and behaviour. Those are the three driving factors. So, everything that we do, every conversation we have, is about those three. If it does not concern those three things, or improves those things, we don't do it. [...] And I know it works because that's what they did down the road in another school, in my last school, it was focused on that and making sure people had time.
>
> (Manuel, deputy head teacher, ICT, Campion)

A key English policy text on behaviour has been the Steer Report (2009) 'Learning Behaviour: Lessons Learned' (see also Steer 2005, 2008) which was commissioned by the Secretary of State for Education in 2007 and which presented an overview of a wide range of issues and practices related to behaviour in English secondary schools. The final report made a total of 47 recommendations, grouped under three overall themes: legal powers and duties, supporting the development of good behaviour and raising standards higher, and suggested that schools must respond to the challenges of behaviour management with a multi-layered, 'whole school' approach. The report gestured towards particular forms of policy enactment for schools and particular kinds of translation activities and noted that:

> The schools that made the best progress tackled the improvement of behaviour as part of a whole-school improvement programme. They improved teaching and learning through focused training and coaching, and planned ways to make the curriculum more motivating.
>
> (Steer 2009: 47)

While the Steer Report is a significant, authoritative and comprehensive policy text and interviewees with a particular interest in behaviour management were usually aware of the reports, few had read the final report or its recommendations. Moreover, alongside Steer, there is currently in play in English education a wide range of sometimes conflicting and contradicting behaviour discourses. These come in a variety of textual forms and from a range of points of articulation and recontextualisation:

> I read the Steer Report; I am largely in sympathy with the views in the Report. I tend to read newspaper articles about turnaround schools and I do a lot of reflecting.
>
> (Nick, deputy head teacher, Atwood)

> It's about deciding how much of the material or how many of the ideas you can use directly in your schools... I think it would be useful if they [the government] produced a lot less... Watching Teachers TV that's actually very good, you get an insight into other schools.
>
> (Matu, deputy head teacher, Science, Wesley)

Whether it is Behaviour for Learning under New Labour or 'discipline' under the Coalition government, these discourses articulate a particular vision of what it means 'to behave' and provide rhetorical resources which can be used to legitimise ensuing policies and practices. These discourses are represented in a diverse body of official texts, commentaries, exemplars, guidance, training courses and materials for teachers. Behaviour for Learning, for example, comes in books, magazines, journal articles, newsletters, CDs, DVDs, downloads, television programmes, software, consultants' reports, LA events, higher education and CPD courses. That is to say, here, policy is re-worked, represented and re-articulated within what Bernstein (1996: 47) calls 'the official recontextualizing field [ORF] created and dominated by the state and its selected agencies and ministries...', but which is now increasingly infiltrated by for-profit providers (see Ball 2009). Discipline is big-money business and the rhetoric of 'crisis' helps produce a market opportunity for the private sector to support the – in this discursive construction, 'failing' – public sector.

Below are three examples: the first a 'for-profit' text, the second available from the DfE and the third offered by a local authority. These indicate the sorts of interpretative and promotional work that is done to announce and signal policy and to translate policy 'into practice'. The first example (Box 5.3), from a private sector provider, also presents a case study where 'Behaviour for Learning' in 2009, becomes 'Improving Behaviour' with an emphasis on 'Tough Care' and 'Rights, Responsibility and Respect' in 2011 – both facilitated by the same trainer.

For-profit provider of behaviour materials

November 2009 'Behaviour for Learning'

Our highly successful training in *Behaviour for Learning* is led out by Peter Hook, one of the Country's most popular and experienced trainers in the field. It has been used by colleagues from over 800 schools across the UK and abroad to help create highly effective learning environments.

We take a highly pragmatic and practical approach to all our courses. *Behaviour for Learning* is no exception.

The training is firmly rooted in, and reflects, the reality of today's classroom. We regularly work in classrooms to ensure all of our advice and support is tried, tested and relevant to experienced and inexperienced teachers alike. There are six key strands of support and training that we can provide to take you on the journey towards a highly effective, practical and sustainable approach to behaviour for learning. Some of these strands can be undertaken on their own to support your existing areas of development or they can be combined to fit in with a wider programme.

(The Critical Difference website,
http://www.thecriticaldifference.com, accessed 20 November 2009)

March 2011 'Improving Behaviour'

You and your colleagues know that securing good behaviour is the bedrock upon which all other improvement activities need to be based. You also know that effective behaviour management is not about new policies. Nor can it be seen as a 'bolt on'. It has to become an integral part of the way your school operates. It is about 'hearts and minds'.

This strand of our work is led out by Peter Hook. Peter is recognised as one of the UK's leading experts on securing good behaviour in schools. Underpinning all of our work is the belief that effective behaviour management has its roots in two key areas – 'Tough Care' linked to a strong focus on 'Rights, Responsibility and Respect'.

(http://www.tcd-ltd.com/behaviour.htm, accessed 16 March 2011)

Box 5.3 For-profit provider of behaviour CPD

Department for Education's behaviour DVD

Improving Behaviour for Learning is an interactive DVD commissioned by the DfES as part of the national strategy for improving behaviour and attendance in secondary schools. This DVD is a drama-based resource that looks at ways of promoting positive behaviour, full attendance and inclusion, and minimising low-level disruption in the classroom.

By viewing lessons taught in a fictional secondary school, teachers can analyse the effect of different teaching styles on pupils' behaviour.

Box 5.4 Department for Education's behaviour DVD

Local authority

Behaviour for Learning (B4L) Service (Redcar and Cleveland)

The Behaviour for Learning Service is part of Inclusion Support Services. It is a strong team of highly experienced specialist staff dedicated and committed to improving outcomes for children and young people in line with the Every Child Matters agenda. The service promotes inclusive education by enhancing the capacity of schools to meet the needs of children and young people experiencing behavioural, emotional and social difficulties. Funding for this service is delegated to schools, enabling them to buy services as required.

The service works in partnership with schools by:

- Offering advice on the development of consistent policies and practice in relation to pupil behaviour in order to raise achievement.
- Providing pupil observation and assessments of individual or group behaviour.
- Contributing to the statutory assessment process for children and young people with special educational needs.
- Offering advice and training for schools (teaching and non-teaching staff) on strategies for preventing and dealing with problem behaviour.
- Offering advice on individual cases where behaviour is a cause for concern which may result in exclusion.
- Undertaking individual support work with children and young people and their parents/carers.
- Undertaking group work with children and young people, e.g. circle time, transition, social and emotional skills, anger management/self control, problem solving, peer mediation schemes.
- Working closely with other services/agencies in the development of joint strategies to promote positive behaviour in schools.

- Contributing to the development of pastoral support programmes and multi-agency meetings for children and young people at risk of exclusion.
- Providing 'health checks' for schools to reduce potential risk of exclusion.

(see www.redcar-cleveland.gov.uk, accessed 16 March 2011)

Box 5.5   Local authority: Behaviour for Learning

Attending to and keeping on top of this burgeoning material created problems for the staff at our four schools. Again, from among many examples:

> I think it's difficult now because there's so many things online that you're expected to refer to. And even in the induction files for new staff there's lots of hyperlinks on the forms rather than I think it must have used to be on the form before.
>
> (Richard, Training School Manager, AST Geography, George Eliot)

> It just becomes a bit wearing because you have to cope with every new thing; you have to read [everything]. Do I read things through properly? Not always. I make a very quick scan and mark it with a decision there and then.
>
> (Philip, head teacher, Wesley)

To a great extent, schools can pick and choose from this abundance of seemingly 'ready-to-wear' material available from state, voluntary and private agencies. Or indeed they can ignore such materials altogether when making decisions about how they will enact or respond to policies such as Behaviour for Learning. However, they cannot escape from making a response in these terms – producing, reviewing and updating both their behaviour policy and those practices that relate to it. The process of selecting out and selecting from and producing local behaviour policies is complex. It is initially dependent on the decisions a school's senior leadership team (and governors) make about school priorities at particular moments in time, coupled with the pressure of meeting government targets, legislative imperatives and the reality of resourcing and supporting these and other new (or reworked) strategies, policies and initiatives as well as local necessities and pressures; that is, what we identified in Chapter 3 as interpretation work.

Behaviour, like other policies, is enacted in particular and distinct institutional contexts with their own histories, resource sets, staffing (recruitment/turnover/experience/values) and dealing with different local social 'problems' and intakes (see also Chapter 2). The challenges of behaviour differ from one school to another, as does the capacity for enactment:

> We do have a rather large cohort of weaker teachers that would get annoyed, you know, wound up by the low level disruption and it would escalate very quickly, rather than being kept in classrooms and dealt with that way.
>
> (Graham, head of sixth form, PE, Campion)

> We've got more [staff and leadership] capacity than a lot of schools in our circumstances... Given the nature of our intake that means we are really addressing quite major issues of kids going off the rails... we have a healthy mix... you know in terms of kids here having different models of how to be... the boys from the estate were really the hardcore and now you just see them levelling off and changing.
>
> (Nick, deputy head teacher, Atwood)

As one head teacher put it very simply:

> I tell you what it is, we respond to the minimum level with certain things, to the maximum level with other things. Depending.
>
> (Philip, head teacher, Wesley)

However, behaviour policies present particular and further challenges to schools. In addition to the policy texts indicated above, legislative frameworks also increasingly impinge upon school behaviour policies, with the effect of a juridification of practice. New legal responsibilities were established by the Education and Inspections Act 2006, which offered 'specific power for teachers to discipline pupils – for breaking a school rule, failure to follow instructions or other unacceptable behaviour' (DCFS 2009: 1). The 2006 Act topped up the disciplinary possibilities outlined in the Education Act 1996 and the School Standards and Framework Act 1998 and specified the responsibility of governing bodies for discipline and the determination by the head teacher of a behaviour policy (Education and Inspections Act 2006: 72–73), an extension and elaboration of section 61 of the School Standards and Framework Act 1998 (p.75).

Schools are also implicated in legislation aimed at tackling and reducing youth crime, disaffection and lack of civic engagement, for example the Violent Crime Reduction Act (2006) (via the power of members of staff to search pupils for weapons and, since January 2011, for all items banned under school rules), the Criminal Justice Act (2003) (via substance abuse) and the Anti Social Behaviour Act (2003) (via truancy). According to the Audit Commission (2004), 'mainstream agencies, such as schools and health services, should take full responsibility for preventing offending by young people' (cited in Solomon and Garside 2008: 26). All these Acts provide supporting legislative powers for school governors and SLTs and this legislation complicates and places further burdens and expectations upon behaviour policies, strategies and initiatives in schools. Schools are placed at the centre of societal policy problems, particularly in terms of issues relating to social disorder and deviance. Local enactments must to some extent take account of these responsibilities alongside and in relation to the pressure to perform.

'Doing' behaviour policy: conflicts in pedagogy

'Behaviour' problems as understood within schools have always been contested and have been differently interpreted at different times. Moreover, behaviour is always both an individual accomplishment, the maintenance of order on a moment-to-moment basis and a set of broader institutional practices. Even if what tends to happen 'in practice', according to Clark (1998: 291), is frequently a focus on the control of the learner rather than attempts at broader educational approaches, such as self-discipline (which address questions of how to act as autonomous and responsible members of a group), these wider more fundamental questions remain salient. Behaviour policies within schools are enacted by assemblages of people – some teachers, some support staff, some 'outsiders' – with their various motivations, philosophies and practices.

Talk about Behaviour for Learning was very evident during our fieldwork and while no school would reject the importance of effective behaviour management and its part in promoting learning, the translation of texts into practices was by no means straightforward. One major constraint lies in the variety of ways in which schools and educational professionals will interpret what is meant by discipline and classroom management as well as what is involved in supporting positive behaviour. Burke (2007: 178) argues that for classroom teachers 'there is a potential balance to be struck between the targets of discipline which aims to control "behaviour", and discipline which aims to promote study' – Behaviour for Learning aims to square the circle. In all of our schools, the professional dispositions of various members of staff seemed to provoke differences in understanding and pedagogy in the field of behaviour management. For example, in George Eliot, this was reflected in different approaches towards punishment as well as a need to manage some discord within the school's adult community:

> I think there is a bit of a discrepancy between members of staff as to what the role of managing behaviour is. Some staff would like, if a student offends, you know, does something wrong, want to see an instant punishment while other staff are more in favour of rehabilitation and the idea of restorative justice... And I think that's probably the biggest difficulty with behaviour is trying to make sure that everybody's happy with what takes place. And I think some of the sanctions that are given out to students probably aren't in the students' best interests.
>
> (Sunny, HoY, History/Citizenship, George Eliot)

Sunny, a pastoral head of year with a background in teaching, was aware that she was caught up in a dilemma. Sometimes teachers would run out of patience with individual students and just want their immediate withdrawal from the classroom. As an experienced classroom teacher, she recognised and acknowledged this situation. Steer (2005) says of incidents like this, that students and teachers have the right to learn together and that any disruptions must be managed:

> Poor behaviour cannot be tolerated, as it is a denial of the right of pupils to learn and teachers to teach. To enable learning to take place preventative action is most effective, but where this fails, schools must have clear, firm and intelligent strategies in place to help pupils manage their behaviour.
>
> (Steer 2005: 3)

In practice and in enacting policy, tensions can occur where some teachers seem more/less tolerant and have different perceptions of what is/is not aberrant behaviour:

> When you're in a lesson or something's happening and you have a student who isn't doing what you're asking them to do and therefore it is having a very, very negative impact on teaching and learning in their classroom – and therefore you want something done, you're not interested – at that particular time you're not interested in anything else other than the fact that they are spoiling things for the 27 other people.
>
> (Sunny, HoY, History/Citizenship, George Eliot)

Reena, a pastoral leader in the same school who was not a qualified teacher and had a professional background in counselling and psychotherapeutic approaches to support work with young people, had a contrasting 'take' on behaviour management in the school. Her approach, her 'sense-making' and her version of policy enactment, was based on and in discourses of self-awareness and the link between cognition, feelings and actions (Goleman 1996; Corrie 2009). She started from a position that was less about raising standards and more about helping students understand and 'own' their actions and feelings:

> The main challenges, I would say, in my experience, anger management, lack of anger management for a better word. It's sort of, the inappropriate responses of young people which leads them to make the wrong choice and get into a conflicting situation. You know, we don't expect them to be perfect, this is all a learning curve for them, but I think, in my experience, that most, the greater contents of my work is around managing temperaments and emotions and finding alternative ways of responding, especially to adults.
>
> (Reena, pastoral HoY 9, George Eliot)

Reena's work involved aspects of restorative justice – an aspect of behaviour for learning that was advocated by the DCSF and the Steer Report (2009). However, this approach, which encourages greater self-knowledge and awareness, takes a bit longer and may not seem as immediate as more punitive sanctions to some classroom teachers – a fact she recognises:

> Working with them together to resolve the conflict. And I could turn round to a young person and say, you know, 'These things that you've said have really upset this person. Can you understand and empathise?' And the number of times I've actually had students saying, 'What's empathy?' and having to say to them, 'Well, can you put yourself in their shoes?' and they think, 'Well, yeah, actually that would really upset me.' So – and I think, to me it's very basic things that need to be put into place at a young age… I think you find, again I have, sometimes may have been in people's bad books because of my philosophy on how to work with young people. And I know a lot of teachers, they want sanctions, sanctions, sanctions. I understand that and, yes, children do have to learn consequences. But, for me, it's not the sanction, it's trying to understand why you've done something and how not to do it again and the sanction would be a part of that.
>
> (Reena, pastoral HoY 9, George Eliot)

Here there is no simple accommodation between policy ideas, principles and the pragmatics of practice – enactments. There are a variety of positions in relation to policy and uneven or unresolved relations between policies. Joshua, an unqualified teacher at Campion who is taking the GTP route[2] to qualified teacher status and who has extensive experience in youth work, specialist education provision and education approaches informed by neurolinguistic programming, also considers himself an 'outsider' in some of the ways of mainstream schooling: 'And also my approach is different. I have been known for many years in many, many different schools as the teacher that doesn't shout.' His 'outsider' position is in some ways reinforced by his current work remit: he is in charge of a nurture group of Year 7 students who are having problems adjusting to their move from primary school and who have one teacher – Joshua – for most of their lessons in their first year of secondary school. He sees his approach as informed by the Every Child Matters policy and its five-point agenda ('be healthy, stay safe, enjoy and achieve, make a positive contribution, achieve economic well-being')[3] but is unconvinced by many aspects of mainstream schooling, saying at one point in his interview 'I really don't want to teach, I love working with young people' (Joshua, GTP, Psychology, Campion). Joshua feels strongly that Campion has 'not got enough of a handle' on discipline and he describes a somewhat stricter, or in any case more consistent, approach to behaviour in 'his' nurture group – an approach enabled to some extent by the peripheral position of the group and its status as 'special' and apart from the workings (and messiness) of the main school. In part here, there is a difference, and sometimes a tension, between teachers whose main work and professional focus is on behaviour and those whose main work and professional focus is on learning, a point we return to below.

Thus, policy enactments in the area of discipline were often a distillation of custom and practice – 'what works' alongside an awareness of the need for consistency, but a variety of psycho-pedagogic theories were also deployed by 'specialist' practitioners. There was a pragmatic recognition of the need to establish and maintain order and control, but for some policy actors there was a need to enact a different version of discipline in a more holistic and student-sensitive manner – an enactment that was being practised somewhat differently in different 'parts' of and places in the school.

In this respect, it is also useful briefly to consider some of the 'specialist' behaviour provision that existed in our case study schools – different 'spaces for behaviour'. Wesley had a 'Learning Zone' on the lower ground floor of one of their buildings which was staffed by a full-time behaviour support officer, and which served as a space for students who were temporarily excluded from their classes – for single lessons, half days or whole days at a time. This process, termed 'inclusion', was managed by Janet who took a maternal but strict approach to her task, a version of 'tough love' perhaps:

> It's almost like it's a safe haven, do you know what I mean? Especially the really badly behaved ones because I'm a constant, you know, every time they're in trouble they end up in here and every time they end up with me. And if they do a full day's inclusion, which, you know, that can happen two, three, four times a term, you don't know how they're going to behave, they sometimes spend an awful lot more time with me than either their tutor or anyone else. So, I've become a sort of homing thing, especially for Year 7s. [...] And I think that's another thing: they know what they'll get when they walk through this door. They know that they will be expected to behave, it doesn't matter what they were doing out there, there's a certain expectation in this room to working, as to how you talk to one another.
>
> (Janet, behaviour support officer, Wesley)

Janet did not have a work background in schools or education, but she used to run her own business and also worked with a Youth Offending Team. Her common sense, no-nonsense persona embodied the behaviour approach of the Learning Zone which was literally and metaphorically a place apart from the rest of the school and the head and other senior managers appeared to let her get on with most things as she saw fit. The Learning Zone was a very ordered and controlled space, Janet insisted on silence between students and she provided various educational materials. However, those materials were rarely linked into students' actual class work that they missed by being in the 'inclusion' unit – so there was order and control, but very little actual learning.

Campion had a similar figure in Lindsey, a behaviour welfare officer whose tiny office was a destination for tearful students, obtaining practical support and phone call discussions with parents. Like Janet, Lindsey was somewhat left to her own devices in interpreting and translating behaviour policy; her approach was 'softer' than that of Janet – an example of heterogeneity and differences in policy enactment within an outwardly 'similar' context. Both Janet and Lindsey were somewhat 'to the side of policy'; as support staff they did not usually attend INSET days and their relationship to policy was a distant one, even if their presence in schools was entirely determined by Behaviour for Learning policies. Nonetheless, they were key actors in the work of reconfiguring the school and shoring up its precariousness. The interview extract with Lindsey below sums up this marginal position which is also central for the 'mainstream' life of the school to function:

> I don't read any [policies]. [...] And not because, well, I mean, obviously I've read through the behaviour policy and I've gone through my staff handbook, but the way I do things is totally different from... Rightly or wrongly, I mean, you know, I do things the way I want to do it. And if you don't like it, it's tough, basically. You know, I can't change now. The kids know me as I am, what they see is what they get, I don't tolerate any nonsense. If they come in and they're f-ing and blinding they're allowed to do so and then, once they've calmed down, and we're having a conversation they can't swear at me, they can't be rude. And, you know, I have a different relationship with the students as opposed to the teachers. You know, kids can say things to me that they couldn't dream of commenting on to a member of staff. And it's like when I'm recommending or talking to them on a personal level, they know that they can trust me and they can tell me anything about their lives and that I won't go and divulge it or disclose to anybody else, unless of course it is a CP [child protection] issue, in which case they do know that, at the beginning of our conversation I will do. And they've come in and talked about their boyfriend problems or, you know, 'Mum was really horrible last night', and whatever else. You know, that's the type of conversations that we can have but they wouldn't have it with a member of staff.
>
> (Lindsey, behaviour welfare officer, Campion)

Behaviour enactments are part of a very particular 'policy geography' and 'policy demography' and are susceptible to a wider than usual variety of discoursive influences.

'Doing' behaviour policy: prescriptive regimes

As is common practice in many English schools, three of the case study schools had produced summaries of their 'regulative discourses' (RDs) (Bernstein 2000: 32) that were laminated and displayed in every teaching area (see

Chapter 6). These summaries were also reproduced in the student planners and diaries and various discipline policies were published prominently on all four schools' websites. These RDs deal with comportment, maintaining order, regulations and sanctions and are part of the everyday life of all schools. As part of daily school life, they are frequently revised and revisited and, in spite of their prominence, they can also be exposed to the vagaries of institutional haphazardness and staff turnover:

> There's usually [a copy of the behaviour policy] up in classrooms and it's got pictures of all the teachers. And half the teachers on it have left, you know. It says if you do this you'll get sent to this person, well this person doesn't work here any more. You know, I just... you put the effort in or you don't. This, kind of, halfway thing just doesn't work at all, it just looks sloppy. But, you know, there are, kind of, you know, you fill in this form and you fill in this form and then every now and again the form changes and... I don't know, I just think sometimes if you just let something run for a bit you might actually not have to introduce anything new.
>
> (Sonja, Mathemathics, Atwood)

As another example, during the period of fieldwork, two of our schools had uniform 'purges' where all staff were expected to monitor aspects such as the wearing of the school tie, length and knot of tie, earrings, hair styles, etc. – enacting policy involves policing policy, too. Regulative discourses on clothing, appearance and comportment are tied into the need to circulate messages about ethos and 'tone'. A tightly monitored uniform policy signals to parents and the local community that the school is orderly, in control and is serious about (a version of) discipline. These sorts of tactics are a form of response to parental and societal concerns about lack of control, unruliness and 'risk'. Uniform purges have always been part of disciplining and control in English schools – although (quite unusually nowadays) one of our schools, Atwood, did not have a uniform at all and thus avoided the sorts of standoffs that regularly plague uniformed schools' disciplinary procedures. Even in the uniformed case study schools, however, there were some issues about what constituted 'appropriate' dress and the need for teachers to be reminded to remind their students of the school rules:

> We have the duty to maintain good standards in relation to the wearing of uniform by students. We must act as a team to achieve this, both inside lessons and out. At the start of a lesson, staff must check that students are in correct uniform. They must also be checked as they leave a lesson.
>
> (Wesley School, Behaviour for Learning Policy Statement)

In a whole variety of ways, different from other areas of policy, behaviour is constituted within a 'field of interpretations' – what is unacceptable or violent behaviour? What is too noisy or disruptive? What is an infringement of uniform? What do institutional policy documents mean? How should I respond? Different individuals (both teachers and non-teachers) and different subject areas and activities may well present conflicting answers to these questions. Having sanctions (or indeed praise) as a main regime to police the enactment of behaviour policy means that consistency is a constant issue:

Annette: What is [Atwood's] behaviour policy?

Trevor: It's up there *(points towards laminated sheet on the wall)* in a nut-shell: praise, warning and concern. But they're revamping it this year, which is a good thing because it doesn't really work [...] it's not consistent throughout the school. I mean, there's a consistent policy but it's not consistently implemented.

(Trevor, NQT Mathematics, Atwood)

At Campion, for example, there is a detailed hierarchy of six different types of detention that precede temporary and then permanent exclusions from school. This level of specification and detail can cause complications and disruptions because it relies heavily on consistency for its effectiveness – and the more complex a system is, the harder it is to enact. In Campion, the main problems are 'low level disruption and lack of consistency' (Dave, Union rep.). Fiona, an assistant head teacher at the school agrees: 'the biggest thing is getting people to be consistent. And you know, what one teacher walks by and ignores, is the next teacher's problem.' However, at Campion, the complexity of the system means that teachers have to do a lot of work following up students who miss various detentions. This 'chasing of students' takes up a great deal of time and understandably, isn't always followed through. A case of too much policy, perhaps:

The theory is behaviour issues are a faculty issue, that's the theory. It doesn't always work like that. And the hierarchy gets kind of lost as to how it will work. In there, at the moment I think I've got four students on report to me for various reasons, but they don't turn up, so we hunt them down.

(Clare, assistant KS4 manager (HoY), Mathematics, Campion)

In line with national policy directives under the Labour government, Campion had shifted its approach towards Behaviour for Learning. Clare explained that 'I like to use academic achievement as a non-confrontational, non-emotional approach to addressing behaviour.' By looking at students' attainments and targets, she highlights 'academic rigour... so you've got a focus and it's a clearer target then as well.' Ewan, the KS3 manager, explains the approach like this:

I think the aim of a school has to be, you know, to provide those students with the qualifications and the skills they need to move on. And I think the head of year role as such, was looking far too solely, if you like, at the welfare and the behaviour and not looking enough at the attainment.

(Ewan, KS3 manager, PE, Campion)

However, Clare also commented that there was a cost in this type of approach:

And I just personally feel that, you know, in my experience in teaching [overseas] I preferred that better balance where it's a more holistic approach to the development of the child and child development as opposed to content driven, you know. Okay, yeah, sure, thinking skills and all that sort of stuff but I just think a lot of the social and emotional things just aren't accounted for.

(Clare, assistant KS4 manager (HoY), Mathematics, Campion)

However, alongside this, Campion had inserted a supplementary programme that was intended to improve behaviour in order to boost attainment – from a different perspective. Campion is located in one of the local authorities in the UK that is pioneering Seligman's (2002) Resiliency Curriculum in their schools. This is a US-developed programme that helps young people listen to their 'self-talk' (inner voice) in order to enhance self-awareness, prevent depression and promote life skills such as persistence, resilience, assertiveness and happiness. This approach has also led to a wide range of research and the production of guides for schools (Weare 2007; Panju 2008; Corrie 2009). The intention is that this more psychotherapeutic approach will hopefully boost attainment in the longer term but is simultaneously concerned with broader ambitions for mental health and emotional fulfilment. But this potentially more progressive approach also contains within itself the capacity to exert different and less overt forms of control that move from 'body to mind' (Slee 1995). While it seems useful to help school students to develop the sorts of life skills that are described above, it could be argued that any reach towards 'control' through pre-determining what students' attitudes should be (assertive, resilient, etc.) also paves the way for identifying students as 'disaffected', 'disturbed' and the like, when they do not seem to internalise and produce these desired responses. It could be that some of these approaches towards behaviour management are versions of an 'invisible pedagogy' (Bernstein 1975), just as much to do with control as more explicit behavioural methods of classroom management. In drawing on a discipline policy 'double-whammy' in this way, here Campion is constructing a disciplinary regime that is attempting to cover all the bases – and asserting a form of 'optimal specification' (Foucault 1979: 98). Resilience provides a different set of texts and discourses about behaviour which can supplement or contradict other 'official' texts. In practice, at Campion, a composite of policy ideas and enactments is produced.

Enacting discipline: enacting 'good' behaviour

With behaviour, there is always a core concern – a need to maintain a semblance of order (or at least controlled disorder). We have already emphasised in several places throughout the chapter that, by and large, schools are well-managed and manage behaviour well. Again, in this sense, our schools are 'ordinary'. There is not a 'crisis' of behaviour – discipline issues and their management have always been part of schooling. In spite of this questioning of some of the urgent government policy activity that periodically 'happens' around behaviour, schools and their leadership teams have to demonstrate a degree of compliance in institutional rhetoric and texts with whatever policy or policy approach is dominant. This is similar to the imperatives of the standards agenda discussed in Chapter 4, but as we have seen, with behaviour more than with attainment, there are different power and knowledge formations that intersect its enactments and a range of disparate moments of interpretation and translation.

The collective efforts in the enactment of behaviour policy by a multitude of actors involves the deployment of a variety of expert knowledges (like Seligman, above), and forms of training and experience, alongside confusion, necessities (legal and institutional) and sets of sometimes discordant, incoherent and contradictory beliefs and values. There is a great deal of pragmatism, borrowing (from policy texts and other schools) and in some cases avoidance of texts. Advice is to be had (and can be purchased) from consultants, local authorities and agencies such as the Specialist Schools and Academies Trust and the National College for Leadership of Schools and Children's Services, etc. There is a bricolage of initiatives, theory and methods that constitute behaviour policies in schools. The policy texts the schools produce and the enactments generated are complex, but sometimes 'untidy' co-constructions – sophisticated, ramshackle and flawed. The policies that emerge are the 'cannibalised products of multiple (but circumscribed) influences and agendas' (Ball 2005: 46). Enactments, therefore, cannot be read-off from texts and neither can they be reduced to anything that might be called an 'implementation gap' – it is not a matter of policies not being 'done' or not being 'implemented' 'properly'. Policy is always contested and changing (unstable) – always 'becoming'. Policy, in the area of behaviour, in our schools always seemed to be not quite finished, or about to be changed. That is, there was a 'complex interplay between discourses and ground-level practices, conflicting choices and pressures, between the "political" [behaviour as an "issue"] and the "technical" [coping at the chalk face]' (Lendvai and Stubbs 2006: 17).

Getting children and students to behave in a positive and reflexive manner in schools is a basic part of the role of the teacher. Experienced teachers who will have an almost effortless 'disciplinary practice' may feel that other aims take priority 'but in the last instance, maintaining control trumps everything else'.[4] However, how different educational professionals 'do' discipline, and how they interpret and enact it in their practices, may vary quite considerably between individuals, subject departments, with different students and at different times of the year. So what may ensue are sets of small struggles and contestations around what schools are attempting – behaviour for learning or behaviour for life? Control and managing behaviour or an approach that is consistent with broader aims of education such as democracy and respect? There will be small struggles about points of enactment – such as issues about what sanctions to apply. There may be stronger points of difference that derive from professional dispositions – for example about discipline as social control (either through behaviourist processes of RD or the surveillance and regulation of dispositions by psychologistic means). While our data illustrates some of the different inflections, discourses and pedagogies that make up this aspect of schoolwork, this is not, in practice, a dichotomised process. For instance, Campion has a Behaviour for Learning policy that carefully mirrors the Steer recommendations, but it also has a complementary and conflicting curriculum approach modelled on Seligman's resilience that is potentially broader in its reach although simultaneously just as invasive and controlling of young people.

In the previous chapter, we indicated the ways in which the technology of delivery worked to establish very traceable links between classroom practice, school procedures and general policy priorities – specifically economic competitiveness. Here the relationships between enactments in schools and the politics of behaviour are evident again but are more convoluted. While they are activated 'loosely' within the discursive parameters of Behaviour for Learning, they can also be characterised as translations in the sense that Latour uses the term, where we are witnessing the continuous transformation of a token by many different people 'who slowly turn it into something completely different as they seek to achieve their own goals' (Latour 1986: 268). In this chapter, as in the rest of this book, we have tried to understand policy enactment in a grounded way and by choosing behaviour policy as our policy example, we were able to explore differences in enactment according to different long-standing – and oppositional – discourses circulating in this arena. As mentioned at the beginning of this chapter, behaviour, unlike assessment and achievement, is a policy site that is very much mediated by time, place and by diverse sets of policy actors with different professional backgrounds, values and practical tactics.

6   Policy artefacts

Discourses, representations and translations

Introduction

In this chapter, we now want to take a different, but complementary, approach to understanding the processes of enactment that are at work in the contemporary secondary school. So far, we have considered policy enactments as sets of 'embodied' practices that are attached to different types and groups of policy actors. We have also written about the ways in which enactments are brought off through sets of technologies that surround some of the current dominant discourses of English schooling: notably standards, assessment and discipline. Let us be clear, these are not discrete processes of enactment; they are interwoven and multi-layered and, in practice, it can be difficult to tease them out as isolated and separate formations. Indeed, to do so may do violence to the act of and the processes of enactment in schools more generally. These dimensions of enactment work together to reconstitute the school, the teacher and the student, as we shall see. In this way, policies 'organise their own specific rationalities, making particular sets of ideas obvious, common sense and "true"' (Ball 2008: 5). The process of producing/making sets of ideas about policies that become part of the 'taken-for-grantedness' of the school frequently involves producing representations and translations, simulacrums of primary policy texts.

In the processes of policy enactments, school leaders and managers will sometimes consciously attempt to 'draw attention' to the substance of policy through the production of visual materials and resources that document/illustrate what has to be done, or what is desirable conduct. These are artefacts that 'mark' policy directionality; that circulate and reinforce and represent what is to be done. Sometimes these artefacts come to stand for/represent the subjects of policy – such as the use of (assessment and progression) grids – 'they can click on a child' – as discussed in Chapter 4. Policies become represented and translated in and through different sets of artefacts, experiences, material resources and in-service activities; these are the micro-technologies and representations of policy that serve as meaning makers and controls of meanings in the social–material world of the school. These artefacts are cultural productions that carry within them sets of beliefs and meanings that speak to social processes and policy enactments – ways of being and becoming – that is, forms of governmentality. In his descriptions of the ways in which power becomes manifested at a micro-level, through certain discourses becoming internalised and 'taken-for-granted', Foucault argues that the result was a form of non-coercive power that would, in certain circumstances, ensure that individuals would govern themselves. What we want to propose here is that, to some extent – and we will return to this question of extent at the end of this chapter – artefacts and materials become part of the tools and techniques of governmentality in the policy work of the school (Foucault 1991).

> Governing people, in the broad meaning of the word, governing people is not a way to force people to do what the governor wants; it is always a versatile equilibrium, with complementarity and conflicts between techniques which assure coercion and processes through which the self is constructed or modified by himself.
>
> (Foucault 1993: 203–204)

Discourses and discursive strategies

In this chapter, we focus on some of the ways in which our four schools are both productive of, and constituted by, sets of 'discursive practices, events and texts' (Fairclough 1995: 132) that contribute to the process of policy enactments and that contribute towards 'doing' school. As Colebatch (2002: 116) says, 'policy involves the creation of order – that is, shared understandings about how the various participants will act in particular circumstances'. In schools, part of the 'creation of order' and thus, governmentality, takes place around the manipulation of signs, signifiers and policy symbols; through the production of cultural artefacts – handbooks, websites, parent newsletters, student diaries and teacher planners – as well as sets of 'activities' such as the prize day, the open day, in-service education, staff briefings, union meetings and similar events. In what follows, we will detail and describe some of these discursive artefacts and activities that reflect, and 'carry' within them, the key policy discourses that are currently in circulation in English secondary schools and thereby do policy work. Before we attempt this, we need to explain our understanding of discursive formations and their work within an institution such as a school.

Foucault writes that discourses are 'the set of conditions in accordance with which a practice is exercised, in accordance with which that practice gives rise to partially or totally new statements, and in accordance with which it can be modified' (Foucault 1986: 208–209). Discursive formations are 'practices that systematically form the objects of which they speak' (Foucault 1986: 49). In these terms, policies can be regarded as representations of knowledge and power, discourses that construct a topic; for example, policies about conduct in schools, as discussed in the previous chapter, carry within them notions of what is to be commended in behaviour and deportment – and what is not

(Bernstein 2000). Policy discourses also act upon and influence one another intertextually. They become worked into/against the everyday practices of school life and become set over and against, or integrated into existing discourses – a heteroglossia of 'tangled plurality' (Foucault 1986: 49).

Policies are discursive formations; they are sets of texts, events and practices that speak to wider social processes of schooling such as the production of 'the student', the 'purpose of schooling' and the construction of 'the teacher'. Foucault (1986: 118) sees discursive formations as:

> a regularity (an order, correlations, positions and functionings, transformations), we will say, for the sake of convenience, that we are dealing with a discursive formation... such as 'science', 'ideology', 'theory', 'or domain of objectivity'.
>
> (Foucault 1986: 38)

Such formations 'converge with institutions and practices, and carry meanings that may be common to a whole period'[1] (Foucault 1986: 118). Thus, in educational discourses, the need to manage behaviour, to promote effective learning, to raise standards, contribute towards what he calls 'a sort of great, uniform text', a version of a 'sovereign, communal, meaning' (Foucault 1986: 118). In other words, discursive formations are 'big Ds' and are made up of sets of contributing discourses. For example, as we shall see, what counts as school is made up of 'groups of statements' (Foucault 1986: 125) that constitute the discursive formation of the 'school'. However, as he also explains, this is not a totalising phenomenon, there is a fragility in all this; discursive formations are characterised by 'gaps, voids, absences, limits and divisions' (Foucault 1986: 119) – a point that we shall also return to later on in this chapter.

Questions of methodology – and methods

While working in our four schools, we have collected examples of 'hard' policy texts and taken photographs of other visual artefacts that the schools produce and deploy to call attention to what has to be done. We have also attended approximately 25 'events' and 'activities' of various kinds in the four schools, where we have recorded sets of field notes (taped and hand-written). While 'what has to be done' in a school covers a vast array of activities – from low level concerns about wearing the 'correct' uniform to the production of success at GCSE level, all the schools in our sample pay serious attention to the production of visual artefacts that address a wide range of policy matters – perhaps in the belief that 'familiarity breeds attention' (Spillane 2004: 76). However, here we want to speculate about this visual data in terms of their discursive effects.

> discourses are composed of signs; but what they do is more than use these signs to designate things. It is this *more* that renders them irreducible to

the language (*langue*) and to speech. It is this 'more' that we must reveal
and describe.

(Foucault 1986: 49)

Koh (2009: 284) argues that 'visual design in education policy documents
and materials is significant' because it is 'situated and intertwined in the
complex interplay of institutional constraints, ideological underpinnings,
political assumptions and priorities'. Koh (2009: 283) talks about a neglect
of the visual mode in policy analysis more generally and the lack of work
'related to the visual component in policy text that increasingly mediates the
process of policy formation and dissemination'. While there is an extensive
pedagogical literature extolling the virtues of display and visuals in promoting learning and understanding for school students, there is little at all on
the role of visuals and cultural artefacts in promoting teachers' mindfulness
of policy and their related practices in their school environments or as 'non-
human' actants in the policy process.

There are difficulties in dealing with this type of data. As Emmison (2004:
249) claims, visual data needs to be coupled with a 'powerful theoretical
imagination' if it is to move beyond the representational/informational form –
a form of 'telling and showing how things are'. As an example, he cites Prior's
(1988: 261) work on contemporary hospital designs that 'illustrate changing
institutional assumptions concerning disease, insanity and the most appropriate forms of treatment and control'. In a similar way, school buildings
can be taken to signify assumptions about power, status and what it means
to be educated – the economics of schooling. A quick consideration of space
and access, even something simple such as where students enter and where
adults (staff and visitors) enter, marks out differences and disparities; most
of our schools (understandably) have rules about what side of the corridor to
walk along and which bits of the building are 'out of bounds' to students (and
parents) – 'techniques of power that are invested in architecture' (Foucault
1993a: 137). These sorts of techniques of power, control and the management
of spatial relations are fairly straightforward to document. We are attempting
something different.

We started to collect visual data as illustrative of the work of the school
in representing its policies (to the internal and external gaze – and these can
be distinctive and different as well as overlapping). In relation to the range
of policies that are in play in each school (Braun *et al.* 2010), the need to
attend to things like 'keeping everyone on board' with policies like achievement, behaviour, learning discourses, all these visuals play some part – but
what? They might be interpretation devices – intended to convey the position of the school leadership's 'take' on policy – they may merely cover the
walls – decorative wallpaper – and claim no attention except for the passing
researcher's camera. What is undeniable is the vast amount and variety of
materials and visuals that are in circulation in each school – in its 'public'
areas: the foyer, the walls of the entrance, the classrooms, as well as in its more

'private' locations: the staff rooms, adult meeting rooms, department offices, withdrawal/referral rooms for recalcitrant students.

There are also difficulties involved in making claims about representativeness or 'truths' about policy discourses through small sets of visual–textual data. We are aware, as Ball and Smith (1992: 18) assert, that 'the sense viewers make of them [photographs] depends upon cultural assumptions, personal knowledge, and the context in which the picture is presented'. So, we, the researchers, may produce a reading of visual data that speaks to us in particular ways through the lens of our research questions and analytical frameworks. As Thomson (2008: 10) says, we bring our own perspectives to bear when reading visual data, a process she describes as characterised by 'slipperiness'. While the visual discourses we identify have regulatory intentions, they will be mediated by other (perhaps residual or antagonistic) discourses that may produce different effects and compete with 'unofficial' visuals – e.g. those that appear on mobile phones. For example, there may be posters, photographs and instructions about the 'correct' uniform wall-papered over the school, but students' sense of style and fashion and some teachers' beliefs and values of the relative unimportance of these 'messages' will mean that there will be fragmented, contested and differentiated outcomes in practice. It may be that what is seen to be 'significant' to the researcher, perhaps because of its ubiquitousness, its coerciveness, might, to the eye of the student or the teacher, simply appear as so much visual noise or simply just space-filling (Messaris 1997). As Berger (1972: 7) puts it, 'the relationship between what we see and what we know is never settled.' One more point: at an earlier stage, when we were presenting part of this work on visual artefacts to a group of critical educators, we were asked about student graffiti – as a form of 'resisting' these cultural productions. None of the posters, displays or notices that we saw in any of the schools was marked or defaced in any way (although if they had been, they may have been promptly removed). In any case, some of the notices and posters that were photographed were displayed in sealed cabinets that would have made any creative 'interaction' impossible.

From the data that we gathered and analysed, both in terms of content and meanings, in this chapter two main collections or heteroglossias are considered: one is to do with the policy 'problem' of the student and the 'teacher' and the discursive formations that surround this identity production, the other is to do with the solutions of policy problems that are posed to the school. Rather than signalling the discursive formations that produce specific policies such as Every Child Matters or Personalised Learning, what follows is focused on the complex overlaps and reiterations in sets of policies that make the school a distinctive institution. To substitute Foucault's discussion of a prison for that of school: the institution is rendered 'an exhaustive disciplinary apparatus; it must assume responsibility for all aspects of the individual; his physical training, his aptitude to work, his everyday conduct, his moral attitude, his state of mind' – and thus, governmentality (Foucault 1979: 235). Discourses that speak to individual policies also contain within them sets of practices that produce the 'school'. As noted already, discourses construct the object of which they speak, here the student, the school, the teacher, and they are productive in that 'they have power outcomes or effects. They define and establish what is "truth" at particular moments' and these truths work to displace other constructions and versions (Carabine 2001: 268).

Discursive productions of the 'good student'

The key policy issues of achievement and behaviour are focused on the 'good student'; via these translations, policies are 'embodied' in a particular moral (and visual) representation of the student subject. The production of the 'good student' is premised on the belief that if students have high academic expectations of themselves they can successfully achieve them. If a student is motivated, believes in her/himself and behaves well, success, it seems, is assured. For example, Archer and Francis (2007: 47) identified some of the key attributes of the 'good student' – that is, 'good, compliant pupils who would not challenge authority' who were 'naturally hard working' and high achieving. These high academic self-expectations are translated and circulated via the use of different sets of visual (and verbal) cues.

Within the 'good student' discourse, notions of having the right attitude manifested in classroom behaviour and work habits in and out of school, along with a high level of motivation are premised as being fundamental to academic success. As Ball (1990: 4) puts it, 'In the process of schooling the student is compiled and constructed both in the passive processes of objectification, and in an active, self-forming subjectification.' For example, George Eliot produced a poster that was laminated and displayed in the hallways and classrooms used by the Year 10 and 11 students (GCSE students). The poster was headed, 'How to get an A* at GCSE' and contained a list of hints including psychosocial, cognitive and 'gaming' technologies to support success (see Box 6.1) – a recipe for 'success' and an articulation perhaps that only an A* marks out the 'successful' student?

This representation and production of the good student (a student who is well behaved and achieves lots of GCSEs, and one because of the other), is being encoded, enacted and embedded in a vast range of visual cues and prompts that all schools produce. For example, schools celebrate pride and achievement by displaying photographs of high achieving students documenting their projected grades. Campion produces a weekly display for the 'student of the week', where achievement, commitment and belief are encouraged; being exhibited in this way both rewards the individual and reproduces the 'good student' (see Figure 6.1). The notice board is centrally located and has some key words that are displayed: these are *enthusiasm*, *commitment*, *positive attitude* and *progress*, one in each corner, with 'excellent effort' under the main heading – 'student of the week'. Interspersed across the board are lists of names of 'good students' for each key stage in the school. Establishing the 'good student' is about establishing a version of school and a version of the student – a pervasive version – and ultimately a totalising and individualising version (Foucault 1979). Atwood School has 'invited' some Year 11 students to feature in posters where they talk about their GCSE targets. These posters are mounted on the walls of the foyer so that every visitor is exposed to these 'calls to achievement', these exhortations to 'do school' in a particular way, and simultaneously are 'reminded' that these are indeed 'good schools' – seeking to meet the grade and perform to the national benchmarks that in turn separate the failing school from the mediocre school, the good school from the outstanding school (Maguire *et al.* 2011).

How to get an A* at GCSE

- Believe in yourself and work with others who are aiming for an A*.
- Do extra reading and examples in your own time.
- Link arguments together to create a train of thought.
- Refine your exam technique so you know exactly what each question in the exam requires.
- Make sure you understand the mark scheme for each paper so you know how to get the top grades.
- Be willing and able to take risks with your work so you are striving to produce something more original.
- Know the key facts thoroughly and know how to select precisely what facts are needed for each answer.
- Learn how to translate skills and knowledge from one area of a subject to another.

Your teacher will help you with:

- Mark schemes.
- Techniques for each type of question.
- Examples of what A* looks like.
- Reading lists and extra materials.
- More analytical work.
- Feedback on your work giving you advice on how to get an A*.

Box 6.1 How to get an A* at GCSE

Figure 6.1 Student of the week

In all this normalisation work, what is also produced by omission is the student who is not valued, who is 'failing' – socially, educationally and morally. Here we see a simple, but effective illustration of the representation and translation of the standards discourse – and through this attempt to 'raise and praise' (while simultaneously 'naming and shaming' by omission) we see the literal/visual process of policy enactment – a visual technology of layers and layered meanings – a method of order and a method of governmentality for students (and their teachers – and sometimes their parents as well). These visual processes that reify external rewards, competition, individualism and particular modes of demeanour, resonate with Bowles and Gintis' (1976) claims, that schools socialise and incorporate young people into capitalist societies through a 'hidden curriculum'. These visual enactments are part of the 'delivery chain', the joining up of the 'good student' to the good economy!

Turning to Behaviour for Learning, this is also bound up with and into discourses of the 'good academically successful student' (Maguire *et al.* 2010); all schools, including our four schools, pay attention to this aspect of their work (see Chapter 5). Our four schools take seriously the policy requirements involved in behaviour and Behaviour for Learning (Steer 2009). In discursive terms, our schools interpret and translate these policies and produce a plethora of documents, posters and regulatory texts that are widely circulated. These discourses are emphatic. It is not about persuasion, but rather it is about constitution; what students must and must not do and how they must do it in order to make up the 'good student'. These 'codes of behaviour' and 'ways of being' are illustrated in posters and artefacts that 'tell' students what to wear, when to arrive, when to leave, where they can and cannot walk, and how to move around the building – thus, discourse is written onto the idealised representations in these visualisations. These are artefacts of governmentality, order and control. To take one example of these 'codes of behaviour', in three of our four schools, there is a compulsory school uniform (see Figure 6.2). The policing of the uniform policy, in part through the creation and reproduction of posters demonstrating the correct uniform and how to wear it, functions as an overt form of policy enactment and governmentality; and the production of the 'good' student who is dressed correctly (and the 'good' teacher who inspects, checks and enacts uniform policy on a daily basis).

These examples of producing the 'good' student who achieves academically and the good student who behaves her/himself and produces an appropriate 'bodily hexis' (Bourdieu 1984), suggest a mutually reinforcing composite subject. What is significant here is the 'joining up', the insertion into the everyday, the exemplifications, the itemisations and the specifications, which borrow stylistically from self-help and improvement – bullet points and other 'popular' imagery. They are also part of a shift in schools and elsewhere from text to image and they are intended to get students to work on themselves – a mentality of rule. In all of the classrooms that we have visited and on the walls of corridors in our four schools, there are artefacts that call up notions of 'how to be' in school – and how to be the 'ideal' student. Indeed, a walk round any

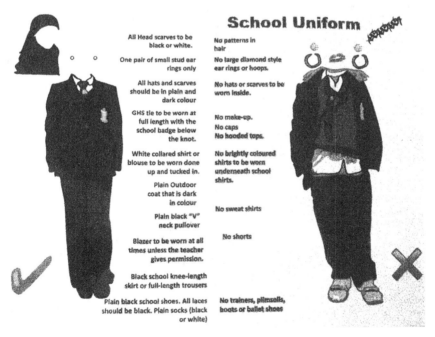

Figure 6.2 School uniform

school will reveal sets of visuals that speak of how to look, how to dress, how to study, how to revise, how to pass exams, how to be successful and who to emulate. The good student is an embodiment of the good school, an assemblage of attitudes, demeanours, gestures and practices. These artefacts relate behaviour policy (and rules) and learning policy, to behaviour and learning (translations) – as we have said, they delineate, hail and engage the students – although so much of the visual apparatus of schools goes unseen in policy analysis work.

Discursive productions of the 'good school'

Discourses are social processes formed within and by wider events, beliefs and 'epistemes' to produce common sense notions and normative ideas. For example, in many ways schools are necessarily captured by a version of 'doing school' that is contained in the dominant discourse of raising attainment.

> The official position is that we know how to improve motivation and overcome poor performance. Provided school leaders learn from the example of high performing heads and adopt the right combination of styles, we can expect the examination results to go up year on year.
>
> (Barker 2010: 89)

In all of these 'official positions' there are assumptions about 'how' to do school and 'what' school is supposed to be for and what it is supposed to be like. These normalising discourses sculpt and shape the ways in which schools select, interpret and translate specific aspects of policy initiatives and policy mandates. Again, drawing on the work of Foucault (1979), normalisation is to do with the constitution of criteria against which all are to be measured and all are to be evaluated and judged. Normalisation goes beyond any binaried account of good/bad. 'It is a dynamic of knowledge, practised and learned, dispersed around various centres of practice and expertise' (Carabine 2001: 278). In our four 'ordinary' schools, where there is a pressing need to keep 'making the grade', some policies will be more urgent than others (standards, GCSE scores, league tables). In all this, there is an imperative towards 'solutionitis': towards solving the policy problem of becoming a 'good' school. This is encoded, circulated and amplified by the textual and discursive work of the school itself in its attempts to reinvent and improve itself – for how could they not respond to these dominant discourses of 'raising standards' and 'constant improvement'.

As we have detailed in Chapter 4, all of our schools deploy the 'obvious' tactics such as targeting particular cohorts of students to coach and mentor, providing booster classes, selecting different subjects and examination boards that may seem 'easier' – what Michael Gove (DfE 2010: 13) calls 'gaming'. All our schools set great store by producing ongoing visual data trails that can then 'show' that progression is taking place. In George Eliot, this includes getting the students to monitor their individual progress by entering their achievements on graphs in their student planners – the visualisation

My Progress During Key Stage 3 – English

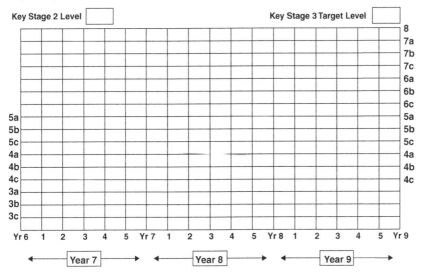

Figure 6.3 Diary progress page

of constant progression and the further constitution of the good school (see Figure 6.3). Students are encouraged to record their national curriculum levels and sub-levels at five points during each key stage. George Eliot's student planner states that 'students should remember that they should aim to progress by two national curriculum levels for each key stage' and then gives some examples of what is expected. In Atwood, Beth, the head of Year 7, demonstrated this attention to the detailed monitoring of student attainment that characterised all our schools. In what she says (below) we see normalising assumptions about the integrity of the levels, the measurement of student capacity and the power of teacher interventions – a very particular discourse of learning and teaching. In this extract, we can also see a dominant discourse about education's purpose – getting points, achieving levels and making the grade (see Chapter 4). This discursive formation is picked up in sets of visuals, recorded artefacts of attainment that simultaneously produce and constitute the school – that make up and are made up by processes of enactment.

> We've got students who came in on a 23–25 Key Stage 2 average points score who need – who are sort of, not proper special needs or proper low ability – but just need a shove to get them into Level 4 territory... I run a girls' group for girls who are, sort of, middle to low Level 5s, but who are specifically targeted for – like, below the radar personality – needing confidence boosting. We have a boys' club for below effort... leading to their low attainment... and then we have a high ability group, who are like

doing a news project. But they're specific high ability who are – who came in on a 33 average points score, which is three Level 5s – but have allegedly dropped back on teacher assessment since they've been at secondary school.

(Beth, HoY 7, English, Atwood)

While here it may seem that we are moving away from the visual, what is particular about the related artefacts that we discuss here is that the visualisation of grids and charts means that you can literally 'see' improvement, comparison, performance over time, 'see' the work done by the school on the student. This work visualises policy, but these visual artefacts and those discussed elsewhere in this chapter, are only meaningful, only 'work' alongside written texts, practices, organisation and talk. Policy is represented, interpreted and translated – policy is enacted – in all these forms together.

The codes and themes that have emerged from our analysis of interview transcripts for this project have been saturated with the significance of league tables and the need for increasing percentage scores at GCSE – the discursive production of the 'good school'. In many ways, our schools seem to be captured by a version of education that is intimately tied into schooling for 'economic competitiveness and an increasing neglect or sidelining (other than in rhetoric) of the social purposes of education' (Ball 2008: 11–12). This is a message that is subtly (and sometimes unsubtly) reinforced by the visual messages produced by the school. For example, Campion School has a weekly e-newsletter that goes to every parent. Last year, from January onwards, the front page of the website was dominated by a central insert, a flashing button that provided a weekly countdown to the start of the GCSE examinations. Thus, all parents, even if their children were not in an examination year, were alerted to and hailed by this discourse. This year, the home page for the school has been taken up with GCSE revision materials, many links to useful sites, and suggestions for parents to help their children prepare for exams. Staff members are alerted to the centrality of this discourse, this version of 'the school' as they move in and out of their staff room.

In the spring term, which leads up to the national examinations in England, during the second year of our project, Campion erected a large notice board at the doorway of the staff room that could not be missed (see Figure 6.4). It highlighted details of targets and in-class groupings for mentoring and coaching for mathematics and English. Similarly, in Wesley, the walls of some individual department rooms were used to 'encourage' the teachers to work to produce the 'good school' by displaying lists of targeted students who needed more support, alongside their photographs. In the main staff room, large photographs (A4 in size) of students who were targets for 'improvement' were displayed; the staff were expected to stick Post-it notes on the photographs detailing positive accounts of progression to encourage one another – while ensuring that these students were 'kept in mind'. Thus, through a combination of different sets of visual artefacts, students and teachers are exposed to the visualisation of policy – in hallways, classrooms, staff rooms and on the

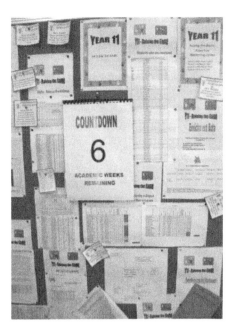

Figure 6.4 Countdown to exams

school website. This repetition, this insistence, this 'management' of the environment to convey policy intentions, repeatedly alerts students and teachers to what is involved in enacting the 'good' school.

Discursive productions of the 'good teacher'

Within the discursive formation of the 'good' school, there is the discourse of the 'good teacher'. If the 'good school' is produced out of high levels of attainment, particularly at GCSE, then so is the 'good teacher'. For example, as Neil, an English teacher at Wesley School explained:

> I was reminded of the Every Child Matters policy, which, again, is a complete farce, because everything about the system encourages, as we've been talking, encourages schools to pour every penny they've got into the C/D borderline students. Everything about the system points them in that direction and then we're meant to go Every Child Matters. It's an absolute farce because clearly every child doesn't matter to the school in the same way, at the same level, because what matters to the school is, can we meet our target, our, well, whatever self-imposed target but a target that we've been told that if we don't meet we're going to get investigated and certain people will lose their jobs and everyone in the school's life

will be made a misery by constantly having to do more and more admin-istration and conform more to a robotic sense of what's good teaching until whoever's investigating us thinks that they're satisfied with it.

This version of the 'good teacher' is exemplified by the sorts of artefacts, post-ers, pictures and charts that make up the visual environment of the school. These ways of doing the 'good teacher' are laid out in staff handbooks, yearbooks for parents and in the students' diaries. This is a form of integra-tion, that is, a political (a common goal, a unity) and educational 'bringing together' of effort, behaviour and focus towards performing the 'good teacher'. Andrew-Power and Gormley emphasise this integrative approach in produc-ing the school:

> In addition to setting the tone, display can also be utilized to embed whole-school policy. This has included whole-school approaches to seat-ing plans, positive behaviour, celebrating achievement and wearing the school uniform correctly.
>
> (Andrew-Power and Gormley 2009: 70)

What is being attempted then is the management and production of the compliant institution and the good school/good teacher; however, in this process, there is not just an attempt to reflect the way things are in terms of contemporary education policy and practice. These discursive attempts work to 'produce' what school is, through calling up a particular version of it. Furthermore, these visual reminders of policy call up some of the more 'opaque relationships of causality and determination between (a) discursive practices, events and texts, and (b) wider social and cultural structures, rela-tions and processes' (Fairclough 1995: 132).

While visual texts make up the school, at least in part, and make up the student and make up the teacher, other processes contribute towards these discourses. For example, in the struggle towards 'making the grade', schools deploy a wide range of activities and events that contribute towards this aspect of their work. There are meetings, staff development days, events and pres-sure groups that all contribute towards the production of the good school, the good teacher and the good student. There are many disciplinary mechanisms that help sustain shared meanings and beliefs in this work, purpose and task of doing school. These bear equally upon student teachers, middle managers and senior leaders. For example, at an in-service education day for all the staff, Milton, the head teacher of George Eliot School, talked about his intention to rework the mission statement to 'tell us something about what we hope for this school' – a new narrative (see Chapter 3).

The head teacher had prepared a draft version of this statement for dis-cussion and the staff moved into break-out groups to consider it – which would eventually be loaded up on the website and inserted into all the school's publicity as the head teacher's vision of the school. In the English department's discussion (which we attended), teachers raised concerns about there 'not being enough focus on the students' and another teacher asked rhetorically, 'who is this for?' Rather than simply address the task they had been given they spent some time correcting the punctuation before turning to consider, somewhat humorously, maxims that could eventually be produced as posters around the school to pick up and reflect the 'mission' statement (as Milton had requested). One teacher commented on the 'lack of morality' in the proposed statement and thought that this gap could be used to produce a maxim. 'Kill or be killed', another teacher humorously retorted, highlighting the head teacher's expressed concerns to raise standards and progress up the local league tables. The staff plenary gave each department an opportunity to feed into the discussion of the statement and then the staff turned to the next matter on the agenda. These processes (a directed agenda, tasks that do not include any discussion about the need for audience for, or purpose of the 'mission' statement even though the teachers did discuss these) contribute towards the management of consent in respect of these discursive formations where everyone and everything has to 'make the grade' and produce the 'good' school, before anything else. What we see here is one example of the mechanisms that are in play, through which the institutional rhetoric is circulated (and perhaps slightly tweaked and a version of 'ownership' maintained) to produce the institutional rhetoric that, in turn, is decanted into sets of tangible artefacts –the process of policy enactment in play.

Enacting policy – and the role of the artefactual

The teachers and the students who embody and make up the school are caught in a complex web of policy discourses through which they are incited to 'do' the good school and 'be' the good teacher and 'perform' the good student. These are exclusionary and selective discourses; only certain 'goods' are sensible or legitimate. Other versions of the good school become unthinkable or doable, and are consigned to the 'field of memory'. So, concerns with students' happiness, or with teachers' well-being, may still exist in the rhetoric of schooling; however, in the policy enactment environment, these discourses become subordinated to the production of order and the ordering of productivity. Within the discursive practices of contemporary schooling and education policy, teachers and students are asked

> not only submit to disciplinary regimes but also participate in their production and administration, through techniques of mutual surveillance; their motivations are shaped by seductive discourses and reinforced by inmate cultures.
>
> (Scott 2010: 227)

As Foucault (1986: 209) explains, discourses are not to be understood as 'determinations imposed from the outside on the thought of individuals, or inhabiting it from the inside'. They work through the ways in which teachers and students are enabled to work on themselves, produce themselves in particular ways through hard work and good behaviour. Furthermore, in these ways of 'governing' schools there are a range of subject positions which signal success and improvement and excellence. They offer the pleasures of performance to those who can inhabit these positions with a sense of achievement, although they are premised on the positioning of 'others' outside of such pleasures. These 'others' may be subject to older and more primitive forms of power or different discourses of 'abnormality' – like 'special educational needs'.

To return to the start of this chapter, we argued that the artefacts and materials that are in circulation in schools can become part of the tools and techniques of governmentality in the policy work of the school (Foucault 1991). We also argued that this is not a totalising phenomenon: discursive formations are characterised by 'gaps' and 'limits' (Foucault 1986: 119). Thus, some of these artefactual processes of policy enactment are less dominant, less attended to, or sometimes 'taken' as 'a bit of a joke' by members of staff and students, as in the discussion of the mission statement. Sometimes, they are displayed in quiet corners where they gradually become bleached to oblivion by the sun, and simply work as 'wall-cover'. However, while this is certainly the case for some (minor) policies, in the main, the 'seductive discourses' and 'inmate cultures' which currently prevail in English schools are embedded in a range of visual artefacts and practices that work to establish and maintain the normalisation of the student, the teacher and the school – discourses that produce material effects and are interwoven into the processes of policy enactments and, ultimately, governmentality. Indeed, to a great extent, policies are not possible without artefacts – artefacts and practices are fundamental to the co-production of school activities – lessons in particular. Most policy analysis omits the artefactual; and in documenting and theorising policy enactments in our four schools, here we have begun to consider the role that artefacts play in this process.

7 Towards a theory of enactment

'The value of hesitation and closer interrogation of utterances of conventional wisdom'[1]

Introduction

In this final chapter, we draw together our responses to the theoretical and empirical question of how schools do policy. While all books come out of proposals and scripted plans for their construction, in the process of doing the writing, the thinking and the analytical work, minds are changed, new directions become evident, different pathways open up while others close down – a somewhat unsettling process. This is even more the case in inductive qualitative research of the kind we are committed to and on which the research we report here is based. Writing is part of the process of analysis – defining codes, explaining their dimensions, applying concepts and developing interpretative memos. In the process of making decisions about what to include, what to exclude, what approach to take and even how to construct the chapters, we have found ourselves confronted in our data with themes and issues that now seem to be more important than they originally looked to be. Equally, we have set aside some ideas that no longer seem as compelling as they once did. In parallel to all of this, we have explored a number of theoretical possibilities in relation to our data.

Now we must attempt to convince you that all of this is greater than the sum of the parts, that it hangs together, that it is a plausible whole that deserves to be taken seriously. We start by revisiting some of the theoretical resources that have helped us unpack 'the how and the what' of policy enactment and, here, somewhat unexpectedly, but perhaps not that surprisingly, the work of Foucault provided us with provocations to think differently about policy work. We will also move, carefully, slowly, towards a very tentative synthesis or model of enactment – an elusive and slippery process: 'For to see what is in front of our eyes requires thinking and thinking about thinking in different ways' (Thrift 2000: 216, cited in Kraftl 2007: 125). This modelling necessarily involves us in specifying the limits of our analysis and identifying some ways in which our work on policy enactment in schools can be taken forward.

Theory and data and data and theory

Starting with our approach then, the primary 'method' of our analysis in this study involves a continuing interplay between data and theory. There is a lot of both here. Theory is indispensable to the understanding of policy work and policy effects. We have used our theoretical resources to think about what is happening in our case study schools and to develop a set of ideas and concepts to represent those happenings – ideas and concepts that we intend to have a more general usefulness. There are various points of focus in this interplay and here we will reiterate some of them. One is the importance of practices, the routine and mundane ways in which policies are enacted – the meetings, events, exchanges and observations that bring policy into the immediate and intimate interactions of daily life at school. Another is the importance of artefacts, of various kinds – posters, planners, texts and materials as both the realisation and representation of policy in relation to practice. In respect to both we have tried to set them within a real and very material version of the school – one with rooms and corridors, windows and furniture, budgets and bodies (specific staff and students). Drawing on Foucault, we see policy as unfolding not through large-scale events, gestures and interventions, but, rather, through a complex 'micro-physics'. In both respects, teachers are 'meaning makers'; they bring creativity and commitment, their enthusiasm, to policy enactment, but this creativity and commitment involve working on themselves, their colleagues and their students in order to 'do' policy and to do it well.

We have also focused in various ways on the discourses that make up policy, and we have sometimes used the concept of discourse in a fairly superficial sense to consider some of the basic ideas in play in behaviour, performance and learning in contemporary policy. We have stressed two points. First, that the primary discourses of policy also produce particular kinds of teacher and student subjects – good teachers and good students, 'ideal learners' as Youdell (2006: 169) calls them, and thus good schools (see Chapters 3 and 6). Nonetheless, we have also indicated some of the ways in which different bits of policy carry within them competing or contradictory subject positions, 'impossible selves' perhaps (Youdell 2006). Second, these primary discourses are set within a history of prior discourses – 'a cemetery of past truths' (Veyne 2010: 39) – which makes it possible, at least at times, or at least in certain spaces, to think about teaching and learning in different ways (see Chapter 5). There is an implicit agonism that sets some of the contemporary discourses over and against these earlier 'flawed' versions of schooling. It is within this agonism, and in relation to the memories of things past, that some ethical and political discomforts arise. However, what is clear in our data is that what we might call resistance, a full-blown reflexively articulated confrontation between agonistic discourses, is rare and fleeting – limited for example to moments of political or trade union action. In the mundane, in relation to the pressures of performance, in response to constant change, there is little space or time or opportunity to think differently or 'against' – although this is a matter we return to at the end of this chapter. Here we do not 'blame' the teacher for a failure of political insight, indeed we recognise, only too immediately, the ways in which we are all deeply implicated in, and bound up and into, the contemporary neo-liberal and globalising settlement and its triumph is that most of the time we do not even notice it is there.

Another point of focus in the interplay of theory and data, which recurs in our analysis, is the complexity and fragility of 'school' in relation to policy enactment and the efforts of configuration and reconfiguration that go into making the school a stable organisation. We have developed a typology of policy work and policy workers (see Chapter 3), which nonetheless needs further elaboration, that is intended to give some substance to the efforts of reconfiguration and, in particular, we have sought to highlight and adumbrate the processes of interpretation and translation that go into doing policy. The typology serves to stress both the management of coherence, what we have referred to as organisational narratives, and the management of change, the manufacture of a set of responses to policy, in practice, in texts, in outcomes and in the fabric of the institutions.

One version of both coherence and management, which is evident in all our schools, is 'deliverology', a very effective joining-up of 'learning' to policy. This is a technology of performance, a *techne* of government and of enactment, which gets policy 'done' in very effective ways by creating an economy of visibility which brings students, teachers and schools directly into the gaze of policy and establishes connections 'between the aspirations of authorities and the activities of individuals and groups' (Rose and Miller 1992: 173). This is a political project for education in relation to national competitiveness and the forces and discourse of globalisation. This purports to make students (and teachers, and all of us) into economically useful citizens, although there are other policies currently in play that construct somewhat different versions of the 'useful' student (and we are thinking in particular of PLTS). In Foucault's words, this 'economic geometry' builds a 'house of certainty' (1979: 202), within which every student is 'known' and positioned and 'treated' accordingly, although we have indicated that certainty is never absolute. The focus here is not learning or understanding but the examination itself. That is the object and method of 'delivery'. What is very evident here is the coherence, repetition and insistence of a particular mechanics of objectification and visibility.

This is also a form of power which is automatic and generalised, a form that has its principle in mechanisms and arrangements rather than persons. The workings of the mechanisms of performance requires the enrolment and coordination of a whole variety of different individuals to enact its techniques and procedures (see Chapter 3 and 4). We can also think about the historical location and consequences of this technology within a whole general regime of policy that is firmly and decisively focused on performance (Ball 2003): what Neave (1998) calls the 'evaluative state' and Clarke (2004) the 'performance–evaluation nexus', involving quality assurance, inspection, audit and the construction of league tables. The generation of these measures, indicators and comparisons provide what Ozga (2008) calls 'governing knowledge'. That is, knowledge of a new kind, a regime of numbers, that constitutes a 'resource through which surveillance can be exercised' (Ozga 2008: 264) – the use of performance information of various kinds as 'a resource for comparison' (p.267), addressed to improvements in quality and efficiency, by making nations, schools and students 'legible' (p.268). National evaluation systems, school performance tables, test comparisons, throughput and equity indicators, etc. (Rinne *et al.* 2002) are increasingly important in the ways that states monitor, steer and reform their education systems at every level and in every sector: 'the technology of statistics creates the capacity to relate to reality as a field of government' (Hunter 1996: 154).

There is yet another way of thinking about the interplay of theory and data, of the joining up of politics and practices, and of the work of reconfiguration and that is by returning to the concept of discourse. By taking discourse more seriously, as a set of regularities, a trace of the 'historical frontier' of an event, as a 'voice as silent as a breath' (Foucault 1972: 25), or as 'what was being said in what was said' (p.28), we can begin to identify a set of 'master' discourses that define schooling. They are learning, curriculum and behaviour. They are what makes 'the school', 'the teacher' and 'the student' into meaningful and recognisable entities. In relation to these (re)configurations, what we take to be policies are power relations, practices and subjectivities which articulate forms of learning and forms of behaviour; that is, specific positions of agency and identity in relation to particular forms of knowledge and practice.

These (re)configurations are founded upon the traces and play of a half-glimpsed and contradictory set of grids and regularities, a 'policy archaeology' as Schureich (1994) calls it, which are 'deposited' and sedimented over time in schools in the form of policies, and which articulate and name epistemologically and ontologically incoherent forms of learning, curriculum and behaviour. These discursive regularities, which are often equally incoherent (certainly under New Labour) but somewhat more visible at the level of government, are constituted in a disparate set of political–economic conditions, assumptions and forces. Over the past 25 years these (ir)regularities which inform, constitute and legitimise educational policy, and indirectly school practices, have been ordered and governed across the tensions between Fordist and post-Fordist versions of the economy,[2] knowledge and the worker, and neo-conservative and neo-liberal versions of government, knowledge and social authority. Within these tensions skills are set over and against curriculum subjects, 'what' against 'how', transmission (teaching) against learning and meta-cognition, 'doing' against 'knowing', 'scripts' against differentiation (Leadbeater 2004), discipline against behavioural management and social and emotional well-being, and to some muted extent, selection against inclusion.

Cutting across these 'educational' regularities is another related set of organisational regularities, which, somewhat more coherently, articulate notions of competition, leadership and enterprise. In policy work in the English school, these are 'named' and enacted as PLTS, SEAL, targets and standards, league tables, exclusion, Every Child Matters, personalisation and student voice. These call upon the readings of and responses of equally incoherent policy and pedagogical subjects. Thus, the problem of enactment, in general terms, becomes the interpretation and translation of this disparate grid of social regularities, into a set of practices which make sense as an organisational vernacular, or at least which hold the inherent incoherences in some kind of institutional 'balance' – what Foucault describes as an apparatus, or *'dispositif'*:

> What I'm trying to pick out with this term is, firstly, a thoroughly heterogenous ensemble consisting of discourses, institutions, architectural forms, regulatory decisions, laws, administrative measures, scientific statements, philosophical, moral and philanthropic propositions – in short, the said as much as the unsaid.
>
> (Foucault 1977, cited in Gordon 1980: 194)

This apparatus is what we have sought to make sense of in our study.

A synthesis of enactment

Some policy makers and some educationalists seek recipes, or at the very least a list of suggestions, for practical tactics in enacting policy – and this desire for sense, order and direction is understandable in the current climate of policy overload and initiativitis – in a period of constant reform and incitement to improve. Schools *need* to and *have* to be able to enact multiple and competing and sometimes capricious policies and, in the main, they want to do this as successfully and as efficiently as they can (Spillane 2004). While we address the question of 'how schools do policy', equally and simultaneously, we want to problematise this question. In what we write we do not want to suggest that a recipe does exist and that, if only it can be identified, then policy enactment will cease to present problems for schools: quite the opposite. Our argument is that policy enactment is not a straightforward and rational process – although sometimes it is made to appear so – and its outcomes are not easy to read off from their policy origins. 'It is not easy (and sometimes impossible) to identify which implementation practices will lead to the desired outcomes and what unintended, and undesired, outcomes will emerge' (Mussella 1989: 100). 'How schools do policy' may be a practical and pragmatic question, but it is also one with ontological overtones. In this we borrow from Foucault who wrote about his work:

> My discourse, far from determining the locus in which it speaks, is avoiding the ground on which it could find support. It is a discourse about discourses: *but it is not trying to find them in a hidden law, a concealed origin*

that it only remains to free; nor is it trying to establish by itself, taking itself as a starting-point, the general theory of which they would be the concrete models.

(Foucault 1972: 205, our italics)

It is not that we do not want to produce a set of ingredients for how schools do policy – rather, it is that we cannot do this. Or rather, it is that we cannot do this in any simple sense. In our attempt to produce a tentative model (for want of a better word) of enactment, again borrowing from Foucault, our aim is 'to reveal a well-determined set of discursive formations that have a number of describable relations between them' (Foucault 1972: 158). We want to point up the impossibility of producing a linear model of enactment practices, any simple story of policies travelling into and through schools, or of policy enactment as a form of osmosis. However, this does not mean that we have nothing to say about these processes. Ozga and Lingard (2007: 78) recognise that educational research 'informs, enables and sustains learning' but 'it cannot, by its very nature, be reduced to totally instrumental activity'. This is the case with our work in our four schools.

At the start of this book, we discussed the distinction between policy implementation and policy enactment. Our point was, and is, that while a great deal of attention has been given to evaluating how well policies are implemented, that is, how well they are realised in practice, less attention has been paid to understanding and documenting the ways in which schools actually deal with multiple, and sometimes opaque and contradictory policy demands, and the diverse ways that they creatively work to fabricate and forge practices out of policy texts and policy ideas in the light of their situated realities – a process of recontextualisation that produces some degree of heterogeneity in practice. What we also said at the start of this book is that understanding this process depends on how policy itself is theorised. As we explained in the first chapter, we take policy making in schools as a complex set of processes of interpretation and translation, which are contextually mediated and institutionally rendered (Braun *et al.* 2011). Thus, policies will be open to situated changes; they may get integrated into older ways of working – the history of prior discourses – and become invisible or asserted within new technologies and new ways of doing school (see Chapter 4). Whatever happens, (most) policies will be struggled over and struggled with by 'those people who are its object' (Ball 1994: 11). Policies are not simply about doing things differently, 'but policies always have objects of intervention and subjects of focus in their discursive formation' (Goodley and Runswick-Cole 2011: 74). Policies call up policy actors – they produce policy subjects.

We say 'most policies', because there is a need to acknowledge that not all policies carry the same degree of compulsion to act; as we have argued, there are some discourses of schooling that bear forcibly and inexcerably upon practice. There are other 'types' of policies that are less prescriptive or weighty, which are designed to fix institutional problems or make schools better places to be in; the 'no bells' policy that one of our schools developed meant that ends of lessons were not interrupted by bells or tannoys, the intention being to help teachers plan for more effective lesson-endings and cut down on disruptions at times of transitions (see Braun *et al*. 2010 for more examples of these different policies in play). Policies work on different levels. There are policies that will be driven by political commitments to structural macrochanges – moves to privatisation come to mind! Others are focused almost exclusively on the classroom interactions between students and teachers – like PLTS. These different 'types' of policies will call up different forms of enactments and those who work in schools will have different orientations towards some of these possible ways of 'doing' school.

Matland (1995: 153) argues that studies of how policies have been put into practice have produced 'long lists of variables that may affect implementation'. Most of these lists detail problems within the policy itself, for example, of it not being clear or coherent, or there not being enough ownership of the policy at the school level. Policies need to be reasonable, they need to be carefully and gradually communicated and they need to respect the expertise and experience of school staff. Policy makers need to work with local officials and agencies on how to support policies in practice. (All this is well known – if not always acted upon – by policy makers.) Matland (1995: 153) adds that all this work on implementing policy 'has given us a field overflowing with diagrams and flow charts with a prodigious number of variables'. Much of this work is based on evaluations of policy work undertaken *after* the event. In contrast, despite Matland's warnings about the 'overflowing' diagrams and charts and tables, we have not been able to resist producing one of our own (see Figure 7.1). Here our purpose is illustrative, an attempt to start to represent some of the material, interpretive and discursive dimensions of policy enactment and the complexity of their inter-relations.

In Figure 7.1 we offer a visual account of our thinking about policy enactment – it is an illustration of our thinking in this book, but also of the development of our thinking during the fieldwork, analysis and writing. The school represents our starting point; it is central but not necessarily in the centre, its history and intake (and connected values) are central too but also fragile. In the diagram, the school looks embattled – all those arrows bearing down on it – but those are also its components, such as the material contexts of staffing, facilities and budgets and the diverse discourses and policies that constitute the school. Performance looms large – although the size of the boxes carries no particular meaning – and its specific construction is shaped by the institutional 'management' of policy. History, intake and values mediate policy, policy contexts and discourses, as they find expression in the school. There is a lot of human action in this diagram: policy interpretation and translation (as well as interpretations of interpretations); professional and emotional dimensions; and the filtering and doing of policy work. There is also resistance, and we left this aspect deliberately unconnected, as its expression in murmurings and discontents (see below) are to

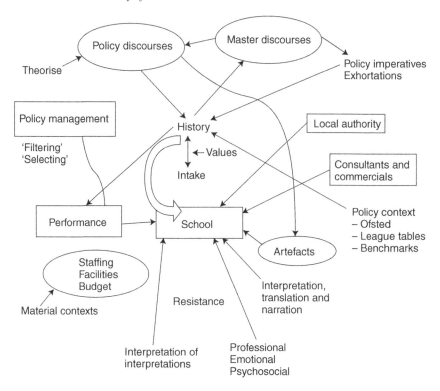

Figure 7.1 Thinking about policy enactment

some extent free-floating, rather than systematic. Neither the model, nor the account of the model we are giving here is comprehensive or finished. Our visualisation is a kind of 'thinking map'; if you have a pen and are happy to write into books, you may want to add to it and make changes; you may want to take issue with our unidirectional arrows and think of some crucial elements that we have failed to consider. A model that is in flux like this and that can develop into its own dynamic is exactly what we had in mind when we started to chart our thinking about policy enactment.

Theorising policy enactment

At the centre of policy enactment is the school – but the school is neither a simple nor a coherent entity, there is a need to understand schools as far more differentiated and loosely assembled than is often the case. Schools are not of a piece. They are precarious networks of different and overlapping groups of people, artefacts and practices. Schools are made up of collections of different teachers, managers, bursars, teaching assistants, mentors, administrators, students, parents, governors and others, who inhabit various ways of being with different forms of 'training', discursive histories, epistemological world views and 'professional' commitments. For example, as we have already detailed, the school bursar will sometimes lead policy decision making related to staffing policy or curriculum innovation, something not usually attended to in accounts of policy work in school (see Chapter 2). In instances like this, pedagogical discourses will sometimes take a back seat to financial imperatives. In other policy arenas, for example assessment in the core curriculum subjects, the 'common sense' across the school will be that these are priority policies that command attention, need additional funding and take precedence in timetabling decision making. Here policy work is 'obvious'. It is non-negotiable. In other areas, such as discipline, tensions in interpretations that lead to agonisms are perhaps more predictable. Schools are also different places at different times of the year, or the day, or parts of the term – more or less fraught or relaxed. Schools are organic organisations that are, in part at least, the product of their context – staff profiles, intake and parental aspirations – as well as being influenced by practical aspects such as the school accommodation, the building and its immediate environment. There is a social context and a materiality to policy.

In the past, much 'implementation' research has concentrated on the role and power of head teachers and senior leaders in school in relation to their capacity to effect change (Fullan 2006); what is still a surprise to us is that these analyses often ignore the work of all the other policy actors (and policy subjects) who make up the 'school'. We have described some of these policy actors: for example, the policy enthusiasts, critics, receivers – not forgetting those who embody specific policies such as the SENCO who is responsible for special educational needs, or senior teachers for whom policy responsibility is a 'career move'. Thus, as we have suggested, some of those who work in schools are policy 'carriers' and sometimes too, policy 'careerists'.

Most of all, as we have already said, threaded through the narratives of this diverse set of policy actors, woven into the texts and practices of policy enactment, we find evidence of powerful discourses of being the 'good' teacher and producing the 'good' student and making the 'good' school. These discourses are embedded in the vast numbers of inter-related policies that come together to address the specifics of and the mechanisms of school performance. Performance and student behaviour is perhaps *the* 'master' discourse of schooling in the twenty-first century that drives policy enactment and takes precedence over everything else in our schools, even though schools are more than policy, and teaching relationships go beyond policy enactments. Even so, to some degree, in a 'fast' policy climate, head teachers and senior leadership teams have to predict and anticipate what will be round the policy corner, so that 'practice may indeed be overtaking policy' (Woods 2011) – which may be the case in relation to PLTS. For the 'ordinary' school that needs to attend to the paraphernalia and to the 'threat' of league tables, examination results, reputation and recruitment, as well as all the tactics of accountability, such as inspections, audits and quality matters – there may be little space left for much else. You might want to interject at this point that we did not attend enough of those other sorts of performances that go on in schools – plays, music, dance and art. These things were in evidence, as were sports, school trips and social events. However, these were not what teachers spoke about in the interviews. But then perhaps, as we note below, we did not ask the right questions of the right people.

Things we did not do in this book

At the beginning of this chapter and the book, we talked about a writing project, a collaborative, ongoing, analytical effort of sense-making, discussion and contestation. We admitted that we could have written a different book, that there are many things we could have said for which we had no room and that there are different ways in which we might have constructed and reworked our analysis. However, our engagement with this research project, the data and our theoretical thinking on policy enactment is not finished and in the same sense, this book is not a finished product but a version of our ongoing work. It is where we have got to. There are some things that we were not able to address because we did not cover them in our fieldwork; things we decided not to ask, or did not realise that it would be useful to ask; and there are points of analysis that we could (and will) pursue in our data that we have not yet had time to address. There are also some aspects of our analysis that we would have liked to write more about, but decided for practical and space concerns not to. In particular, there are areas and departments in the four schools which we did not get to know as well as others. Our fieldwork was guided by the three substantive policy domains we wanted to explore (standards, behaviour and personalised learning), although we sought to locate these within a broader context of policies in school, and thus we have fairly extensive 'coverage' of key subjects such as English and Maths, but have comparatively fewer insights into some of the other curriculum areas.

We interviewed between 20 and 24 individuals in each of the schools in depth and whilst this, together with our observations and document collection, provided us with a large amount of data, it still means that there are many individuals working in the schools that we have not met, not talked to and who may not even have been aware of the research happening in their school. These gaps and omissions do concern us and we had many discussions within the team asking ourselves whether our findings would have been 'different' if we had looked in different places. The answer to this question must inevitably be yes, our data set would have been a different one, but here we can only write (and theorise) about the things we have done. So there are policies and policy trajectories which we did not follow in the fieldwork and members of staff whom we did not interview. There are questions too about the identities of teachers (embodied, social, cultural, professional) and possible disjunctions between how they see themselves and perform 'the teacher' that we do not have the space to fully explore. There are questions about classed, 'raced' and gendered regimes in schools that interpolate policy enactment and that need further analysis.

In Chapter 2 we briefly pointed towards psychosocial and affective dimensions as part of school contexts which are not covered by what we have termed 'professional' factors. Psychosocial dynamics are an analytical field that we expect to do some future work on in relation to policy enactment. Perhaps affect and emotional ties – to your school, department, colleagues and students – can be one of the keys to individuals' willingness to take on (and put up with) policies and frequent policy changes, and relate to what we have identified as 'enthusiasms', just as these ties, or their absence, are crucial for many teachers to function, thrive in or quit certain schools or teaching more generally. Psychosocial activities such as laughing at and about policy and school leaders, gossiping, complaining with colleagues, can all help to reduce the anxiety and the 'threats and fears' involved in policy work in schools; they can buffer policy effects to some extent, and can bind colleagues together in ways that are not always acknowledged in some of the current work on schools (although these informal social relations are evidenced in the classic ethnographies of the school such as those by Hargreaves (1967); Lacey (1974); Ball (1981)).

There are many other beginnings in our text which we would like to pursue. For example, the idea of narration; the work of policy translation and its many forms and practices; the 'relations' of policy to material context – space, sunlight, visibility, departmental geography, the condition of buildings. We have also done far less work than we intended on the local policy documents produced in the schools. We have collected a huge volume and variety of such texts, which are themselves a form of policy enactment, but have only begun to scratch the surface of this collection in terms of analysis. We also became interested in commercial texts, of various kinds, which were 'bought' for policy purposes, which need to be better incorporated into an understanding of the interpretation, translation and enactment of policy.

Whilst these are all aspects of policy enactment that we were not necessarily setting out to examine at the outset of the project, one of the areas that we were planning to take on in greater depth as part of the study and which nevertheless only got fairly scant attention in this book is Personalised Learning. As we indicated in Chapter 1, PL was a high profile central government policy at the time of the project's inception, with the DCSF describing it as the requirement for schools to take 'a highly structured and responsive approach to each child's and young person's learning' (DCSF 2008a: 5). Emanating from the 'Teaching and Learning in 2020 Review Group' (DfES 2006), Personalised Learning was presented as a 'big idea' in school reform and, as researchers, we were interested in it as a polyphonic, multiple policy agenda. However, in our four case study schools, Personalised Learning was much less visible than government literature and messages would suggest. By and large, interviewees felt that 'personalising learning' was an integral part of all schooling, part of prior and enduring practices, and that teachers' commitments to their students as individuals, the principles of comprehensive education that allow for various pathways and levels within schools, as well as some additional activities such as the promotion of Personal Learning and Thinking Skills, and Every Child Matters, already covered the government's PL brief.

As a consequence, at least in our case study schools, PL was an example of a policy that received very different attention at government than at school policy levels and whilst this lack of take-up is interesting in itself, the wealth of findings in other areas of policy generated by the research led us to somewhat 'neglect' our initial commitment to investigate PL. Also though, PL is an example of a 'personal' policy – associated in particular with the enthusiasm of one Secretary of State for Education, David Milliband, and his advisors, and a policy almost entirely limited to exhortation and modest monetary 'incentives'. It could be taken 'less' seriously by schools; it could be filtered out or double-counted.

We want to reiterate that this book is not primarily about any individual or even collective policy; it is also not about a comprehensive and definite representation of 'our' four schools – rather, what this book is about is the practices of policy enactment. While we have sought to tell you something about how policy is in 'real' schools, we are also unashamedly theoretical.

Next steps

> All my books... are little tool boxes... if people want to open them, to use this sentence or that idea as a screwdriver or spanner to short-circuit, discredit or smash systems of power, including eventually those from which my books have emerged... so much better!
>
> (Foucault 1975, cited in Morris and Patton 1979: 115)

As we suggested at the start of this book, theorising policy enactment was always going to be complex and slippery and in many ways an incomplete and impossible project. Nevertheless, we want this book to contribute towards debates around policy enactment and contribute to the conceptual frameworks within which these conversations occur. We want to offer the reader the possibility of thinking about policy enactment in new ways, to put policies in context and understand more about the processes behind their enactment. As we said in the first chapter, we want to provoke questions and problems and generate a new space, and perhaps some tools, for further exploration.

Any further research needs to take context more seriously. The material, structural and relational contexts of schooling need to be incorporated into policy analysis in order to make better sense of policy enactments at the institutional level. One of our key 'findings' is the significance of different 'types' of contextual factors as constraints and pressures as well as enablers of policy enactment – sometimes all of these simultaneously. As we argue in Chapter 2, policy making and policy makers tend to assume 'best possible' environments for 'implementation': ideal buildings, students and teachers and plentiful resources. Policy makers do not necessarily take into account the reality of school – the finances, the physical space, the student body, the profile and willingness of the staff. Overall, then, policy makers and researchers need to give serious attention to the messy complexity of schools and not impose a 'theory from above'. Just as one-size-fits-all policies run aground when hitting the rocks of real life, so do attempts to produce sets of definitive statements about policy enactment.

It would be useful too to look at some of the exceptions that may prove the rule in enacting policy, what Flyvberg (2006: 229) calls 'atypical or extreme cases' – for example, what happens in schools that are perceived as 'unsuccessful'? Under even greater pressure, would their relationships with policy be different? And what of so-called 'outstanding' schools – is there more space for policy autonomy? Are they freed up from the pressures, constraints and 'threats' that we have charted in the 'ordinary' school? It could be useful to map different sets of policy enactments through deploying some of our theoretical resources, for, as we have already said, policies are themselves not of a piece, and the policy climate is constantly changing.

One of the 'silences' that is a constant presence in our work is the persistent sociological question of the relationship between power, agency and the space for alternatives. We have given this question some attention in different places in this book – and certainly in our discussions and coding of the data that we collected. For instance, in the process of doing this research project, some of the questions asked most frequently at the seminars where we have presented our work, have centred around any evidence of and degrees of resistance to various policies in our four schools. Our audiences were sometimes visibly frustrated by our inability to 'do' resistance in our data. As Foucault (1976: 95) writes:

> Where there is power there is resistance and yet or rather consequently this resistance is never in a position of exteriority to power... [it] depends on a multiplicity of points of resistance: these play the role of adversary, target, support, or handle in power relations. These points of resistance are present everywhere in the power network... there is a plurality of resistances, each of them a special case.

So why have we not given more attention to this plurality? There are some problems with resistance and resistance theory in the contemporary English school setting. One problem is simply that of how to recognise it – in grand gestures and/or in instances of personal unease? Another lies in how resistance is constructed and understood; it may merely be a sociological trope, a conceit or simply a desire. Giroux's (1983) critique of resistance theory warns that some oppositional behaviour may in practice have oppressive outcomes. As we have already said, we do think what we were able to recognise examples of the refusal of some policies, but not that much. Rather in our data we found evidence of discontents, murmurings, indifference and disengagements – what Goffman calls 'role distancing' – that is, some 'disdainful detachment of the performer from a role he is performing' (Goffman 1961: 110). We also found evidence of psychosocial forms of policy buffering, as we have already mentioned. Clearly, we need to do a great deal more in detailing the micro-politics of resistances, resistances within accommodations, and so on. Again, perhaps we need to look for resistance in different places?

To reiterate another central theme within our analysis, schools are 'not of a piece', and as such, it is not surprising that they are made up of competing and conflicting values, principles and desires. While there are policy impera-tives, there will always be some alternative spaces for thinking differently: 'schooling serves a whole range of purposes and encompasses a whole range of practices, not all of which are oppressive or connected with the requirements of a capitalist economy and some of which can contribute to the promotion of social justice' (Gewirtz and Cribb 2009: 90). Yet, at the same time, schools develop routines and procedures to ensure their management and enactment of some high-stakes policies, through what Olsen and Sexton (2009) describe as a form of 'threat rigidity'; that is, a form of control and management that exerts pressure to conform to the dominant policy agenda. 'Threat rigidity' may be more evident in the 'ordinary school', one that is more susceptible to pressures of performativity (Maguire *et al.* 2011; Perryman *et al.* 2011).

When we seek to sum up the outcomes of policy enactments in our schools, we are left with an analytic conundrum rather like one of those optical illu-sions, that can be seen as a vase or a face. Do we emphasise interpretational variations and spaces of difference or the colonisation of practice by performa-tivity and the triumph of modernisation? If pushed to respond we might have to say that our analyses would suggest that some profound changes are taking place in what it means to be educated, and what it means to be a teacher and a learner – as effects of policy. However, despite their profundity these changes are also incomplete, other versions of education can still be glimpsed, other rationalities are still being murmured.

Appendix
Case study schools and interviewees

Atwood School

Pseudonym	Position/subject
Ajay	Student teacher
Atanu	HoY 9, Geography
Beth	HoY 7, English
Caroline	Assistant head teacher, SLT, History
Catherine	Deputy head teacher, SEN
Charlie	LSA
Daniel	Governor
Debbie	Deputy head teacher, History
Eric	Assistant head teacher, Geography, BTEC Tourism
Gillian	NQT Science
Greg	Bursar
Heather	Future Leader (English)
Joe	Head of Sociology
Kelechi	Student teacher
Ken	Head teacher
Naomi	RE
Nick	Deputy head teacher
Nicola	Head of English
Patricia	LA advisor
Roy	LA advisor
Sheila	LSA
Sonja	Mathematics
Stewart	Science, NUT rep.
Tanveer	AST Science
Trevor	NQT Mathematics

Campion School

Pseudonym	Position/subject
Adrian	Head of Mathematics
Alice	Teaching and Learning Coordinator, Technology
Anjali	KS4 manager, English
Bob	LA advisor
Carla	Head of English
Cheryl	TA
Clare	Assistant KS4 manager (HoY), Mathematics
Daisy	NQT Mathematics
Dave	Art, Union Rep.
Ewan	KS3 manager, PE
Fiona	Assistant head teacher, PE
Gareth	Deputy head of sixth form, History
Geoff	LA advisor
Graeme	Head teacher
Graham	Head of sixth form, PE
Joshua	GTP, Psychology
Lesley	Deputy head teacher, Psychology
Lindsey	Behaviour welfare officer
Manuel	Deputy head teacher, ICT
Molly	GTP English
Roger	Mathematics
Terry	Bursar

George Eliot School

Pseudonym	*Position/subject*
Aabid	Joint head teacher, Social Sciences
Ashley	Head of English
Deborah	LA advisor
Eman	English
Frances	Head of Access, Way to Work
Frank	AST Science, Union rep.
Jamie	NQT Business Studies
Justin	Deputy head teacher, SLT
Kristi	Student teacher
Laura	Teaching and Learning Coordinator, AST Social Sciences
Lyn	Assistant head teacher
Madhari	Deputy head of Mathematics
Mai	NQT Mathematics
Martin	Head of Mathematics
Milton	Head teacher
Nigel	Learning mentor
Oscar	Science
Owen	Deputy head teacher
Rachael	Head of PE
Reena	Pastoral HoY 9
Richard	Training School Manager, AST Geography
Siobhán	Business Manager
Sunny	HoY, History/Citizenship
Zohra	Student teacher

Wesley School

Pseudonym	Position/subject
Alisa	School business manager
Amy	NQT Sociology
Darshan	Mathematics
Diane	LA advisor, behaviour
Douglas	HoY, Mathematics
Duncan	Assistant head teacher, Geography
Hazel	Deputy head teacher, Science
Imraan	Head of Business Studies/ICT
James	Assistant head teacher, Social Science, Politics
Janet	Behaviour support officer
Jean	LA advisor, English
Karen	Head of language support
Kathleen	NQT Dance
Matu	Deputy head teacher, Science
Neil	English, 2nd in department, Union rep.
Patrick	SIP
Paul	Head of English
Philip	Head teacher
Raaida	Head of Mathematics
Robert	AST Art
Wendy	Head of Sociology

Notes

1 Doing enactments research

1 Sometimes heavy doses of sense need to be imported into these texts by teachers.

2 Taking context seriously

1 In 2010 in state-funded secondary schools, 15.4 per cent of pupils were known to be eligible for FSM (www.education.gov.uk/rsgateway/DB/SFR/s000925/index.shtml) (accessed 1 December 2010).
2 Future Leaders is a leadership training programme targeted at urban schools (www.future-leaders.org.uk).
3 Building Schools for the Future was launched in 2004 with the aim to rebuild or refurbish every secondary school in England over a 15–20 year period. Local authorities entered into public–private partnerships, known as Local Education Partnerships with private sector companies. Funding for BSF came from PFI (see below) and government capital funding, and was targeted at local authorities with the most deprived schools first, through a standard formula of GCSE results and free school meal uptake. The scheme was discontinued in July 2010 after a change of government from Labour to a Conservative–Liberal coalition (www.partnershipsforschools.org.uk/about/aboutbsf.jsp).
4 The Private Finance Initiative (PFI) is a procurement method which secures private sector investment in public sector infrastructure in return for part-privatisation. PFI contracts typically also contain provision by the private contractor for associated services such as maintenance. It is a way of funding capital investments without immediate recourse to the public purse. For the duration of the contract, the PFI building is leased by the public body (www.hm-treasury.gov.uk/ppp_index.htm).
5 LA consultants at the time of our fieldwork were employed through a DCFS initiative called the National Strategy, aimed at improving teaching and learning in schools through professional development (www.nationalstrategies.co.uk).

3 Doing enactment: people, meanings and policy work

1 The two terms are often used interchangeably. Here we want to use them to tease out different, but overlapping and inter-related, aspects of policy enactment.
2 In Bernstein's terms (Bernstein 1996), such a pedagogy rests on an implicit hierarchy, implicit sequencing rules and implicit criteria within which power is unseen and progress relies on forms of self-regulation and self-organisation.
3 Such assignments can become parts of 'policy careers'.
4 It is important to recognise that these narratives are also rehearsed for the research interview as a preferred presentation of the school and the ordering work of the head teacher to the researchers.

5 'Knowledge Management (KM) comprises a range of strategies and practices used in an organization to identify, create, represent, distribute, and enable adoption of insights and experiences. Such insights and experiences comprise knowledge, either embodied in individuals or embedded in organizational processes or practice' (Wikipedia).

6 RAISEonline provides interactive analysis of school and pupil performance data, see http://www.ofsted.gov.uk/Ofsted-home/About-us/FAQs/RAISEonline2.

7 Ofsted might also be considered as a policy actor in this sense, it/they are often an absent presence in policy planning and in the construction of responses.

8 See http://web.me.com/dylanwiliam/Dylan_Wiliams_website/Welcome.html.

9 See http://www.teachernet.gov.uk/management/newrelationship (accessed 24 August 2010).

10 We interviewed the CEO of the company about their work with schools.

11 We also found some 'standards enthusiasts' – Lesley, Anjali, Caroline (see Chapter 4).

12 See http://www.kappanmagazine.org/content/92/1/81.abstract (accessed 2 December 2010).

13 An AST is a teacher who has passed a national assessment and been appointed to an AST post. ASTs concentrate on sharing their skills, through outreach work, with teachers in their own and other schools.

14 This is the loosest and most diverse of our categories and contains within it a set of diverse positionings in relation to policy which vary in terms of subject, status, specialism, confidence, commitment and capability.

15 A fast-track promotion scheme, see http://www.future-leaders.org.uk (accessed 28 October 2010).

16 See http://www.infed.org/thinkers/gardner.htm.

17 There may well be some schools positioned very differently in relation to policy (e.g. in the private sector) in which continuity and coherence are normal.

18 John Law, 'Actor Network Theory and Material Semiotics', version of 25 April 2007, available at http://www.heterogeneities.net/publications/Law2007ANTandMaterialSemiotics.pdf (downloaded 10 August 2010).

19 Satisficing, a portmanteau 'combining *satisfy* with *suffice*', is a decision-making strategy that attempts to meet criteria for adequacy, rather than to identify an optimal solution.

4 Policy subjects: constrained creativity and assessment technologies in schools

1 See www.guardianpublic.co.uk/pac-barber-conference-deliverology (accessed 4 April 2011).

2 This is an ironic reference to the Every Child Matters initiative.

3 See http://lottaguru.com/jeffrey-pfeffer-on-creating-performance-culture (accessed 4 April 2011).

4 The QCA has been abolished by the Coalition Government, the TDA has been folded into the DfE.

5 Normalisation involves the construction of an idealised norm of conduct and then rewarding or punishing individuals for conforming to or deviating from this.

6 While this was one point of focus for our study and our interviews, we were overwhelmed with data of all kinds that 'spoke' to the ways in which performance was a major preoccupation in the case study schools.

7 These anxieties are likely to affect others as the new metric 'refocuses' pressures and expectations to include sciences, languages and humanities.

8 This would fit within the discussion of neo-liberalism and 'mercantile society' in the conclusion.

9 The 'achieving' or *strategic* approach to learning can be summarised as a very well-organised form of surface learning, in which the motivation is to get good marks. The exercise of learning is construed as a game, so that acquisition of technique improves performance (see www.learningandteaching.info/learning/deepsurf.htm, accessed 16 February 2010, and Marton and Säljö (1976).

10 See http://nationalstrategies.standards.dcsf.gov.uk/node/18522 (accessed 11 February 2010).
11 This is an education for an imaginary fordist, basic skills economy perhaps?
12 This is education for a post-fordist economic imaginary perhaps?
13 See also Stoll, L. and Stobart, G. (2005).
14 Two contrasting master narratives of teaching are embedded here, distinct groupings and specific regularities of statements – see Chapter 7.

5 Policy into practice: doing behaviour policy in schools

1 We did ask about behaviour policy in the interviews, so these mentions were not necessarily spontaneous.
2 Graduate Teacher Programme, a teacher training programme designed for graduates who can achieve qualified teacher status while training and working in a paid teaching role.
3 Every Child Matters was a policy initiated by the DCFS in the Children Act 2004 and has been incorporated in the Early Support programme of the Coalition government: http://www.education.gov.uk/childrenandyoungpeople/sen/earlysupport/esinpractice/a0067409/every-child-matters (accessed 16 March 2011).
4 These points were raised by John Coldron in an email discussion in response to our earlier paper at BERA 2009 (Ball *et al.* 2009).

6 Policy artefacts: discourses, representations and translations

1 Although in Foucault's work, these were long – epistemes extending for hundreds of years.

7 Towards a theory of enactment: 'the value of hesitation and closer interrogation of utterances of conventional wisdom'

1 Slee, R. (2011), p. 13.
2 See Jessop (2002) for a full discussion.

References

Andrew-Power, K. and Gormley, C. (2009) *Display for Learning*, London: Continuum.

Anti Social Behaviour Act (2003). London: The Stationery Office.

Archer, L. and Francis, B. (2007) *Understanding Minority Ethnic Achievement: Race, Gender, Class and 'Success'*, London: Routledge.

Atkinson, P. and Coffey, A. (2004) 'Analysing documentary realities', in D. Silverman (ed.) *Qualitative Research*, London: Sage, pp. 56–75.

Audit Commission (2004). Online. Available at: http://www.legislation.gov.uk/ukpga/2003/38/contents (accessed 15 February 2011).

Bach, S., Kessler, I. and Herron, P. (2006) 'Changing job boundaries and workforce reform: the case of teaching assistants', *Industrial Relations*, 37(1): 2–21.

Ball, S.J. (1981) *Beachside Comprehensive: A Case-study of Secondary Schooling*, Cambridge: Cambridge University Press.

Ball, S.J. (1990) 'Introducing Monsieur Foucault', in S.J. Ball (ed.) *Foucault and Education: Disciplines and Knowledge*, London: Routledge, pp. 1–8.

Ball, S.J. (1993) 'What is policy? Texts, trajectories and toolboxes', *Discourse*, 13(2): 10–17.

Ball, S.J. (1994) *Education Reform: A Critical and Post-structural Approach*, Buckingham, Philadelphia: Open University Press.

Ball, S.J. (1997) 'Policy sociology and critical social research: a personal view of recent education policy and policy research', *British Education Research Journal*, 23(3): 257–74.

Ball, S.J. (2001) 'Performativities and fabrications in the education ceremony: towards the performative society', in D. Gleeson and C. Husbands (eds) *The Performing School: Managing, Teaching and Learning in a Performance Culture*, London: RoutledgeFalmer, pp. 210–26.

Ball, S.J. (2003) 'The teacher's soul and the terrors of performativity', *Journal of Education Policy*, 18(2): 215–28.

Ball, S.J. (2005) *Education Policy and Social Class: The Selected Works of Stephen J. Ball*, London: Routledge.

Ball, S.J. (2008) *The Education Debate*, Bristol: Policy Press.

Ball, S.J. (2009) 'Privatising education, privatising education policy, privatising educational research: network governance and the "competition state"', *Journal of Education Policy*, 42(1): 83–99.

Ball, M.S. and Smith, G.W.H. (1992) *Analyzing Visual Data*, London and New Delhi: Sage.

Ball, S.J., Maguire, M.M., Braun, A., Perryman, J. and Hoskins, K. (2011) 'Assessment technologies in schools: "deliverology" and the "play of dominations"', *Research Papers in Education*, 1–21, iFirst.

Ball, S.J., Hoskins, K., Maguire, M. and Braun, A. (2011a) 'Disciplinary texts: a policy analysis of national and local behaviour policies', *Critical Studies in Education*, 52(1): 1–14.

Barber, M. (2007) *Instruction to Deliver: Tony Blair, the Public Services and the Challenge of Delivery*, London: Methuen.

Barber, M. (2010) 'Rising to the challenge of delivering results', in J. Adetunji, *'Deliverology' is the Way Forward, says Barber*. Online. Available at: http://www.guardianpublic.co.uk/pac-barber-conference-deliverology (accessed 4 April 2011).

Barker, B. (2010) *The Pendulum Swings: Transforming School Reform*, Stoke-on-Trent: Trentham Books.

Barthes, R. (1970) *S/Z*, Paris: Seuil.

Beck, U. (1992) *Risk Society: Towards a New Modernity*, London: Sage.

Berger, J. (1972) *Ways of Seeing*, London: Penguin.

Bernstein, B. (1975) *Class, Codes and Control. Vol. 3: Towards a Theory of Educational Transmissions*, London: Routledge and Kegan Paul.

Bernstein, B. (1996) *Pedagogy, Symbolic Control and Identity*, London: Taylor & Francis.

Bernstein, B. (2000) *Pedagogy, Symbolic Control and Identity: Theory, Research and Critique*, Oxford: Rowman and Littlefield.

Bibby, T. (2010) *Education – An 'Impossible Profession'? Psychoanalytic Explorations of Learning and Classrooms*, London: Routledge.

Blair, T. (2005) Monthly Press Conference, Downing Street, 24 October 2005.

Boje, D.M. (1991) 'The storytelling organization: a study of story performance in an office-supply firm', *Administrative Science Quarterly*, 26(1): 102–26.

Boje, D.M. (1995) 'Stories of the storytelling organization: a postmodern analysis of Disney as "Tamara-land"', *Academy of Management Journal*, 38: 997–1035.

Bonnett, A. and Carrington, B. (2000) 'Fitting into categories or falling between them? Rethinking ethnic classification', *British Journal of Sociology of Education*, 21(2): 487–500.

Bottery, M. (2000) *Education, Policy and Ethics*, London: Continuum.

Bottery, M. (2000a) 'The directed profession: teachers and the state in the third millennium', *Journal of In-service Education*, 26(3): 475–86.

Bourdieu, P. (1984) *Distinctions: A Social Critique of the Judgment of Taste*, trans. R. Nice, Cambridge, MA: Harvard University Press.

Bowles, S. and Gintis, H. (1976) *Schooling in Capitalist America: Education Reform and the Contradictions of Economic Life*, London: Routledge and Kegan Paul.

Braun, A., Maguire, M. and Ball, S.J. (2010) 'Policy enactments in the UK secondary school: examining policy, practice and school positioning', *Journal of Education Policy*, 25(4): 547–60.

Braun, A., Ball, S.J, Maguire, M. and Hoskins, K. (2011) 'Taking context seriously: towards explaining policy enactments in the secondary school', *Discourse*, 32(4): 585–96.

Britzman, D. (2003) *Practice Makes Practice: A Critical Study of Learning to Teach*, rev. edn, Albany: State University of New York Press.

Brown, A.D., Stacey, P. and Nandhakumar, J. (2008) 'Making sense of sensemaking narratives', *Human Relations*, 61(8): 1035–62.

Buckles, J. (2010) 'Off the straight and narrow: formulating a policy process that re-engages agency and democracy'. Paper presented at the BELMAS seminar on critical approaches to policy and leadership, Wokefield Park, July 2010.

Burke, J. (2007) 'Classroom management', in J. Dillon, and M. Maguire (eds) *Becoming a Teacher: Issues in Secondary Education*, Buckingham, UK: Open University Press/McGraw Hill, pp. 175–86.

Cabinet Office (2006) *The UK Government's Approach to Public Service Reform*, Prime Minister's Strategy Unit, Public Service Reform Team.

Callon, M. (1986) 'Some elements of a sociology of translation: domestication of the scallops and the fishermen of Saint Brieuc Bay', in J. Law (ed.) *Power, Action and Belief: A New Sociology of Knowledge?*, London: Routledge and Kegan Paul, pp. 196–233.

Carabine, J. (2001) 'Unmarried motherhood 1830–1990: a genealogical analysis', in M. Wetherall, S. Taylor and S.J. Yates (eds) *Discourse as Data: A Guide for Analysis*, London: Sage, pp. 267–310.

Clark, C. (1998) 'Discipline in schools', *British Journal of Educational Studies*, 46(3): 289–301.

Clarke, J. (2004) *Changing Welfare, Changing States: New Directions in Social Policy*, London: Sage.

Coburn, C.E. (2005) 'Shaping teacher sensemaking: school leaders and the enactment of reading policy', *Educational Policy*, 19(3): 476–509.

Cole, R. and Weiss, M. (2009) *Identifying Organizational Influentials: Methods and Application Using Social Network Data*. Online. Available at: http://www.insna.org/PDF/Connections/v29/2009_I-2_P-45-61.pdf (accessed 19 May 2011).

Colebatch, H.K. (2002) *Policy*, 2nd edn, Buckingham: Open University Press.

Connolly, P. (1998) *Racism, Gender Identities and Young Children*, London: Routledge.

Conservative Manifesto (2010) *Invitation to Join the Government of Britain*, London: Conservative Party.

Craft, A. (2005) *Creativity in Schools: Tensions and Dilemmas*, London: Routledge.

Criminal Justice Act (2003). Online. Available at: http://www.legislation.gov.uk/ukpga/2003/44/contents (accessed 15 February 2011).

Corrie, C. (2009) *Becoming Emotionally Intelligent*, 2nd edn, London: Network Continuum.

Currie, G. and Brown, A.D. (2003) 'A narratological approach to understanding processes of organizing in a UK hospital', *Human Relations*, 56(5): 563–86.

Department for Children, Schools and Families (DCSF) (2005) *Higher Standards, Better Schools for All: More Choice for Parents and Pupils*, Norwich: The Stationery Office.

Department for Children, Schools and Families (DCSF) (2007) *Behaviour Improvement Policy*. Online. Available at: http://www.dfes.gov.uk/behaviourimprovement/funding/index.cfm (accessed 12 January 2008).

Department for Children, Schools and Families (DCSF) (2007a) *DCSF Guidance to Schools on School Uniform and Related Policies*. Online. Available at: http://www.education.gov.uk/consultations/index.cfm?action=conResults&consultationId=1468&external=no&menu=3 (accessed 5 November 2010).

Department for Children, Schools and Families (DCSF) (2007b) *Safe to Learn: Embedding Anti-Bullying Work in Schools*. Online. Available at: www.teachernet.gov.uk/wholeschool/behaviour/tacklingbullying/safetolearn (accessed 18 March 2011).

Department for Children, Schools and Families (DCSF) (2008) *Drug Education: An Entitlement for All*. Online. Available at: www.teachernet.gov.uk/_doc/13032/ACFE3AC.pdf (accessed 16 March 2011).

Department for Children, Schools and Families (DCSF) (2008a) *Personalised Learning: A Practical Guide*, Nottingham: DCFS Publications.

Department for Children, Schools and Families (DCSF) (2009) *A New Relationship with Schools: The School Improvement Partner's Brief*, 3rd edn, London: DCFS.

Department for Children, Schools and Families (DCSF) (2009a) *Behaviour Challenge Strategy*. Online. Available at: http://webarchive.nationalarchives.gov.uk/20091003041141/http://www.teachernet.gov.uk/wholeschool/behaviour/bc (accessed 18 February 2011).

Department for Children, Schools and Families (DCSF) (2010) *Standards Site: Gaining Ground, Improving Progress*. Online. Available at: http://www.standards.dfes.gov.uk/sie/966151 (accessed 4 August 2010).

Department for Education (DfE) (2010) *The Importance of Teaching: The Schools White Paper 2010*, Cm 7980, London: The Stationery Office.

Department for Education (DfE) (2011) 'Education Bill gives Secretary of State new powers to intervene in underperforming schools', press notice, 27 January 2011. Online. Available at: http://www.education.gov.uk/inthenews/pressnotices/a0073822/education-bill-gives-secretary-of-state-new-powers-to-intervene-in-underperforming-schools (accessed 15 February 2011).

Department for Education (DfE) (2011a) *The Education Bill* (introduced 26 January 2011). Online. Available at: http://dfe.gov.uk/aboutdfe/departmentalinformation/educationbill/a0073748/education-bill (accessed 16 February 2011).

Department for Education and Skills (DfES) (2005) *14–19 Education and Skills, White Paper*, London: HMSO.

Department for Education and Skills (DfES) (2005a) *Learning Behaviour (The Steer Report)*, London: HMSO. Online. Available at: www.dfes.gov.uk/behaviourandattendance/about/learning_behaviour.cfm (accessed 10 January 2008).

Department for Education and Skills (DfES) (2006) *2020 Vision: Report of the Teaching and Learning in 2020 Review Group*, Nottingham: DfES Publications.

Dilley, R. (1999) *The Problem of Context*, Oxford: Berghan Books.

Dorling, D., Rigby, J., Wheeler, B., Ballas, D., Thomas, B. and Lupton, R. (2005) *Poverty, Wealth and Place in Britain 1968–2005*, Cambridge: Policy Press.

Education and Inspections Act (2006) *Chapter 40*. Online. Available at: http://www.legislation.gov.uk/ukpga/2006/40/contents (accessed 16 October 2010).

Elmore, R.F. (1996) 'School reform, teaching and learning', *Journal of Education Policy*, 11(4): 499–504.

Elmore, R.F. (2009) *Building a New Structure For School Leadership*. Online. Available at: http://www.ashankerinst.org/Downloads/building.pdf (accessed 3 February 2011).

Emmison, M. (2004) 'The conceptualization and analysis of visual data', in D. Silverman (ed.) *Qualitative Research: Theory, Method and Practice*, London: Sage, pp. 246–65.

Fairclough, N. (1989) *Language and Power*, London and New York: Longman.

Fairclough, N. (1995) *Critical Discourse Analysis*, London: Longman.

Fairclough, N. (2003) *Analysing Discourse: Textual Analysis for Social Research*, London: Routledge.

Fenwick, T. (2010) '(un)Doing standards in education with actor–network theory', *Journal of Education Policy*, 25(2): 117–33.

Fenwick, T. and Edwards, R. (2010) *Actor–Network Theory in Education*, London: Routledge.

Fielding, M. (2004) 'Transformative approaches to student voice: theoretical underpinnings, recalcitrant realities', *British Educational Research Journal*, 30(2): 295–311.

Fielding, M. (2007) *Taking Education Really Seriously: Four Years Hard Labour*, London: RoutledgeFalmer.

Fielding, M. (2008) *The Human and Intellectual Cost of High Performance Schooling: On the Necessity of Person-centred Education*, London: Routledge.

Fielding, M. (2011) 'Is state school too dangerous for rhapsody?', *The Guardian*, Thursday 24 March 2011. Online. Available at: http://www.guardian.co.uk/education/mortarboard/2011/mar/24/is-state-school-too-dangerous (accessed 31 March 2011).

Flyvberg, B. (2006) 'Five misunderstandings about case-study research', *Qualitative Inquiry*, 2(2): 219–45.

Foucault, M. (1972) *The Archaeology of Knowledge*, New York: Vintage.

Foucault, M. (1975) 'Of power and prisons', in M. Morris and P. Patton (eds) (1979) *Michel Foucault: Power, Truth, Strategy*, Sydney: Feral Publications, pp. 109–47.

Foucault, M. (1976) *The History of Sexuality: Will to Knowledge*, vol. 1, London: Penguin.

Foucault, M. (1977) 'The Confession of the Flesh, an interview', in C. Gordon (ed.) (1980) *Power/Knowledge: Selected Interviews and Other Writings*, London: Vintage.

Foucault, M. (1979) *Discipline and Punish: The Birth of the Prison*, London: Peregrine Books.

Foucault, M. (1980) 'Two lectures', in Gordon, C. (ed.) (1980) *Power/Knowledge: Selected Interviews and Other Writings, 1972–1977*, London: Vintage.

Foucault, M. (1983) 'The subject and power', an afterword to H. Dreyfus and P. Rabinow, *Michel Foucault: Beyond Structuralism and Hermeneutics*, Sussex: The Harvester Press.

Foucault, M. (1986) *The Archaeology of Knowledge*, London and New York: Tavistock Publications.

Foucault, M. (1991) 'Governmentality', trans. R. Braidotti and revised by C. Gordon, in G. Burchell, C. Gordon and P. Miller (eds) *The Foucault Effect: Studies in Governmentality*, Chicago, IL: University of Chicago Press.

Foucault, M. (1993) 'About the beginning of the hermeneutics of the self' (transcription of two lectures in Dartmouth on 17 and 24 November 1980), in M. Blasius (ed.) *Political Theory*, 21(2): 198–227.

Foucault, M. (1993a) 'Space, power and knowledge (a conversation between M. Foucault and P. Rabinow)', in S. During (ed.) (1999) *The Cultural Studies Reader*, 2nd edn, London and New York: Routledge/Taylor & Francis, pp. 134–45.

Foucault, M. (1996) 'The impossible prison', panel discussion, trans. C. Gordon, S. Lotringer (ed.) *Foucault Live: Collected Interviews 1961–1984*, New York: Semiotext(e), pp. 275–86.

Fullan, M.G. (2001) *Leading in a Culture of Change*, San Francisco, CA: Jossey-Bass.

Fullan, M.G. (2003) *Change Forces with a Vengeance*, London and New York: RoutledgeFalmer.

Fullan, M.G. (2006) *Turnaround Leadership*, San Francisco, CA: Jossey-Bass.

Gewirtz, S. and Cribb, A. (2008) 'Taking identity seriously: dilemmas for education policy and practice', *European Educational Research Journal*, 7(1): 39–49.

Gewirtz, S. and Cribb, A. (2009) *Understanding Education. A Sociological Perspective*, Cambridge: Polity.

Gewirtz, S., Ball, S.J. and Bowe, R. (1995) *Markets, Choice and Equity in Education*, Buckingham: Open University Press.

Gibson, A. and Asthana, S. (1998) 'Schools, pupils and examination results: contextualising school "performance"', *British Educational Research Journal*, 24(3): 269–82.

Gilbert, R. (1992) 'Text and context in qualitative educational research', *Linguistics and Education*, 4: 37–57.

Gillborn, D. and Youdell, D. (2000) *Rationing Education: Policy, Practice, Reform and Equity*, Buckingham: Open University Press.

Gillies, D., Wilson, A., Soden, R., Gray, S. and McQueen, I. (2010) 'Capital, culture and community: understanding school engagement in a challenging context', *Improving Schools*, 13(1): 21–38.

Giroux, H. (1983) 'Theories of reproduction and resistance in the new sociology of education: a critical analysis', *Harvard Educational Review*, 53(3): 257–93.

Goffman, E. (1961) *Encounters: Two Studies in the Sociology of Interaction*, Indianapolis: Bobbs-Merrill.

Goffman, E. (1971) *Relations in Public: Microstudies of the Public Order*, London: Allen Lane.

Goleman, D. (1996) *Emotional Intelligence: Why it Can Matter More Than IQ*, London: Bloomsbury.

Goodley, D. and Runswick-Cole, K. (2011) 'Problematising policy: conceptions of "child", "disabled" and "parents" in social policy in England', *International Journal of Inclusive Education*, 15(1): 71–86.

Goodson, I. (1983) *School Subjects and Curriculum Change*, Beckenham: Croom Helm.

Gordon, C. (ed.) *Power/Knowledge: Selected Interviews and Other Writings 1972–1977. Michel Foucault*, London: Harvester Press.

Grantham, A. (2001) 'How networks explain unintended policy implementation outcomes: the case of UK rail privatization', *Public Administration*, 79(4): 851–70.

Guardian, The (2010) 'Full list of scrapped school building projects', *The Guardian* (published 6 July 2010). Online. Available at: http://www.guardian.co.uk/education/interactive/2010/jul/05/building-schools-for-the-future-michael-gove (accessed 25 March 2011).

Hall, S. (1997) *Representation: Cultural Representations and Signifying Practices*, London: Sage, in association with the Open University.

Hardy, I. and Lingard, B. (2008) 'Teacher professional development as an effect of policy and practice: A Bourdieurian analysis', *Journal of Education Policy*, 23(1): 63–80.

Hargreaves, D.H. (1967) *Social Relations in a Secondary School*, London: Routledge and Kegan Paul.

Hartley, D. (2007) 'Personalisation: the emerging "revised" code of education?', *Oxford Review of Education*, 33(5): 629–42.

Hodder, I. (2003) 'The interpretation of documents and material culture', in N.K. Denzin and Y.S. Lincoln (eds) *Collecting and Interpreting Qualitative Materials*, London: Sage, pp. 155–75.

Hoffman, M. (2010) 'Disciplinary power', in D. Taylor (ed.) *Michel Foucault: Key Concepts*, Durham: Acumen.

Hoyle, E. (1974) 'Professionality, professionalism and control in teaching', *London Educational Review*, 3(2): 15–17.

Hunter, I. (1996) 'Assembling the school', in T. Barry, A. Osborne and N.S. Rose (eds) *Foucault and Political Reason*, Chicago: University of Chicago Press, pp. 143–66.

Jeffrey, B. (2002) 'Performativity and primary teacher relations', *Journal of Education Policy*, 17(5): 531–46.

Jessop, B. (2002) *The Future of the Capitalist State*, Cambridge: Polity.

Jones, K. (2003) *Education in Britain: 1944 to the Present*, Cambridge: Polity.

Kelchtermans, G. (2003) 'Teachers' emotions in educational reforms: self-understanding, vulnerable commitment and micropolitical literacy', *Teaching and Teacher Education*, 21(8): 995–1006.

Kingsolver, B. (2009) *The Lacuna*, London: Faber and Faber.

Koh, A. (2009) 'The visualization of education policy: a videological analysis of learning journeys', *Journal of Education Policy*, 24(3): 283–315.

Koyama, J. (2010) *Making Failure Pay: For-profit Tutoring, High-stakes Testing and Public Schools*, Chicago: University of Chicago Press.

Kraftl, P. (2007) 'Utopia, performativity, and the unhomely', *Environment and Planning D: Society and Space*, 25(1): 120–43.

Lacey, C. (1974) *Hightown Grammar: The School as a Social System*, Manchester: Manchester University Press.

Latour, B. (1986) 'The power of association', in J. Law (ed.) *Power, Action and Belief: A New Sociology of Knowledge?*, London: Routledge, pp. 264–80.

Latour, B. (2005) *Reassembling the Social: An Introduction to Actor–Network Theory*, Oxford: Oxford University Press.

Lauder, H., Jamieson, I. and Wikeley, F. (1998) 'Models of effective schools: limits and capabilities', in R. Slee, G. Weiner and S. Tomlinson (eds) *School Effectiveness for Whom?*, London: Falmer, pp. 51–69.

Law, J. (2007) *Actor Network Theory and Material Semiotics*, version of 25 April 2007. Online. Available at: http://www.heterogeneities.net/publications/Law2007ANTandMaterialSemiotics. pdf (accessed 10 August 2010).

Law, J. (2008) 'Actor–network theory and material semiotics', in B.S. Turner, *The New Blackwell Companion to Social Theory*, 3rd edn, London: Blackwell, pp. 141–58.

Leadbeater, C. (2004) *Personalisation Through Participation: A New Script for Public Services*, London: Demos.

Lendvai, N. and Stubbs, P. (2006) 'Translation, intermediaries and welfare reform in central and south eastern Europe'. Paper presented at the 4th Annual ESPAnet Conference 'Transformation of the welfare state: political regulation and social inequality', University of Bremen, Germany, September 2006.

Levin, B. (1998) 'An epidemic of education policy: (what) can we learn from each other?', *Comparative Education*, 34(2): 131–41.

Loveday, B. (2008) 'Performance management and the decline of leadership within public services in the United Kingdom', *Policing: A Journal of Policy and Practice*, 12(1): 120–30.

Lupton, R. (2004) *Schools in Disadvantaged Areas: Recognising Context and Raising Performance*, CASE Paper 76, London: LSE.

MacBeath, J. (2008) 'Stories of compliance and subversion in a prescriptive policy environment', *Educational Management Administration Leadership*, 36(1): 123–48.

Maguire, M. (2007) 'Gender and movement in social policy', in C. Skelton, B. Francis and L. Smulyan (eds) *The Sage Handbook of Gender and Education*, London, Thousand Oaks and New Delhi: Sage, pp. 109–24.

Maguire, M., Ball, S.J. and Braun, A. (2010) 'Behaviour, classroom management and student "control": enacting policy in the English secondary school', *International Studies in Sociology of Education*, 20(2): 153–70.

Maguire, M., Perryman, J., Ball, S.J. and Braun, A. (2011) 'The ordinary school – what is it?', *British Journal of Sociology of Education*, 32(1): 1–16.

Mahony, P., Menter, I. and Hextall, I. (2004) 'The emotional impact of performance-related pay on teachers in England', *British Educational Research Journal*, 30(3): 435–56.

Malin, N. (2007) *Evaluating Sure Start*, London: Whiting & Birch.

Mannheim, K. (1952) 'The problem of generations', in P. Kescemeti (ed.) *Essays on the Sociology of Knowledge*, London: Routledge and Kegan Paul.

Marton, F. and Säljö, R. (1976) 'On qualitative differences in learning: 1 – outcome and process', *British Journal of Educational Psychology*, 46(1): 4–11.

Matland, R.E. (1995) 'Synthesizing the implementation literature: the ambiguity-conflict model of policy implementation', *Journal of Public Administration Research and Theory: J-PART*, 5(2): 145–74.

Messaris, P. (1997) *Visual Persuasion: The Role of Images in Advertising*, Thousand Oaks and London: Sage.

Mintron, M. (1997) 'Policy entrepreneurs and the diffusion of innovation', *American Journal of Political Science*, 41(3): 738–70.

Moore, A. (2004) *The Good Teacher: Dominant Discourses in Teaching and Teacher Education*, London: Routledge.

Moore, A. (2006) 'Recognising desire: a psychosocial approach to understanding education policy implementation and effect', *Oxford Review of Education*, 32(4): 487–503.

Morgan, M., Ludlow, L., Kitching, K., O'Leary, M. and Clarke, A. (2010) 'What makes teachers tick? Sustaining events in new teachers' lives', *British Educational Research Journal*, 36(2): 191–208.

Mussella, D.F. (1989) 'Problems in policy implementation', in M. Holmes, K.A. Leithwood and D.F. Mussell (eds) *Educational Policy for Effective Schools*, Toronto: Ontario Institute for Studies in Education, pp. 93–111.

Neave, G. (1998) 'The evaluative state reconsidered', *European Journal of Education*, 33(3): 265–84.

Olsen, B. and Sexton, D. (2009) 'Threat rigidity, school reform and how teachers view their work inside current education policy contexts', *American Educational Research Journal*, 46(1): 9–44.

Ozga, J. (2000) *Policy Research in Educational Settings: Contested Terrain*, Buckingham: Open University Press.

Ozga, J. (2008) 'Governing knowledge: research steering and research quality', *European Educational Research Journal*, 7(3): 261–72.

Ozga, J. and Lingard, B. (2007) 'Globalisation, education policy and politics', in B. Lingard and J. Ozga (eds) *The RoutledgeFalmer Reader in Education Policy and Politics*, London: RoutledgeFalmer, pp. 65–82.

Panju, M. (2008) *Seven Successful Strategies to Promote Emotional Intelligence in the Classroom*, London: Continuum.

Paton, G. (2009) 'Schools focus on average pupils to "flatter league tables", claim Lib Dems', *Daily Telegraph*, 11 February 2009.

Perryman, J., Ball, S.J., Maguire, M. and Braun, A. (2011) 'Life in the pressure cooker: school league tables and English and Mathematics teachers' responses to accountability in a results-driven era', *British Journal of Educational Studies*, 59(2), 179–95.

Phillips, N., Lawrence, T.B. and Hardy, C. (2004) 'Discourse and institutions', *Academy of Management Review*, 29(4): 635–52.

Powell, S. and Tod, J. (2004) *A Systematic Review of How Theories Explain Learning Behaviour in School Contexts*. Online. Available at: http://eppi.ioe.ac.uk/cms/Default.aspx?tabid=123 (accessed 23 February 2011).

Power, M. (1994) *The Audit Explosion*, London: Demos.

Prior, L. (1988) 'The architecture of the hospital: a study of spatial organization and medical knowledge', *British Journal of Sociology*, 39(1): 86–113.

Probyn, E. (1993) *Sexing the Self: Gendered Positions in Cultural Studies*, New York: Routledge.

Putnam, R.D. (2000) *Bowling Alone: The Collapse and Revival of the American Community*, New York: Simon and Schuster.

Reay, D. and Wiliam, D. (1999) 'I'll be a nothing: structure, agency and the construction of identity through assessment', *British Educational Research Journal*, (25): 3.

Reay, D., Crozier, G. and James, D. (2011) *White Middle-Class Identities and Urban Schooling*, London: Palgrave Macmillan.

Richardson, H. (2010) 'Head teachers' search powers to be toughened', *BBC News*, 7 July 2010. Online. Available at: http://www.bbc.co.uk/news/10528023 (accessed 30 March 2011).

Rinne, R., Kivirauma, J. and Rinne, H.S. (2002) 'Shoots of revisionist education policy or just slow readjustment? The Finnish case of educational reconstruction', *Journal of Educational Policy*, 17(6): 643–58.

Riseborough, G. (1992) 'Primary headship, state policy and the challenge of the 1990s', *Journal of Education Policy*, 8(2): 123–42.

Rizvi, F. and Kemmis, S. (1987) *Dilemmas of Reform*, Geelong Vic: Deakin University Press.

Rizvi, F. and Lingard, B. (2010) *Globalizing Education Policy*, London and New York: Routledge.

Roffey, S. (2011) 'Why are MPs more interested in naughtiness than in what causes it?', *The Guardian*, Tuesday 15 February 2011. Online. Available at: http://www.guardian.co.uk/education/2011/feb/15/school-behaviour-discipline-white-paper (accessed 30 February 2011).

Rose, N. and Miller, P. (1992) 'Political power beyond the state: problematics of government', *British Journal of Sociology*, 43(2): 173–205.

Rutter, M., Maughan, B., Mortimore, P. and Ouston, J. (1979) *Fifteen Thousand Hours: Secondary Schools and Their Effects on Children*, London: Open Books.

Sanguinetti, J. (1999) 'Teachers under pressure: discursive positionings and micropractices of resistance'. Paper given at the Australian Association for Research in Education Conference, Melbourne, November 1999.

Sarup, M. (1978) *Marxism and Education*, London: Routledge and Kegan Paul.

School Standards and Framework Act (1998) *Chapter 31*. Online. Available at: http://www.legislation.gov.uk/ukpga/1998/31/data.pdf (accessed 16 March 2011).

Schureich, J. (1994) 'Policy archaeology: a new policy studies methodology', *Journal of Education Policy*, 9(4): 297–316.

Scott, S. (2010) 'Revisiting the total institution', *Sociology*, 44(2): 213–31.

Seligman, M.E.P. (2002) *Authentic Happiness: Using the New Positive Psychology to Realize your Potential for Lasting Fulfilment*, New York: Simon and Schuster.

Siskin, L.S. (1991) *Realms of Knowledge: Academic Departments in Secondary Schools*, Washington DC and London: Falmer.

Skelton, C. and Francis, B. (2003) *Boys and Girls in the Primary Classroom*, Maidenhead: Open University Press.

Skelton, C. and Francis, B. (2009) *Feminism and 'The Schooling Scandal'*, Abingdon: Routledge.

Skocpol, T. (1992) *Protecting Soldiers and Mothers: The Political Origins of Social Policy in the United States*, Cambridge, MA: Belknap Press of Harvard University Press.

Slee, R. (1995) *Changing Theories and Practices of Discipline*, London and Washington: Falmer.

Slee, R. (2011) *The Irregular School: Exclusion, Schooling and Inclusive Education*, London and New York: Routledge.

Solomon, E. and Garside, R. (2008) 'Ten years of Labour's youth justice reforms: an independent audit', *Centre for Crime and Justice Studies*, London: King's College.

Spillane, J.P. (2004) *Standards Deviation: How Schools Misunderstand Education Policy*, Cambridge, MA: Harvard University Press.

Spillane, J.P., Reiser, B.J. and Reimer, T. (2002) 'Policy implementation and cognition: reframing and refocusing implementation research', *Review of Educational Research*, 72(3): 387–431.

Steer, A. (2005) 'Learning behaviour: the report of the practitioners', *Group on School Behaviour and Discipline*, London: DfES.

Steer, A. (2008) 'Four interim reports on behaviour', UK Government. Online. Available at: www.teachernet.gov.uk/wholeschool/behaviour/steer/fourreports (accessed 30 February 2011).

Steer, A. Sir (2009) *Learning Behaviour: Lessons Learned. A Review of Behaviour Standards and Practices in our Schools*, Nottingham: DCSF Publications.

Stoll, L. and Stobart, G. (2005) 'Informed consent? Issues in implementing and sustaining government driven educational change', in N. Bascia, A. Cumming, K. Datnow, K. Leithwood and D. Livingstone (eds) *International Handbook of Education Policy*, Dordretch: Springer.

Supovitz, J.A. and Weinbaum, E.W. (eds) (2008) *The Implementation Gap: Understanding Reforms in High Schools*, New York: Teachers' College Press.

Taylor, S., Rizvi, F., Lingard, B. and Henry, M. (1997) *Educational Policy and the Politics of Change*, London: Routledge.

Thomas, R.M. (2005) *High-Stakes Testing: Coping With Collateral Damage*, New York: Routledge.

Thomson, P. (2008) 'Children and young people: voices in visual research', in P. Thomson (ed.) (2008) *Doing Visual Research with Children and Young People*, Abingdon: Routledge, pp. 1–20.

Thomson, P. (2009) *School Leadership: Heads on the Block?*, London and New York: Routledge.

Thrift, N. (2000) 'Afterwords', *Environment and Planning D: Society and Space*, 18: 213–55.

Thrupp, M. and Lupton, R. (2006) 'Taking school contexts more seriously: the social justice challenge', *British Journal of Educational Studies*, 54(3): 308–28.

Thrupp, M. and Lupton, R. (2011) 'Variations on a middle class theme: English primary schools in socially advantaged contexts', *Journal of Education Policy*, 26(2): 289–312.

Timmermans, S. and Berg, M. (1997) 'Standardization in action: achieving local universality through medical protocols', *Social Studies of Science*, 27 April 1997: 273–305.

Trowler, P. (2003) *Education Policy*, London: Routledge.

Usher, R. and Edwards, R. (1994) *Postmodernism and Education*, London and New York: Routledge.

Vander Schee, C. (2009) 'Fruit, vegetables, fatness, and Foucault: governing students and their families through school health policy', *Journal of Education Policy*, 24(5): 557–74.

Veyne, P. (2010) *Foucault*, Cambridge: Polity.

Vincent, C., Ball, S.J. and Braun, A. (2008) 'It's like saying "coloured": understanding and analysing the urban working classes', *The Sociological Review*, 56(1): 61–77.

Violent Crime Reduction Act (2006). Online. Available at: http://www.legislation.gov.uk/ ukpga/2006/38/contents (accessed 15 March 2011).

Wallace, M. (1991) 'Coping with multiple innovations in schools: an exploratory study', *School Organisation*, 11(2): 187–209.

Watson, M. and Hay, C. (2003) 'The discourse of globalisation and the logic of no alternative: rendering the contingent necessary in the political economy of New Labour', *Policy and Politics*, 31(3): 289–305.

Weare, K. (2007) *Developing the Emotionally Literate School*, London: Paul Chapman.

Woods, P.A. (2011) *Transforming Education Policy: Shaping a Democratic Future*, Bristol: Policy Press.

Woolgar, S. (ed.) (1988) 'Knowledge and reflexivity: frontiers in the sociology of knowledge', London: Sage, cited in M. Grenfell and D. James with P. Hodkinson, D. Reay and D. Robbins (1998) *Bourdieu and Education: Acts of Practical Theory*, London: Falmer, p.124.

Wright, N. (2001) 'Leadership, "bastard leadership" and managerialism: confronting twin paradoxes of the Blair education project', *Educational Management and Administration*, 29(3): 275–90.

Youdell, D. (2006) *Impossible Bodies, Impossible Selves: Exclusions and Student Subjectivities*, Dordrecht: Springer.

Index

Lightning Source UK Ltd.
Milton Keynes UK
UKOW06f0808260615

254169UK00006B/46/P